I0595548

Arthur Sherburne Hardy

Life and Letters of Joseph Hardy Neesima

Arthur Sherburne Hardy

Life and Letters of Joseph Hardy Neesima

ISBN/EAN: 9783337017972

Printed in Europe, USA, Canada, Australia, Japan

Cover: Foto ©Thomas Meinert / pixelio.de

More available books at **www.hansebooks.com**

LIFE AND LETTERS

OF

JOSEPH HARDY NEESIMA

BY

ARTHUR SHERBURNE HARDY

BOSTON AND NEW YORK
HOUGHTON, MIFFLIN AND COMPANY
The Riverside Press, Cambridge
1892

Copyright, 1891,
By ARTHUR SHERBURNE HARDY.

All rights reserved.

SIXTH EDITION.

The Riverside Press, Cambridge, Mass., U.S.A.
Electrotyped and Printed by H. O. Houghton & Co.

PREFACE.

Although personally acquainted with Mr. Neesima and familiar with the main events of his life, the reading of his letters and journal made upon me a fresh and deep impression. It seemed to me that no pen could reveal the personality of the man or tell the story of his life so effectively as his own. To say that one possesses certain qualities is well; to see these qualities in action is better. With no thought of the public ear, Mr. Neesima, in his correspondence and journals, disclosed himself with the simplicity and modesty peculiar to him, and with the truthfulness of one who, unconscious of an audience, asks for no verdict. I have therefore endeavored to let him speak who speaks best, and this volume is essentially an autobiography. From the large amount of material at hand all that does not contribute to a vivid impression of Mr. Neesima has been, I trust, rejected; the intent being, not to write the history of the Japan mission, but to show forth this man in the light of his own acts, utterances, and thought.

One other purpose has rendered this work a sacred one to a son. Mr. Hardy was averse to everything of the nature of a biography of himself. It is some-

times saddening to think that a long life of unre-
corded benefactions should have no memorial. But
this thought is not true to fact. No word of a loving
heart, no act of a helping hand, is lost; and their results, as wrought into the lives of men, are worthier
memorials than the page that rehearses them or the
tablet that commemorates them. Still, in the preparation of these pages, which necessarily record one
act of a life which, to those who knew it, was but the
sum of such, it has been a pleasure to the son to
throw as it were this side light upon a noble nature
without violating a father's wishes.

ARTHUR SHERBURNE HARDY.

HANOVER, N. H., *May* 21, 1891.

CONTENTS.

CHAPTER VII. 1885–1890.

LIFE OF JOSEPH NEESIMA.

CHAPTER I.

In the summer of 1864 the brig Berlin, owned by Thomas Walsh & Co., of Nagasaki, arrived at Hakodate, consigned to Frederic Wilkie, Esq., in command of William B. Savory, of Salem, Mass. Just before leaving on the return voyage to Shanghai, Captain Savory was informed by Mr. Wilkie that a young Japanese, the friend of a native clerk in his office, was anxious to escape from Japan to the United States, where he hoped to obtain an education. Reminding the captain that serious consequences were likely to follow his detection in the act of taking a native out of the country, Mr. Wilkie called the young man, then about twenty-one years of age, into his office, and Captain Savory, through the clerk, Mr. Munokite, who acted as interpreter, offered him a passage to Shanghai provided he could reach the brig without assistance from those on board, and promised to do what he could towards securing his transfer to some vessel returning to the United States. As a result of this proposition, Mr. Munokite assisted his friend on board the Berlin during the night of July 18th. Owing to the presence of Japanese custom officers on the vessel, the runaway was secreted in one of the cabin staterooms, and given to understand by signs that he must remain in hiding until the brig was under way. "I shall never forget," writes Captain Savory in 1883, "the first interview I had with him, or how happy he felt when he saw the shores of his country fading from his view, knowing that he was safe from all harm. His sole aim then was to learn the English language, that he might be able to translate the Bible into his own tongue for the benefit of his countrymen."

On arriving at Shanghai the Berlin was ordered to Nagasaki. Knowing that his young *protégé* could return to Japan only at the risk of his life, Captain Savory secured his transfer to the ship Wild Rover, owned by Alpheus Hardy & Co., of Boston, U. S. A., under the command of Capt. Horace S. Taylor, of Chatham, Mass. In September, 1864, Captain Taylor sailed for Foochoo, but remained in Chinese waters through the winter, touching at Hongkong, Saigon, Shanghai again, and Manilla, from which latter port he set sail April 1, 1865, for Boston, where he arrived in August, after a four months' passage.

When this young Japanese came on board the Wild Rover, at Shanghai, he could speak but a few English words, although having some knowledge of the written language. On being asked his name he replied, "Neesima Shimeta." "I shall call you Joe," was the captain's laconic announcement.

Shortly after reaching Boston, Captain Taylor informed his owner that he had a Japanese boy on the ship who was anxious to secure an education, and at Mr. Hardy's request Neesima was sent for. During the voyage he had acquired the ship's vocabulary, but was still unable to make known his wishes in intelligible English. To every question asked by Mrs. Hardy he replied only in monosyllables. It was impossible to elicit from him his reasons for leaving Japan, and beyond the statement of Captain Taylor, a very reticent man, nothing could be learned of his aims or desires. The experience of the Mission Board in aiding foreigners under similar circumstances had not been encouraging. Neesima was therefore sent to the Sailor's Home, and requested to put in writing the reasons which led him to flee his native country.

On October 11th Mr. Hardy received the following statement : —

"I was born in a house of a prince [Itakura] in Yedo. My father [Neesima Tamiharu] was writing-master of the prince's house and his writer, and my grandfather was an officer of whole,[1] the prince's servant. I began to learn Japan, and China too, from six years age, but at eleven years age my mind had changed quite to learn sword-exercise and riding horse. At sixteen years age my desire was deepened to learn China and cast away sword-exercise and other things. But my prince picked me up to write his daily book, although it would not have been my desire. I was obliged to go up his office one another day, and I must teach small boys and girls too, instead my father at home. Therefore I could not get in China school to learn China, but I read every night at home. A day my comrade lent me an atlas of United States of North America, which was written with China letter by some American minister.[2] I read it many times,

---

[1] That is, a steward, in charge of the private servants and attendants of the prince, — pages, carriers, cooks, kago bearers, etc., — an office of considerable dignity and responsibility.

[2] What is here called an "atlas" was a *History of the United States* written by Dr. Bridgman, of Shanghai, in China. After Dr. Bridgman's death, his widow visited Dr. Brown, in Yokohama, and left with him a few copies of her husband's history, which were distributed by

and I was wondered so much as my brain would melted
out from my head, picking out President, Building,
Free School, Poor House, House of Correction, and
machine-working, etc. And I thought that a governor
of our country must be as President of the United
States. And I murmured myself that, O Governor
of Japan! why you keep down us as a dog or a pig?
We are people of Japan. If you govern us you must
love us as your children. From that time I wished to
learn American knowledge, but alas, I could not get
any teacher to learn it. Although I would not like
to learn Holland, I was obliged to learn it because
many of my countrymen understood to read it. Every
one another day I went to my master's house to
learn it.

"Some day I had been in the prince's office and I
got none to write at all. Therefore I ran out from the
office and went to my master's house. By and by my
prince stepped into the office, wanting to see me; but
he saw nobody there, and he stayed me until I came
back into. When he saw me he beated me. 'Why
you run out from the office? I would not allowed you
to run out from there.' After ten days I ran out from
there again, but he would not know about it. But
alas! in the next time he found out again I ran out
from the office, and he beated me. 'Why you run
out from here?' Then I answered to him that 'I
wished to learn foreign knowledge, and I hope to understand it very quickly; therefore, though I know I
must stay here, reverence your law, my soul went to
my master's house to learn it, and my body was obliged
to go thither too.' Then he said to me very kindly

Dr. Brown. It was doubtless one of these copies which fell into Neesima's hands.

that 'you can write Japan very well, and you can earn yourself enough with it. If you don't run out from there any more I will give you more wages. With what reason will you like foreign knowledge? Perhaps it will mistake yourself.' I said: 'Why will it mistake myself? I guess every one must take some knowledge. If a man has not any knowledge I will worth him as a dog or a pig.' Then he laughed very hard about it, and said to me: 'You are stable boy.' Beside him, my grandfather, parents, sisters, friends, and neighbors, beated or laughed for me about it. But I never took care to them, and held my stableness very fast. After few months I got many business in the office, and I could not get out from there. Ah! it made me many musings in my head and made me some sickness too. I would not like to see anybody, and would not desire to go out to play myself, but I liked only to stay in a peaceful room. I knew it is bad sickness, therefore I went to some doctor, hoping to get some medicine. After he stay my sickness many times, he told me, 'Your sickness comes from your mind, therefore you must try to destroy your warm mind, and must take walk for healthfulness of your body, and it would be more better than many medicines.' The prince gave me many times to feed my weakness, and my father gave me some money to play myself. But I went every day to my master's house to learn Holland. I read up Holland grammar, spending many times, and I took a small book of nature, and I pleased to read it so much as I would say that this book would be more better than doctors' medicine to my sickness. When my sickness got better, after few months, the prince picked me up again to write his daily book. and I must stay in the office every day against his order. Ah! I could not get out from there to learn Holland, but I got many times to read book at night, and I read through the book of nature at home, taking a dictionary of Japan and Holland. Alas! the study of night-time caused me weak eyes, and I was obliged to stop it too. After ten weeks my weak eyes recovered entirely, and I began to read the book again; but I could not understand some reasonable accounts in it. Therefore I purposed to learn arithmetic. But I had not any times to learn it. A day I asked to the prince, 'Please get me more time to take knowledge.' Then he let me get out from there thrice a week, although it was not enough to me. I went to some arithmetical school to learn it, and understood addition, subtraction, multiplication, division, fractions, interest, etc. Then I took the book again, and understood some reasonable accounts in it.

"Some day I went to the seaside of Yedo, hoping to see the view of the sea. I saw largest man-of-war of Dutch lying there, and it seemed to me as a castle or a battery, and I thought too she would be strong to fight with enemy. While I look upon her one reflection came down upon my head: that we must open navy, because the country is surrounded with water, and if foreigners fight to my country, we must fight with them at sea. But I made other reflection too: that since foreigners trade, price of everythings got high, the country got poorer than before, because the countrymen don't understand to do trade with the foreigners. Therefore we must go to foreign countries, we must know to do trade, and we must learn foreign knowledge. But the government's law neglected all my thoughts, and I cried out myself: Why government? Why not let us be freely? Why let us be as a bird in a cage or a rat in a bag? Nay! we must cast away such a savage government, and we must pick out a president as the United States of America. But alas! such things would have been out of my power.

"From that time I went to a marine school of government to learn navigation a week thrice. After many months I understood little algebra, little geometry, to keep log, and to take sun, to find latitude. Ah! the study of night-time caused me weak eyes again, and I could not study at all during the time of one year and a half which would not come again in my life. After my eyes got better I was obliged to go in the prince's office. That time was very hot and sickly season of Yedo. A day the sun shined very hard, and in the evening it had rained very heavy. Then I felt cold and chilled myself. The next morning my head began to ache, and my body was so hot as a fire would burn within me. I could eat nothing, but drank cold water only. After two days measles raised up all over my body. When the measles got better my eyes began to spoil, and I played and spent many times very vainly. A day I visited my friend, and I found out small Holy Bible in his library that was written by some American minister with China language, and had shown only the most remarkable events of it. I lend it from him and read it at night, because I was afraid the savage country's law, which if I read the Bible, government will cross whole my family. I understood God at first, and he separated the earth from firmament, made light upon the earth, made grass, trees, creatures, fowls, fishes. And he created a man in his own image, and made up a woman, cutting a man's side bone. After he made up all things of universe, he took a rest. That day we must call Sunday or Sabbath day. I understood that Jesus Christ was Son of Holy Ghost, and he was crossed for the sins of all the world; therefore we must call him our Saviour. Then I put down the book and look around me, saying that: Who made me? My parents? No, God. Who made my table? A carpenter? No, my God. God let trees grow upon the earth, and although God let a carpenter made up my table, it indeed came from some tree. Then I must be thankful to God, I must believe him, and I must be upright against him. From that time my mind was fulfilled to read English Bible, and purposed to go to Hakodate to get English or American teacher of it. Therefore I asked of my prince and parents to go thither. But they had not allowed to me for it, and were alarmed at it. But my stableness would not destroy by their expostulations, and I kept such thoughts, praying only to God: Please! let me reach my aim.

"And I began to read English from some Japanese teacher. A day I walked some street of Yedo, and suddenly met a skipper of a schooner, who knew me well and love me too. I asked to him, 'When your vessel going?' He answered, 'She will bound to Hakodate within three days.' I told him, 'I got warm heart to go thither. If you please, let me go thither.' He said me: 'I will take you to go thither, but perhaps your prince and your parents will not allow it to you. You must ask first to them.' After two days I took up some money, little clothing, and little books, and left quite my home, not thinking that if this money was gone how I would eat, or dress myself, but only casting myself into the providence of God. In the next morning I went on board of the schooner that would bound to Hakodate. When I came to Hakodate I searched some teacher of English, but I could not find him with many ways. Therefore my head was quite changed to run away from the country. But one thought stayed me, that my grandfather and parents would sorrow about it, and it balanced my mind little while. But after one reflection came upon my head, that although my parents made and fed me, I belong indeed to Heavenly Father; therefore I must believe him, I must be thankful to him, and I must run into his ways. Then I began to search some vessel to get out from the country.

" After many labor I got into an American vessel which would bound to Shanghai. After I came in Shanghai river, I joined to the ship Wild Rover, and had been in the China coasts with her about eight months ; with the passage of four months, I come in Boston harbor by the kindness of God. When I saw first the ship's captain, H. S. Taylor, I begged to him if I get to America : 'Please ! let me go to school and take good education ; therefore I shall work on the board as well as I can, and I will not take any wages from you ;' and he promised me if I get home he will send me to a school and let me work on the board as his servant. Although he not give me any money, he bought for me any clothing, cap, shoes, and any other thing. At sea he taught me to keep log, to find out latitude and longitude. When I come here the captain let me stay on the board long while, and I had been with rough and godless men who kept the ship, and every one on the wharf frightened me. No one on the shore will relieve you, because since the war the price of everythings got high.　Ah! you must go to sea again.　I thought too I must work pretty well for my eating and dressing, and I could not get in any school before I could earn any money to pay to a school.　When such thoughts pressed my brain I could not work very well, I could not read book very cheerfully, and only looked around myself long while as a lunatic.　Every night after I went to bed I prayed to the God: Please! don't cast away me into miserable condition.　Please! let me reach my great aim!　Now I know the ship's owner, Mr. Hardy, may send me to a school, and he will pay all my expenses. When I heard first these things from my captain my eyes were fulfilled with many tears, because I was very thankful to him, and I thought too: God will not forsake me."

To this remarkable statement was due the beginning of that interest which Mr. and Mrs. Hardy felt in Neesima, an interest which deepened with the years, and which subsequent events amply justified.

During the voyage from Japan, Captain Taylor had told Neesima that the owner of the ship might find him some employment in Boston, and possibly provide for his education.　In this hope, but perplexed by the difficulty of pursuing his studies while earning his living, Neesima had written the following on some scraps of paper which he confided to the captain before reaching Boston:—

" I must tell you that I am most concerned for it that I will not reach my great aim, because I made such thoughts as hereafter:—

" Though the ship's owner will be very kindly to me, perhaps he will not send me to school so long as I may reach my great aim, because he will spend his moneys very vainly for me, and I guess he will spend least twenty dollars a month for my eating, dressing, useful things of my study; and if he spend so much moneys for me, he will give me some great work to do. I must work almost all day. Although I will not loathe such work, perhaps it will hindered good time of my study. · If I not understand good know-ledge I may not come back to Japan to see my prince, family, friends, because of my shameful condition, and they will worth me as a dog or a cat because I left home very wickedly, hoping to get some know-ledge.

"I am concerned about it as much as my brain would melted out, and when such musings fell on my head I could not read book at all, I would not do anything very cheerfully, and I looked around myself long time as a lunatic, because it confused my mind very much. But I know not yet will I take what course of my life, and I know not too any trade to earn myself. Alas! I am poor and foolish. I have no one around me to relieve me except you. Then I wish heartily to you that *please* let me direct into some good way which I may reach my aim. If you let me reach my aim I will never forget your kindness and virtuousness.

"Although I will go down behind a grave, my soul will go to heaven to tell to God about it and let him bless you with the truth of God.

"Please let me hear that Mr. Hardy will let me go to what kind of school, and I wish that he gave me remainder of his table for my eating, old one of his clothing for my dressing, ink, pen, paper, pencil, for using of my study."

The above was not seen by Mr. Hardy at the time,

but was sent to him seventeen years later by the widow of Captain Taylor.

On learning that Mr. Hardy had decided to send him to school, Neesima wrote him the following letter:

I am very thankful to you. You relief me, but I can't show to you my thankfulness with my words. But I at all times bless to God for you with this prayer: O God! if thou hast eyes, look upon me. O God! if thou hast ears, hear my prayer. Let me be civilized with Bible. O Lord! thou send thy Spirit upon my Hardy, and let him relief me from sad condition. O Lord! please! set thy eyes upon my Hardy, and keep out him from illness and temptation.

Your obedient servant,
JOSEPH NEESIMA.

In 1885, when, after a lapse of twenty years, this runaway occupied a position of honor and influence in his native land, he sent to those whom he loved to call his American parents, and whose name he had adopted, a fuller account of his early life and the circumstances under which he left Japan. From this narrative, which affords an interesting picture of his Japanese home, the following pages are taken: —

KYŌTO, JAPAN, *Aug.* 20, 1885.

To MR. AND MRS. ALPHEUS HARDY,

To whom I owe more than to my own parents for their boundless love and untiring interest manifested in my welfare, both temporal and spiritual, I most gratefully and affectionately dedicate this brief narrative of my younger days.

Their ever grateful child,
JOSEPH HARDY NEESIMA.

"I was born in a family which served a prince of Japan, who had his palace in the city of Yedo (called Tokyo, the eastern capital, since 1868), within a short distance of the Shogun's castle, and his possession of land in a province of Kodzuke, the castle town of which is called Annaka, and is situated on one of the two roads directly extending from Yedo to Kyoto. It is a humble town having a population not exceeding four thousand, and lies seventy miles nearly north of the capital. His palace at Yedo was surrounded by the extensive houses of his retainers, which exactly formed a square inclosure.

"I was born within this inclosure on the 14th of January, in the year of 1843.[1] Previous to my birth four girls were born. So I was the first son in the family. In those days, when the feudal system was still in full sway, boys were much preferred to girls in those families which are entitled to wear two swords as a mark of the rank called Samurai by the native tongue; for there must be a male heir to the family in order to perpetuate its rank and allowance in case of the father's death. For that reason my birth caused great joy to the family, and particularly to my grandfather. When he heard a boy was. born he exclaimed *Shimeta!* which is a most joyous exclamatory phrase often used by our people when they come to realize some long cherished hopes or wishes.

"Just about that time it was a part of our New Year days, as our old lunar month came a month later than our solar year.[2] It was then a high time with us.

---

[1] Old Japanese style. According to our mode of reckoning, February 12, 1843.

[2] The Gregorian calendar was not adopted by the Japanese govern-

Every house was decorated by some complicated fantastic ornaments called *Shime.* At the day dawn, just before the ornaments were removed from the house, a male babe was introduced into the family. On account of the *Shime,* a good omen, I was doubtless named after it, and was called Shimeta, a man of the Shime. But a story went round among our neighbors that I was named after my grandfather's exclamation *Shimeta!* when I was born. It may have a double meaning. At any rate I was called Shimeta, and it was written after the family name Neesima, according to our usage. Of course I have no knowledge of the events that happened in my home during my babyhood. But, so far as I recollect, I was a pet child of the family, especially of my grandfather. I was chiefly brought up on his lap. I have, also, some faint recollection of being carried occasionally by my grandmother. I was often taken out of doors on my sisters' backs, when my mother busied herself at home with sewings and mendings.

"At my fourth year my brother was born. I can well remember how happy I was with that occasion. I also remember what a tiny babe he was, and I thought how nice it would be when he grew a little larger and I might spin a top or fly a kite for him.

"At my fifth year I was taken to the temple of a god,[1] who was supposed to be my life guardian, to

ment until 1872. Prior to this time the civil year was a lunar year of 12 months of 29 and 30 days alternately, a mode of reckoning introduced from China in 602 A. D., and requiring, at definite periods, the interjection of an intercalary month of varying length in order to harmonize the lunar and solar periods.

[1] Every Japanese child is placed by his parents at an early age under the protection of some Shinto deity, whose foster-child he be-

offer to him the thanks of the family for his protection over me. It was a most joyous occasion to the family. My father bought for me two little swords to wear then. A nice suit of silk dressing was also made for me to wear on that occasion. I was accompanied by my parents and grandparents to present myself at the temple. When we came home I was loaded with candies, little kites, tops, and all sorts of playthings.

" I remember quite well what impressive thing the death of a person was when my grandmother departed to the world beyond. She was a woman of an amiable disposition, and used to give much alms to the poor in her latter life. She was often told by some Buddhist priests that her future abode should be the happy *Nirvāna*, on account of her constant almsgiving. I recollect very well what she said at her deathbed : 'O, I am going ! O, I am going !' I supposed then that she was intending to go to the happy *Nirvāna*, to be received into the bosom of the merciful Buddha. I also remember what confusion took place in my home at her funeral, how our neighbors came to our house, how they tried to console the bereaved family, and how generously my grandfather provided for them many kinds of sweetmeats, rice, *sake*, etc. I was then six years old. When her funeral took place I followed in the procession, partly walking and partly being carried on a man's back. We started from home early in the morning on account of the distance of the temple, in the yard of which she was to

comes. Until fifteen years of age, Neesima worshiped the family gods which stood upon a shelf in one of the rooms of his father's house ; but subsequently, seeing they did not partake of the food provided for them, refused to do so.

be buried with her ancestors. We were all received in the large hall of the temple, where numbers of the priests appeared in purple, red, and black robes, making a solemn ceremony by beating drums, striking cymbals, and repeating some sacred writings of Buddha.

"While I was quite young my father used to take me out to temples of the different gods to worship, as certain days of the months or years are especially devoted to them. On those occasions the temple grounds were generally crowded by all sorts of peddlers, selling pictures, kites, tops, divers kinds of playthings, cakes, candies, fruits, flowers, shrubs, etc.

"I must not forget to mention here what devoted pagan worshipers my father and grandfather were. They never missed going to the temples to worship on special days, and also kept numerous gods at home. A dozen of them were kept in the sitting-room, a dozen more in the parlor, with the tablets of their ancestors, and at least a half dozen in the kitchen. They offered them tea and rice in the morning and lights in the evening. At each offering they made the most profound bows before them, and made some prayers in behalf of the family. So far as I can recollect, they must have been thoroughly convinced that the life and prosperity of the family were depending on them. Being quite young and thoughtless, I supposed that my grandfather and father were the best people that ever lived in the world. Of course, I followed their example set before me, and often bowed myself down before these dumb idols, having some childish ambition that I might acquire some wisdom and skill to become an accomplished samurai.

"As my father was a teacher of penmanship, he

was especially devoted to a god of penmanship and learning, and went to his temple and prayed to him that his son might become skillful in penmanship. I knew most too well how desirous he was that I should become his successor and helper in teaching. I really disliked to devote myself to that tedious business, but I was compelled by him to spend half a day throughout years of my younger days in writing those perpendicular characters over and over after the copies carefully written by him.

"With regard to the home education I received in my younger days, I might here narrate one instance. One day I was naughty and refused to make an errand for my mother, and when she gave me a scolding I returned her an improper word. My grandfather heard it, came directly after me and caught me without saying a word, rolled me up in a night coverlet, and shut me up in a closet. After an hour's confinement I was released from the punishment, which was, I believe, the first one I ever received from my grandfather. I thought then he was too severe for a trifling offense, and went to a corner of the parlor to weep. After a while he came to me and urged me gently that I must no longer weep. Then he told me a story of the bamboo-shoot, in a most tender and affectionate manner I ever heard before. It was told in a native poem which means as follows : ' If I do not care for it, I would never use my rod for shaking the snow off from the down-bent branch of a young bambooshoot.' Then he asked, ' Do you understand its meaning, my dear ? ' and explained its meaning himself. ' You are young yet, and just as tender as a bambooshoot. If your evil inclinations spoil you, as a slight pressure of snow might easily break down the tender shoot, how sad I should be, my dear. Do you suppose I am unkind to you by thus punishing you ?' I remained speechless then, but I understood full well what he meant, and what kind intention he had for correcting me. I was really ashamed of my naughtiness, and thought that my grandfather was very kind in thus punishing me. I believe this talk made a deep impression on my young mind, and helped me to behave much better than before. However, I was just gay and playful as other boys were. I was very fond of spinning tops, rolling hoops, and flying kites. I was especially fond of the latter play, and when I went out to fly my kite often forgot to come home at the regular mealtime, which troubled my mother exceedingly. On that account my father refused to buy any more kites for me ; so I secured everything necessary for making one without his knowledge, and made a first-rate one myself. How gay I was then I can hardly describe, when I saw it going straight up toward the blue sky. I was also very fond of running and jumping. A scar on my left temple is a reminder of an accidental fall which was a great humiliation to me, and confined me at home nearly two months.

"Since then I gave up those boyish rough plays, and became fond of staying at home, either for studying or writing. I took also some drawing lessons from our neighbor, and drew birds, flowers, trees, and mountains, after the regular Japanese style, without a perspective. I was just over nine years old then.

"Being the heir to the family, I was specially warned by my mother to make most profound bows to those higher officers employed by my prince. It was her ambition that through their favor I might be promoted to a rank much higher than my father's. But I did not pay any attention to such a matter, as some young fellows of our neighbors did, — that is, to be very polite in bowing, and expert in using flattering terms. My boyishness disliked it. Furthermore I was very shy, and had some slight impediment in my speech. I could hardly speak distinctly when I was obliged to converse with strangers. Sometimes I refused to speak even to our neighbors. It caused a great anxiety to my mother. Either through her influence or my father's decision, I was sent to a school-of-etiquette, to learn to make the most profound bows, most graceful manners and movements, etc., in a company of noblemen, and to acquire also the polite style of conversational phrases. My teacher seemed to me a man of real genius. He told me many interesting stories, and invited me to come to him as often as I could. I believe I spent more than a year in acquiring the old-fashioned politeness, although I was not aware at the time of its benefit.

" All the events of my younger life took place within the square inclosure belonging to my prince. It was a mere little spot, but to me it was no small world. Whatsoever events took place, or whatsoever gossip was circulated, all seemed to my boyish mind no small affair. And above all, the prince seemed a regular terror to us. He could either behead us or expel us at his own pleasure, as disgraced servants. Any little favor conferred upon us from him was considered by us a great luck. So everybody belonging to him desired to secure his favor through his elder men, who were really the governors of his whole estate. My father used to take me to one of these elder men while I was quite young ; afterward I went to his house alone, without being accompanied by my father, because I was invited by him to come there as often as I would. As he was childless, he was always delighted to have me come and play with him when he had nothing in particular to do. Staying there towards evening, I often slept on his lap and was carried home in his arms. When I began to draw some pictures, I used to take them to show to him, and he was really delighted to see the progress I made. He often invited me to come to his house when he had company. As I had acquired some manner of politeness at the school of etiquette, especially in the cup-bearing and waiting upon gentlemen at their meals or banquets, I was quite serviceable to him on such occasions. He often took me with him when he went out to worship his ancestors or his guardian gods. I was really attached to him, because he loved me as if I were his own son. He was a good horseman and expert in shooting arrows. Moreover, he was a man of some character. He often rebuked his prince for his extreme arbitrariness, and also for his excessive drinking. So the prince felt uncomfortable to keep him near him, and sent him off to his castle town Annaka to represent him to the people, although it was called by the prince a promotion. What a painful day it was for me when he was ready to leave Yedo for Annaka! I went as far as an outskirt of that immense city, with my father and many others, to see him off. I wept bitterly when I took my last farewell. He was somewhat affected, but manfully concealed it and showed me an affectionate and touching smile. His last word to me was, 'Good-by, Shimeta; be a good boy. When you grow up larger, come up to Annaka to see me.' Then he bade his attending servants to start for the journey. He was then carried away on a *kago* [palanquin], being followed by many attendants, and I came home with my father dreadfully tired and disappointed. This was one of the great events that happened to me within the first decade of my life. The marriages of my two elder sisters took place within this decade.

" Just about this time the country was in a most painful condition. The people were accustomed to peace under the reign of the Tokugawa family, nearly three centuries. Their laws were rigid and fixed. Their executive officers were extremely suspicious and fearfully oppressive. The ambition of the people was completely crushed down. Many samurai had almost forgotten how to use their swords. Coats of mail were stored in warehouses merely as curiosities, and were useless from decay. In fact the people had become cowardly, corrupt, and effeminate. Licentiousness prevailed almost universally throughout the country. Truly some reformation was needed. A few far-sighted patriots lamented over this sad state, and cherished some hope for a regular renovation. But it was almost beyond their expectations to see it. Just about that time [1853] the famous American fleet commanded by Commodore Perry made a sudden appearance in our waters. It caused an awful commotion in the country.—The people were frightened by the terrible sound of the American cannon. However, most of the leading princes of the country raised a most impatient war-cry against the Americans, and urged the government of the Shogun to expel them from our waters at once. But we had no forts, no warships, no cannons, no trained army to fight with. The Shogun's chief counselors were quick enough to see how useless it would be to attempt to expel the Americans from our waters. They knew also that the motive of the Americans was entirely peaceful, and agreed with them to open a few ports for commerce. This very treaty with the Americans was soon followed by treaties with some European powers. But the action of the Shogun's counselors offended these impetuous princes. All sorts of charges were brought upon his government. He was called by them a coward, a slave to the foreign barbarians, etc. The party spirit was soon kindled. The leading princes of Kyūshū and Shikoku islands leagued together and rose up against him. They sent out a number of their spirited young samurai all over the country to stir up the hatred of the people against the misgovernment of the Shogun, and also against the foreign nations. The cry to restore the imperial reign and expel the foreign barbarians then became almost universal. It was indeed the starting-point of our late revolution, which happily resulted in the restoration of the imperial reign, and also in the freer opening of the foreign intercourse, instead of expelling foreigners from our shores.

"I must not forget to mention something of my prince in connection with this extraordinary period of our national history. He was quite accomplished in Chinese classics, and was well known in the country as the finest scholar among the princes. He was a man of far sight, and quite fixed in his purpose. About five or six years before the American fleet appeared in our waters, this prince, who spent most of his time in his own secluded palace, perceived that the military system of the country must be improved, and the people must be better educated and well informed.

He selected a few promising young men out of his own retainers and sent them to a military school just established under the auspices of the Shogun's government. He gave out an order to his retainers and compelled every one of them, except some aged ones, to take lessons in sword-fencing and horseback riding. Furthermore, he established a Chinese school and made education compulsory to his younger subjects. As he was subject to excessive drinking, and was very fond of giving costly gifts to his favorite friends and subjects in his younger days, he found his treasury almost empty when he came to equip his retainers with foreign arms. There was no other way for him to procure money than to impose an extra-duty on the farmers and merchants living in his dominions, for purchasing cannon and muskets of the European model, just introduced to the country by the Hollanders. He confiscated all the bronze bells from the Buddhist temples found in his dominion, and cast a number of the field-pieces and mortars out of them. By making such an extraordinary effort he was enabled to provide a sufficient number of cannon and muskets of the new model for the use of all his retainers. Accepting the order of the prince, I began to go to riding and fencing schools at the eleventh year of my age. I did not enjoy the horseback riding so much as I did the sword-exercise. Horses were not well trained ; some of them were just ugly as can be, and I was often carried on their backs instead of riding upon them.

"At the age of fourteen I gave up these exercises and devoted myself closely to the study of the Chinese classics. Just about this time my prince invited a native scholar [Dr. Sugita], who was well versed in

Dutch, to his court, to teach his subjects that strange language. He selected only three youths out of his subjects to take lessons from him. I was one of the three chosen by him and the youngest of all. I studied Dutch with him nearly one year. His scholarship was soon made known to the Shogun's government, and he was appointed to go to Nagasaki to receive instruction from the Hollanders in engineering and navigation. After he went away I gradually lost my interest in studying Dutch, and suspended it temporarily. In the meanwhile I made considerable progress in Chinese. On that account, as a special favor, I was promoted by my prince to be an assistant teacher in his Chinese school, and became more interested in studying that language. At that time the prince became seriously ill and died. It caused me a great disappointment and sorrow. His younger brother succeeded him and became our prince. But he was far inferior to his deceased brother in every respect. He cared nothing for improving the condition of his retainers. All the affairs of the prince's court assumed a different aspect. He found his enjoyment chiefly in eating and drinking. He often listened to his favorite mistress for promoting or rejecting his officers. I felt then all my hope for carrying out my study was gone. However, I was not idle in securing my purpose, and endeavored to keep up my study as much as I could. My father became doubtful whether it would be wise to pursue my study any further. He was afraid of my being influenced by those mannerless and careless fellows he often found among our students. Beside that, he was still cherishing a hope that I should become his successor in the penmanship school. So he began to interfere with my study and to urge me to assist him in teaching the penmanship. But I was very unwilling to do so.

"In those days it was almost next to an impossibility for a son to disobey his father's command. So I was bound to obey him. The only hope I had for obtaining my aim was to secure some favor from my Chinese teacher, and also from that gentleman in Annaka whom I have previously mentioned. While I was seriously contemplating on the subject, those friends were taken away from me by death, one after another, within a few months. How disheartened I was then! I often exclaimed within myself: ' My prince is gone, and my teacher also. The friend at Annaka, on whom I hung the last cord of my hope, is also taken away from me. What unfortunate fellow I must be! Who will help me to continue my study? What will be my fate in future?' I felt I was left almost alone and helpless in the world.

"When I completed my fifteenth year I was obliged to commence my service to the prince. It was my duty to sit in the little office connected with the front entrance hall of his palace. There were always more than half a dozen persons in the office. Our business was to watch the hall, and whenever the prince went out or came home we were all obliged to sit on one side of the hall in a row and bow ourselves profoundly before him upon the matted floor. Beside that, we used to keep some records for him. But our chief occupation was to spend our time in silly gossip, talking, laughing, and frequent tea-drinkings. I found it almost unbearable to keep company with them. Yet there was no way for me to excuse myself from its participation. Furthermore, I was much prevented by them from studying in the office. Early in the spring of my seventeenth year, my prince was ordered by the Shogun to go to Ōsaka to keep watch of that great castle built by our renowned hero Hideyoshi, who conquered and governed the whole empire of Japan about three centuries ago. Of course the prince took with him a number of his retainers. My father was one of them. He followed the prince as his scribe, and left his school in my charge. I was also ordered by the prince to be a scribe in his court at Yedo during his absence. While I was so much pressed by a double duty, both at home and in the prince's court, a fresh desire for knowing the European nations came to me, and I found it almost irresistible. Dutch was then the only European language we could study. I found a good teacher in that language within a mile from my home. I used to go there whenever I could spare a little time, although I was much tied up to many duties. But when I became intensely interested in the new study, I began to neglect my duties, so inexcusably imposed upon me by my prince and my father. I often absented myself from the office, although I was required to be there. I did this purposely, because I wished to be discharged from my service on account of my disregarding the prince's order. But as there was no one to take my place there, I was still kept in the office. My frequent absences gave the superior officer, who kept the prince's palace during his absence, great inconvenience. He found much writing to be done, but on coming to the office he did not find me there, and often scolded me. But I did not mind it. I simply requested him to discharge me from the service at once. Finding me beyond his control, he often summoned my grandfather to his office and scolded him also. So my grandfather began to meddle with my study. But I remained as obstinate as ever, and kept up my study even in this trying way. When my father returned he resumed his service, and I was released. Still I could not get rid of the service of the prince altogether.

"Just about that time the country was in fearful commotion. Assassination and bloodshed occurred here and there almost every day. Being frightened by this, my eoward prince selected a number of the younger persons from his retainers to be his lifeguards. Unfortunately, I was chosen to be one of them. Whenever he went out of his palace I was obliged to follow him. Early in the spring of my eighteenth year I followed him as far as Annaka. Of course he was carried in a *kago*, and we, his lifeguards, were obliged to follow him on foot. It required in me no small amount of patience to be forced into such a servitude. When I came home from Annaka I was utterly disgusted with the prince's service. I often planned to run away from home in order to get rid of it, but I was not bold enough to do so. I was too fondly tied up to my home, and was much afraid of causing great sorrow and disgrace to my parents and grandfather. While I was in this hard fix I was not discouraged with the hopeless outlook, and attempted to secure a favor from one of the prince's elder men. Through his influence I was partially exempted from the prince's service. How glad I was then when I found more leisure hours to study. At that time I had just acquired Dutch enough to read a simple treatise on physics and astronomy. But I was utterly ignorant of mathematics, and the simplest calculations in this treatise were beyond my comprehension. So I was prompted to go to the Shogun's naval school just established in Yedo, and take lessons in arithmetic from its very rudiments. I believe it was then the only school in the country where I could find efficient teachers in mathematics. There I had chances to hear from my teachers of the foreign steamers, and sometimes I wished to see them. One day I happened to walk on the shore of Yedo Bay and caught a sight of the Dutch warships lying at anchor.—They looked so stately and formidable! When I compared those dignified sea-queens side by side with our clumsy and disproportioned junks, nothing further was needed to convince me that the foreigners who built such war-ships must be more intelligent and a superior people to the Japanese. It seemed to me a mighty object lesson to rouse up my ambition to cry out for the general improvement and renovation of my country. I supposed the first thing to be done would be to create a naval force, and also to build vessels of the foreign style to facilitate the foreign commerce. This new idea prompted me to pursue the study of navigation.

" In a course of two years' hard work I finished my arithmetic, algebra, and geometry, and also acquired the rudiments of theoretical navigation ; but my study was sadly interrupted by severe measles. My illness was a very serious one, and utterly enfeebled me. I was obliged to stay away from my school nearly three months. While I was yet feeble I began to study algebra in a Dutch book, and got through with it before I found myself strong enough to go out of doors. But this apparent little gain caused me great loss. Weak eyes, headaches, and sleeplessness came upon me one after another, and I was obliged to give up my studies for some time.

"In the winter of the same year I had the first opportunity to take a voyage on a steamer to Tamashima, a seaport a little beyond Okayama. The schooner belonged to the prince of Matsuyama, who was closely related to my prince. On that account he gave me a free passage. It took us a little over three months to come back to Yedo. I enjoyed it exceedingly, and was also benefited by staying away so far from my prince's square inclosure where I spent all my younger days, and where I supposed that the heavens were but a little square patch. It was my first experience in mingling with different people and seeing different places. Evidently the sphere of my mental horizon was much widened by that voyage. I visited the city of Osaka, where I had my first opportunity to taste beef. Being filled by a fresh idea for freedom, I planned to get rid of my obligation to my prince by connecting myself with the Shogun's government. The way to secure it was to be employed by him as a navigator, but that plan was soon banished from my thought when I found out something of the life of those employed in the Shogun's navy. Their base and licentious life shocked me. I did not like to mingle with them. So I found no way to sever myself from my prince. Still my strong desire to obtain freedom became a real incentive to disregard and disobey him. I refused his order decidedly when I was compelled to take up a musket and prepare myself to be his soldier.

"The war-cloud was then becoming intensely thick in the country. My prince was obliged to stand up for the cause of the unfortunate Shogun against the rising imperial party. As for me, I had full sympathy with the latter party, and often wished to join them.

Yet a tender cord which bound me to my parents and grandfather tied me also to their prince. This was to me another severe trial. I became extremely nervous and irritable, and I might have been utterly ruined if I had not found a consoling friend to rescue me from this trouble. He often invited me to his house to study Dutch with him, and as he was farther advanced in the study he was a great help to me. He lent me a number of books to read, and among them I found a Japanese translation of the story of Robinson Crusoe. It created in me a desire to visit foreign lands. Being pleased with it, I showed it to my grandfather and urged him to read it. When he read it through, he gave me a solemn warning, saying, 'Young man, don't read such a book; I fear it will mislead you.' At that time I received permission from my prince to go to a private school, and stayed there a part of the time when he did not require my service. Some time afterwards my friend lent me a number of Chinese books. One of them was a historical geography of the United States written by the Rev. Dr. Bridgman of the North China mission. Another was a brief History of the world written by an English missionary in China. Another was Dr. Williamson's little magazine; and what excited most my curiosity were a few Christian books, published either at Shanghai or Hongkong. I read them with close attention. I was partly a skeptic, and partly struck with reverential awe. I became acquainted with the name of the Creator through those Dutch books I studied before, but it never came home so dear to my heart as when I read the simple story of God's creation of the universe on those pages of a brief Chinese Bible History. I found out that the world we live upon was created by his unseen hand, and not by a mere chance. I discovered in the same History his other name was the 'Heavenly Father,' which created in me more reverence towards Him, because I thought He was more to me than a mere Creator of the world. All these books helped me to behold a being somewhat dimly yet in my mental eye, who was so blindly concealed from me during the first two decades of my life.

"Not being able to see any foreign missionaries then, I could not obtain any explanations on many points, and I wished at once to visit a land where the gospel is freely taught, and from whence teachers of God's words were sent out. Having recognized God as my Heavenly Father, I felt I was no longer inseparably bound to my parents. I discovered for the first time that the doctrines of Confucius on the filial relation were too narrow and fallacious. I said then : 'I am no more my parents', but my God's.' A strong cord which had held me strongly to my father's home was broken asunder at that moment. I felt then that I must take my own course. I must serve my Heavenly Father more than my earthly parents. This new idea gave me courage to make a decision to forsake my prince, and also to leave my home and my country temporarily.

"While I was walking on the streets of Yedo one morning, I met quite unexpectedly a friend whose acquaintance I formed during my voyage to Tamashima. He informed me that the prince's schooner was going to leave Yedo for Hakodate within three days. Knowing that I was still interested in navigation, he asked me whether I would take a short voyage to Hakodate with her. Possibly it was a mere compli-

mentary question on his part, but to me it was a question
of no small interest. He went off on his way quickly,
and I my own, without saying anything definite on
the subject. But soon after the separation a thought
flashed on me like lightning, that I must not miss this
opportunity for going to Hakodate, and from thence
attempt an escape to a foreign land. Then the question was how to avail myself of this opportunity. I
knew almost too well that my prince would not give
me permission to go so far as Hakodate. I thought
then the most feasible way to execute my object would
be to secure the favor of the Prince Matsuyama, the
owner of the schooner, before I said anything either
to my prince or to my parents. Without coming
home I went directly to a confidential counselor of
the prince to ask him to secure the prince's favor for
me, to give me a free passage to Hakodate in his vessel. He was much pleased to see me, as I was previously acquainted with him, and presented the case at
once to his prince in my behalf. The matter was arranged with the prince that he should hire me to be
employed in his vessel on her passage to Hakodate,
and should ask my prince's leave that I might go.
The prince complied with all my requests with great
pleasure, and sent a messenger to my prince to obtain leave for me from his service. The messenger
was particularly instructed by him to obtain a favorable reply without the least delay. Of course my
prince could not refuse this special request of Prince
Matsuyama, and gave a favorable answer to the messenger at once. This settled my case fairly, and no
one could prevent my departure for Hakodate.

" When the news reached my father he was utterly
confounded ; and although he was quite unwilling to

let me go, he could not change the order of the prince. It surprised every one of my neighbors and acquaintances. There was no time to be lost for my preparation; but, through the great diligence of my mother and my sisters, I was quite well equipped to start at once. Two days after the matter was decided that I must depart from home, my grandfather provided a generous dinner, and invited our neighbors and friends to partake of it with us. When we were all seated in a circle in our parlor, having one of those low dinner-tables before each one, and were ready to commence eating, he passed around a cup of cold water for us to sip from, after the manner of our solemn departing ceremony, generally performed when we expect no fair chance of seeing each other again. What a trying hour it was to my inexperienced heart! for every one who was present wept, and none raised up their faces except myself and my grandfather. He skillfully concealed his tears and appeared unusually cheerful; and I kept myself very brave. When the dinner was over my grandfather said to me : ‘My dear child, your future will be like seeking a pleasure on a mountain of full blossoms. Go your way without a least fear.’ This unexpected parting from his lips gave me a full courage to start from home like a man. Then I bowed to him, to my parents, my sisters, and all who were invited there, and left my dear home which I did not expect to see again before I should see the wide world.

“My younger brother followed me on the street of Yedo to a considerable distance. When I looked back to speak to him I found him sadly weeping. Then said I : ‘Why do you weep, my brother? You are like a girl. You had better go home from here.’

So I sent him back, giving him my parting instruction to be ever diligent in his study. (This was my last sight of my brother. He died in the year 1871, three years before I returned to my home.) Early the following morning we sailed out of Yedo bay, leaving that great city beyond the horizon, glancing now and then at the snow-capped, beautiful Fusiyam. in the distance. We stopped here and there on the way to Hakodate for the merchandise of the prince. At the entrance of our harbor we might have experienced a sad shipwreck, being helplessly carried by the strong tide against a reef, if we had not received kindly help from the shore to tow us out of danger. It was in the early part of the spring of 1864 when we left Yedo, and within a month we reached Hakodate in safety. Here I was planning to get access to some foreigners, that through their favor I might attempt an escape. Through a friend of mine I was introduced to Père Nicholi, a Russian priest, to be his teacher of the Japanese language, so that through his influence I might attain my object.

" Being far away from home, I became more careful in my observations ; what struck me most was the corrupt condition of the people. I thought then a mere material progress will prove itself useless r long as their morals are in such a deplorable sta Japan needs a moral reformation more than mere material progress, and my purpose was more strengthened to visit a foreign land.

" After my being with the Russian priest nearly a month at his house, I gradually introduced to him my secret object, and asked his assistance to carry it out. I told him then what Japan needs most is moral reformation, and so far as I am convinced the reformation must be brought through Christianity. He was much pleased with my talk, but warned me against such a project as I had revealed to him. He urged me to stay with him, and told me he would be glad to give me lessons on the Bible as well as ir English. Being discouraged with his warning, I begar to seek some friends in the foreign concession. The very first friend I found there was a Japanese clerk employed by an English merchant, who showed me a strangely kind attention at a brief interview. I liked him very much and asked him the favor to be received at his office quite often. He told me he would welcome me at any time when he was free from business, and, furthermore, he agreed to teach me English. But after a few interviews with him I revealed to him my long-cherished plan. He was much pleased with it and promised me he would keep it in mind. Having an intense desire to carry out my project, I assumed the costume of the common citizen, and tried to keep myself unnoticed when I went out on the street at Hakodate. I laid aside my long sword, which was then regarded as a mark of the samurai class. I also dressed my hair more simply. It was not more than a week after my confidential conversation with him, when he told me I might equip myself at once for leaving the country. An American captain had given him a consent to take me as far as China. It was his plan that, if I got away as far as China, there might be a better opportunity for me to find a passage to the United States. How glad I was then when I was informed of this fair chance of my seeking something in an unknown land beyond the sea!

"Just at that time Père Nicholi was absent from

his house for his summer vacation, and had left it entirely to my charge. Having stayed there nearly two months, I had formed a number of acquaintances, some of whom were high officers of the local government, but to only a few of them did I reveal my plans. When I was almost ready to embark in an American vessel, I made a pretense of being called back to my home, lest my sudden disappearance from Hakodate might rouse suspicion in some of the officers that I was to take refuge in a foreign vessel, and a government ship would be sent to chase after me. At this time any one attempting to leave the country without permission of the government, if retaken, suffered death penalty.

"While I was making a hasty preparation I found a little spare hour to get my photograph taken by a Russian artist, to be sent to my parents with my farewell letter. Thereby I gave them notice of my departure for a far-off land, having America in view.[1]

"At the appointed hour I called on my Japanese friend at the foreign concession, who agreed to take me over to the American vessel, which was ready to sail on the following morning for Shanghai. He was there waiting for me, and gave me a warm welcome. He made some hot lemonade for us to drink before we started together on that midnight adventure, and told me I must not be nervous about my hazardous risk. But to my remembrance I was not nervous at all. Before I reached his place I heard a dog barking in the distance, and perceived at once that my Japanese

---

[1] This letter was not delivered, lest the friend to whose care it was committed, and the father also, might be subjected to severe punishment by the government; and three years elapsed before the father of Neesima heard from his son.

shoes attracted the attention of the animal ; so I took them off on the spot, in order to detect how far or in what direction that barking creature might be. When I told my friend where I had left my shoes, he rushed out in his bare feet and brought them back to me. Then we went down together to a wharf where he had ready a small boat. While we were standing on the wharf we heard somebody coming, so I hurried to the boat and laid flat down on the bottom, to make an appearance that I was one of the bundles that contained a few articles of my own. It proved to be a watchman, and the chance was he would catch both of us. But, providentially, he was a coward, and dared not approach close enough to detect us. He only saw my friend on the wharf about to untie the boat, and asked him in a trembling voice, 'Who is here?' 'It is I,' replied my friend calmly, and said further that he had necessary business with the captain of an American vessel which could not be delayed until to-morrow. My friend was well known to the watchman, who recognized him at once, and his brief explanation, spoken in such a quiet and confidential manner, was quite enough to be a passport to let him off from the wharf even in a midnight hour. As we rowed away we saw the thousands of lights on the shore. The people were celebrating a festival of one of their heathen gods. As the American vessel was lying quite far from the shore, it required in us considerable effort to reach it. The captain was waiting for us, and we were taken on board the Berlin without the least delay. Giving me a warm grip of hand, my friend bade me farewell and rowed to the shore alone, and I was taken to a store-room of the cabin and locked up. I went to sleep at once, and had a splendid night, being aroused by the brisk steps of sailors overhead in the morning. I heard also some Japanese talking with the captain in the cabin, — customhouse officers, come on board to examine the vessel before she left the harbor. It was useless for me to rise, because I was locked up in my room; so I remained quietly waiting for the captain's summons.

"At that moment all the past events of my life came to my recollection. What troubled me most was my filial affection to my parents and grandfather, so touchingly roused up then. However, it was too late for me to look back, and I was glad for my success so far. It was no small undertaking for me to start a new life who had no experience in hardships, and to launch myself into the almost boundless ocean to seek something to satisfy my unquenchable appetite. What kept up my courage was an idea that the unseen hand would not fail to guide me. I had also an idea of risking my life for a new adventure, and said within myself: if I fail in my attempt altogether, it may be no least loss for my country; but if I am permitted to come home after my long exile to yet unknown lands, I may render some service to my dear country.

"Toward noon the captain unlocked my door and called me up on deck. Then the vessel was quite far off from the harbor, and that beautiful city Hakodate was almost sunk beyond the horizon. We were sailing along the coast, and the blue mountains were more or less within our sight for twelve days. When we came to leave the blue peaks of those mountain islands beyond the expansive horizon, I climbed up into the rigging to catch their last sight. I felt then somewhat sensitive, but some thoughts of the future gave me fresh courage, and I looked forward to China instead of looking homeward. Three days after I lost sight of our mountain island our vessel was towed up to Shanghai by a small tugboat.

"Here I must mention my experience on the voyage. As I was unable to pay my passage, I agreed with the captain to work for it. So I commenced my service in the cabin. Alas! I could not speak a single word in English. So the captain was kind enough to teach me the names of the objects found in the cabin. It was a regular object lesson. He pointed out an object, speaking its name distinctly that I might catch it. There was one passenger on board. I know not whether he was an American or an Englishman. He also taught me English. Sometimes he treated me very kindly, and sometimes very roughly. I was once beaten by him because I did not understand what he ordered me to do. Then I was terribly enraged, and rushed down to my room for my Japanese sword to revenge myself. When I caught my sword and was about to dash out of the room, a thought came to me at once that I must take a serious consideration before I should take such an action. So I sat down on my bed and said within myself: This may be a mere trifling matter; I may possibly meet still harder trials hereafter. If I cannot bear this now, how can I expect to meet a serious one? I felt quite ashamed of my impatience, and resolved that I should never resort to my sword for any causes.

"Another event took place on the voyage to China. When I had emptied a dish tub, after washing dishes, I carelessly threw a tablespoon overboard. The Chinese steward frightened me by saying, 'The captain will beat you.' I thought it might be a costly silver spoon. Then I took out all the Japanese money I had, went to the cabin, and confessed to the captain by making motions with my hands and shoulders, begging him to take the money for the lost spoon. To my great surprise he smiled at me and refused to take it from me. And here I must not fail to mention the name of the captain who so kindly offered to take me to China at the risk of losing his vessel, viz. : Captain William T. Savory, a citizen of Salem, Mass. At Shanghai I was transferred to another American ship called Wild Rover, commanded by Captain Horace S. Taylor, a native of Chatham, Mass. As Captain Savory was obliged to go back to Japan in the same vessel, he requested Captain Taylor to take charge of me.

"A few days after I came to the ship Wild Rover I presented my long sword to the captain, requesting him to take me to the United States, and I agreed to work out my passage without pay. So I began to work in his cabin. Not being able to call me by my Japanese name, the captain gave me a 'new name,' Joe. Hence my American parents called me Joseph. The ship remained in Shanghai until the first part of September, then sailed to Foochoo for lumber, to be brought to the former port again. Then she went to Hongkong, and from there to Saigon, where she took a cargo of rice for Hongkong. While there I wanted to buy a copy of the Chinese New Testament, but found that my Japanese money would not pass there. So I requested the captain to buy my small sword for eight dollars. Some time after I obtained that money, the captain gave me permission to go on shore with the Chinese steward to get a sight of the city. Then I had a fine chance to purchase a copy of the New Testament in a Chinese bookstore. Soon after the ship unloaded she sailed for Manilla to get a full cargo of hemp for the homeward voyage. When we were ready to sail out from the harbor of Manilla there was a report that an English steamer was lying in wait for American vessels at the entrance of the harbor. We had no idea that the civil war in the United States was over then, and the captain feared that English boat might do some mischief to the ship. He busied himself on deck with his spyglass, and the mates were hurrying down to the magazine to take out powder and balls to be used for self-defense. However, we sailed forward towards the suspicious ship and passed her without the least disturbance. It was the first of April, 1865, when we left Manilla, and it took us just four months to reach Boston. We did not stop on the way, as we had plenty of provisions and water.

"During the voyage my business was to wait upon the captain at his meals, to keep the cabin in order, etc. I often pulled ropes when I was free from the captain's service. The most enjoyable part of the voyage was my daily calculation of the ship's position with the captain. He was extremely kind to me, and treated me as if I were one of his own brothers. He never spoke any cross words to me. Every one on board treated me pleasantly. I often wished to go to the forecastle to see the sailors, but I was not allowed to do so. The captain warned me to keep far from them. We enjoyed fine weather and fair winds throughout the voyage, with the exception of one or two rough storms. When just off the Cape of Good Hope we saw a waterspout; it was the finest sight I ever saw. Then we caught the trade winds, and sailed daily thirteen miles an hour on an average.

" When we came near Cape Cod we were informed by a fisherman that the civil war was ended, and President Lincoln assassinated. As we slowly entered the harbor of Boston, and saw the beautiful, busy city, with the gilt dome within a short distance, the captain ordered the crew to let go the anchor. Down it went, and all on board rejoiced that the voyage was ended.

" But to me it was more than mere rejoicing, for I found soon afterward that the end of the voyage was going to be my happy destiny. Through the kindness of the captain I was introduced to the owner of the ship and his wife. They became at once my fostering parents, in the land of my adoption, through whose untiring care, wise guidance, and constant prayers, I was permitted to realize some dreams I used to dream at home so often and so vaguely in my younger days."

To these " younger days " Neesima often referred in his journals of later years. Of his mother he says : —

" She was a very kind-hearted woman, always ready to help her neighbors along, though she found so much to do in her own family. . . . One day she was sick in bed. I was very anxious for her, and wished to procure some remedy, though she had something from the doctor. So I went to the temple and prayed to the god that he would cure my mother. I bought a little bit of cake, which was a portion of the morning offering, and gave it to her for a remedy, hoping earnestly that it might do some good to her. I knew not, indeed, whether nature cured her, or whether her will or faith in the god made her whole, but she became better soon after she received that cake. She truly believed that the god had granted my earnest request for her and restored her health so soon. I had done the same thing for my neighbors, and was often successful in curing them."

Of his grandfather, for whom he entertained the warmest love, he says : —

"He performed his duty faithfully as steward for forty years. He often entreated the prince to dismiss him from office because, being well stricken with years, he found its duties rather tedious. After several entreaties he was permitted to retire with honor and a pension, when seventy-eight years of age, just one year before my leaving home. He took especial pains to instruct me, and in the evening took me on his lap and told me stories of heroes and good men who lived long ago. He instructed me to obey my parents, to be kind to my friends, to keep my tongue quiet, to be humble, not to steal, nor lie, nor flatter. He loved me very deeply, very intensely, and very affectionately. Oh, I could not forget what he did for me."

Of himself he writes : —

" I was obedient to my parents, and, as they early taught me to do, served gods made by hand with great reverence. I strictly observed the days of my ancestors and departed friends, and went to the graveyards to worship their spirits. I often rose up early in the morning, went to a temple which was at least three and a half miles from home, where I worshiped the gods, and returned promptly, reaching home before breakfast. I did that not only because I expected some blessing from the god, but that I might receive praise from my parents and neighbors. . . . When Commodore Perry came to Yedo Bay and forced us to open the port to the American people, we desired very strongly to expel him from the coast, though we had not any means to do so. We had been sleeping in peace over three hundred years, and had reached the lowest degree of effeminacy. Our swords began to rust in their sheaths. We sent them to the factories to be repaired for use. Gunsmiths who had been poor for so long for want of business suddenly began to clothe themselves in soft garments, while theatre men, who lived by the mercy of the fashionable people, were deprived of their luxury. Every-one who had the privilege of wearing swords began to devote himself to sword exercise, drilling, and horse riding. Although I was then quite young, yet I desired to be a brave soldier, or a man of honor, like those whom I found so often in our ancient history. I frequently went to the temple of the god of war, prayed sincerely that he should give me strength, and often performed very foolish ceremonies for his service. Once, when I was reading a life of a Chinese hero, I came across a famous phrase which he proclaimed when he quitted the sword-exercise : ' A sword is only designed to slay a single man, but I am going to learn to kill ten thousand enemies.' That is, he was inclining to study some work of stratagem. Though I was not able to measure my own quality, yet I desired to follow his example, and wished to kill many thousands of enemies, not by a sword, but by stratagem. This thought helped me to quit sword-exercise and to confine myself entirely to study. I studied very diligently, and often went to bed after cock-crow. I hated the western nations because they were foreigners, and disliked at first to study the language, which seemed to me so curious and strange. My prince was very kind to me . . . but providence did not spare his life. He died by a disease of the throat when I was sixteen years of age. It caused me a great sorrow, and destroyed entirely my dawning hope to study. When his younger brother took his place, he changed most everything which his departed brother had established. The school was entirely neglected, and many scholars left it because the prince expressed his hatred towards them instead of encouraging them. He chose the most ignorant and foolish persons among his people for his cup-bearers, and discharged all the best men whom his brother had employed. He appointed me an assistant of his secretary, and kept me busy like a slave. Besides the secretaryship on one hand, I had forty or fifty little pupils on the other, and could scarcely find a time to study Chinese. It was a very trying work indeed to teach such young playful pupils. When I treated them too gently they began to think I was too easy, and did not study very hard; and when I whipped them they became more obstinate, and some of them kept crying a long while and did not study at all. I was very much disgusted in teaching them, because my heart was not in it, but on study. I frequently thought that I should run away from home and go to a place where I might further my knowledge. I could not keep down my rambling thoughts, and often desired to perform that plan."

Neesima's diary prior to his arrival in Boston, and the notebooks written while pursuing his studies at home, are exceedingly interesting. On the long voyage from Hakodate to Boston he filled several books with his attempts at English composition. Everything was new to this boy, whose world had hitherto been the "square inclosure" of his prince. Every mechanical contrivance about the ship, the capstan, force pump, pulley tackle, steering-gear, etc., was accurately delineated in perspective, and to these drawings was added a detailed explanation of the principles involved and the uses subserved. Under the picture of a windlass occurs the first sentence in English: "I will write the figure of everything in this ship if my eyes does get better." The Japanese junk in which he made the voyage to Takashima, and afterwards to Hakodate, touched at several ports along the coast, either for trading purposes, to make surveys, or to seek shelter. His journal describes these ports minutely, and contains maps of their harbors, the names of their governors, the condition of the castle defenses, a history of the outlying provinces, with statistics of their products, exports, taxes, and population, as also his own personal observations on the moral condition of the people. He keenly regrets the prevalence of drunkenness and prostitution, and the conviction that no merely material progress would be sufficient to secure his country's prosperity sharpens his hunger for Christianity. At Hakodate he went daily to the Russian hospital for the treatment of his eyes, and records his surprise on finding that the poor were received and cared for without money and without price.

It appears from his own statement that he was, from a Japanese point of view, well educated. His knowledge of the Chinese classics was extensive; he was an expert penman and a natural artist. Before leaving Hakodate he had mastered in Dutch the elements of arithmetic, algebra, geometry, and navigation, and acquired the rudiments of physics and astronomy. His notebooks on the former subjects are almost treatises. He rewrites in his own language every demonstration, and solves innumerable problems and exercises. At every page one is impressed by the earnestness and persistence with which this young mind pursues its quest of truth and knowledge in spite of ridicule, blows, and bodily infirmity. Here, too, is the record of the struggle with parental obedience, of the fears of failure and disgrace. From every easy avenue open to ambition and advancement he turned aside. From the strong influences of the religious and social systems in which he had been reared he broke away, because they failed to satisfy him. His eye was fixed upon no narrow horizon of personal advantage. With a far-sightedness which is marvelous in one so young and inexperienced, he discerned dimly the true source of future good for his native land, and following steadfastly the light of that conviction went steadily on his own way, the true patriot, braving the death which would have been the only welcome home in the event of failure.

CHAPTER II.

SCHOOL AND COLLEGE DAYS.

Having decided, not without some hesitation, to undertake Neesima's education, Mr. and Mrs. Hardy accompanied him to Andover, Mass., late in September, 1865. Plans for his future study were necessarily vague, but the mastery of English was clearly indispensable to all progress, and he was therefore placed in the English department of Phillips Academy. Fearing that as a foreigner he might be subjected to annoyance, Mr. Hardy consulted Dr. Samuel H. Taylor, the principal of the academy, with reference to his location in some private family, and was recommended to Mr. and Miss Hidden, who lived in a pleasant house on a small farm in the outskirts of the village. Mr. Hardy called at once upon Miss Hidden, who received his proposition with surprise. Her brother was in delicate health, they lived quietly without servants, had never taken boarders, and could not for a moment entertain the idea of receiving a Japanese unaccustomed to American ways of living and unable to speak the English language. Neesima's manuscript account of the circumstances under which he left Japan was, however, left with Miss Hidden. As before, this simple narrative opened the hearts of its readers, and on the following day Mr. Hardy was notified that the Hiddens would receive Neesima. One half of their large house was occupied by Mr.

Ephraim Flint, Jr., then completing his theological course in the seminary. Both Mr. Flint and his wife took the greatest interest in the young stranger, and gave much of their time to his instruction. This interest developed into a warm friendship, and in later years Neesima often visited Mr. Flint at Hinsdale, Mass., where he was settled, and where he died, much mourned and beloved.

Neesima remained in Andover until the fall of 1867, when he was sent to Amherst to take such studies as would best fit him for his future work. His time at Andover was devoted to English, natural science, and mathematics, and, on leaving the academy, Dr. Taylor writes of him: "What he has done he has done well." His eyes were not strong, and he was at this time under the care of a Boston oculist. Any bodily weakness alarmed him, and the struggle between the desire to improve his opportunities and the fear of jeopardizing by overwork his "great aim" is often recorded in his journal.

On the flyleaf of this journal he writes, on reaching Andover, the verse which of all others occurs most frequently in his private papers: "For God so loved the world, that he gave his only begotten Son, that whosoever believeth in him should not perish, but have everlasting life." "This verse," he said in later years, "is the sun among all the stars which shine upon the pages of God's holy word;" and the vital principle of religion was ever for him the conviction of the love of God for man. On the opposite page of the journal is found this prayer: —

"O Lord, Thou picked out me from darkness, forsaking my parents whom I did love, and bringeth me here, passing boundless ocean very safely, no hurri-

cane, no tempest,—but always fair wind.—O Lord,
Thou let me acknowledge thy holy Word every day,
and maketh me warm bed to lie down in, and prepar-
eth me nice table to eat enough. O Lord, no man
can do such goodness and mercy for me but Thou only.
O Lord, wash away my sins, take up my evil heart
and give me right spirit to understand and remember
thy holy Word; and let my eyes and ears be good to
see and hear thy holy Word more and more. O God,
wilt Thou help me to destroy many gods and idols?
Please destroy them with thy power and let me be
comforted. O Lord, I will never keep thy name in
vain, and I will try to obey thy commandments as I
can. I ask Thee for my helpers, teachers, parents,
and all brethren; keep out from them illness and
temptation. For thine is power and glory and kingdom forever. Amen."

FROM MARY E. HIDDEN TO MR. HARDY.

ANDOVER, January 2, 1866.

At my brother's request I reply to your note, which
was received in due time. Joseph was glad to get
some word from you, and has rather been looking for
you since the week after the term closed, not feeling
certain what disposition was to be made of him. I
gathered from what you said that his entering school
here was somewhat of an experiment. You doubtless
have been apprised of his efficiency through Dr. Taylor, but he has another teacher to whom he recites
every evening, and who speaks of him as going ahead
very fast. This is the gentleman who lives in the
other part of the house. Both he and his wife have,
from the first, taken great interest in this young Japanese, and seem to consider him a door of usefulness

opened them in their at present somewhat private life; and really the benefit he derives from Mr. Flint is far greater than from the teacher in the academy, though he needs contact with school life. We find Joseph a gentleman, and it is to our shame as a Christian community that we are not more in advance of this "heathen brought to our own door," as one has said.

When, by his own artless conversation we are led to see how he has resisted temptations thrown in his way, and shown himself an example of good report, we are led to feel that the hand of God is upon him, and that he may yet become a chosen vessel in the redemption of his people from darkness and idolatry to the glorious Gospel of the Blessed God.

He has been very busy through the vacation with his studies. We can hardly avoid giving him considerable attention, as something needs to be explained or corrected very often. He is very grateful for any favors shown him, and is ready to do any in return. He is very skillful with his China-brush, and I have suggested to him to send to you a specimen of his drawing. . . . He has a profound sense of gratitude for what you are doing for him, and seems only to wish to be *comfortable*. His aim appears to be the good of his people, and his health he feels to be an important consideration.

I have no fancy or desire to take boarders, and should not in this instance except for the peculiar circumstances. We have made him a regular member of the family; he sits with us all the time and shares all the privileges of the family. It is not often that we find one who can be received in this way without a feeling of intrusion, but he is an exception.

TO MR. HARDY.

ANDOVER, *January* 1, 1866.

I am very well and had a most comfortable New Year. O, I may say I never had such a comfortable New Year in my life, because I had enough of all things that I wanted without any trouble and labor. O dear Sir, I feel your kindness and goodness from the top of my head to the extreme of my feet, and I wish you to know that since I came here how happy I am, and how successful as follows: —

In the school I had recitations in arithmetic from decimal fractions until duodecimal, and I heard many scholars read or spell in English. O dear Sir, it seems to me I have found a kind and godly neighbor called Mr. Flint, who lives in Mr. Hidden's house. He teaches me every evening the arithmetic, and I have recited to him through reduction, signs, definitions, vulgar fractions, decimal fractions, addition, subtraction, multiplication, division, interest, and compound interest, until commission. A few days ago he gave me a small geography, and hears me recite about it; and lets me write some compositions, and corrects them for me; and Mrs. Flint explains to me the New Testament every evening, too. I have memorized Beatitudes, Lord's Prayer, golden rule, 22nd Chap. Math. 37th verse, 3d chap. St. John 16th verse, 1st and 23d Psalms, and Ten Commandments, and I have read in the New Testament until the 17th Chap. Luke; and I have read out from the Old Testament the escape of Israelites from Egypt; their stay in a wilderness, eating and dressing by God's miracle; Moses' death; Daniel in the lion's den; three wise men in the strongest fire; the strongest man Samson; the miracle for a widow and Naaman in the time of Elijah; and I have stopped in his room every evening to recite out these things.

Mr. Hidden and his sister take care about me very kindly, and I feel very comfortable, as if I had been in my father's home. I think all these things belong to the providence or mercy of God, and I must glorify, love, and obey Him. I hope and believe too He will bless you and your whole family. I would like to see you sometime.

TO MR. HARDY.

ANDOVER, *January* 20, 1866.

I am very well through God's mercy and your care. Dear Sir, I am not able how to explain my great thankfulness to you, but in my mind only. When I rest from my study I always remember God's mercy and your care, and give thanks to Him, and pray to Him for you, "Bless him who helps the poor for thy name's sake." Please tell me when your friend will go out from Boston to Yokohama. I hope to send letters to my father and my friend who lives in Hakodate to let them know of my present success. . . . .

TO THE JAPANESE FRIEND WHO AIDED HIM TO ESCAPE FROM HAKODATE.

ANDOVER, *February* 23, 1866.

I am very well through God's mercy since I commenced my hazardous adventure. When I called on Him who made heaven and earth and sea and all that in them is, my sorrow turned into joy and my misery changed to success. Oh, I may surely say that it is very wonderful and marvelous that such success has fallen on me. I passed through many thousand miles of water very safely, without hurricane, tempest, or any trouble. Also, a kind and religious man . . . hears me recite in arithmetic . . . and his wife explains to me the most holy and valuable book in the world, entitled the New Testament, and tells about one Saviour Jesus Christ, who was sent down from his father to enlighten the darkness and save sinners. In the Academy I am studying reading, spelling, English grammar, and arithmetic; also, I have a Bible lesson every Sabbath. All the teachers and scholars, and many who know about me, are interested in me and love me, and some give me things to please me. But these things they don't do for my sake, but for the Lord Jesus Christ. O dear friend, think you well who is Christ; the same is the light that shines in darkness. It is not the light that comes out from the sun, moon, stars, and candles; but this the true light that shines on the benighted and wicked world, and guides us unto the way of salvation. The light of candle is blown away, but this is the true light of eternal life and we can in no wise blow it out. And we may take this light through Jesus Christ. "For God so loved the world that he gave his only begotten Son, that whosoever believeth in him should not perish, but have everlasting life. For God sent not his son into the world to condemn the world, but that the world through him might believe." See John, 3d chapt. 16–17 verses, New Testament.

O dear friend, I have nothing to repay your kindness, but will send only "study the Bible," and my photograph. Please care for your health and study the book I have mentioned above. O alas! it is not the country's law to study the Bible and worship one tender and merciful Father who made us, loved us, and gave his only begotten Son through whom we may be saved. But the law ought to be broken because it is made by the Devil, the King of the world. The world was not made by the Devil, but by our true Father who gave unto us his true law.—O friend, whether then is right to hearken unto the Devil more than unto God, please judge you. If the fierce Devil persecute you for righteousness' sake, don't trouble yourself. I am sure your God will protect you from evil, and though your body should be killed, your soul would be received unto Him, and you would dwell in the brighter place with eternal life. I would like indeed to go there with you.

Your truly friend,

NEESIMA SHIMETA.

TO MRS. HARDY.

ANDOVER, *April 9, 1866.*

. . . I am very glad springtime has come and weather becomes warmer and pleasanter day by day, birds singing here and there, and grass becoming green on the wayside, fields, and hills. I hear farmers will sow seed in the ground pretty soon. I say myself, I must try to sow seed in my heart and mind, that I may bear fruit unto everlasting life. When I grow weary by study I take a walk for exercise. Now it is too warm to wear my overcoat, and the overcoat which you gave me for spring wear is very suitable for this season. I feel very happy for your charitable love. I have spent this vacation in reading, writing composition, drawing, and translating the Gospel of John in the Japanese language. Please accept these, in which I have written account of the Japanese religions, and care for your health, and give my regard to Mr. Hardy and your whole family.

TO MRS. HARDY.

ANDOVER, *July* 24, 1866.

So you (like the Samaritan) relieve me from the misery, and help me to get good education, therefore I will call you my neighbor. Nay, I will call you my mother whom God gives me. I pray to Him for you day and night that He may bless your family bountifully. He knows our hearts and desire If we ask Him faithfully, He will answer us with best thing. . . . O, be cheerful to help me (a poor boy, like a wingless bird). Our Father which art in Heaven will rejoice your charitable deed, and will reward to you with the best thing. . . . I am very glad I got through arithmetic in this term. I will take algebra and grammar in the next term. My eyes are not very well, but I expect they shall be strong if I stop my study little while and take much exercise in this vacation. This afternoon I must go to the exhibition of the Academy, therefore I have not much time to write many things to you. Please give my love to Mr. Hardy and tell him be very careful for this hot season.

TO MRS. HARDY.

ANDOVER, *September* 10, 1866.

. . . Mrs. Hidden's aunt, called Mrs. C——, commenced to be weak from the last spring and grew worse and worse. Now she is in the point between life and death. In the evening of the last Sunday I went in her chamber and waited on her a little while. Though her mind turned aside, she seemed to me more quiet than any rest time. I told her: "Mrs.

C——, I pray to God for your blessing and I believe He will answer my prayer. Won't you pray to Him? I think He will hear your prayer and bless you." Then she answered: "Joseph, I thank you for your kindness," bursting in tears; and she cried out quite loud, "O Lord, have compassion on me, and show me thy mercy through Jesus Christ." She cried twice in this manner. At that time Mrs. Hidden was down stairs. She heard then this crying, and thought very strangely, and came up to her chamber door and asked me: "What matter is it?" I told her she made prayer. She said: "Does she make prayer? I never heard her make prayer, nor noticed it in my life. I am very glad about it." Then she asked her: "Do you trust in Jesus?" She said: "Yes, live or die, I trust in Him." She is aged about three score and ten, but never said anything regard Jesus, nor made prayer; but from my single question in that Sabbath evening she turned her heart unto Him who takes sins away from the world. . . . I believe the Lord will hear her earnest prayer and guide her into everlasting habitation. . . .

TO MRS. HARDY.

ANDOVER, *October* 27, 1866.

. . . I am very well through the tender care of God. I enjoy very much my studies in this term. My eyes are quite well, so that I can study during the day, and in the night, least one hour and half or two. In the beginning of this term I took Romans for my evening study, and read through it a week ago. Mr. Flint interested me very much and explained it for me. Now I am reading first Corinthians. Last Friday Capt. Taylor's wife wrote a letter to me, and

told me he will sail to China again and he would like
to see me before his voyage.   Therefore I wanted to
see him very much.   But I thought within my heart
that I must spend some money for going up and coming back.   But in the Saturday morning Mrs. Flint
gave me a ticket, and Mr. Hidden presented to me
one dollar bill to spend it in Boston.   After our morning prayers in the Academy I went to Boston . . .
then I went to Charlestown to see Capt. Taylor.   He
was there on board the ship and seemed very glad to
see me.   Forenoon I stayed there with him, and it
was very pleasant to me to spend a few hours with my
old acquaintance.   Afterwards he took me to Boston
to get dinner, gave me his thin overcoat which is very
suitable for this season, and bought for me a very nice
hat, though I did not tell him about it.   After a quarter of five o'clock he came to the depot with me,
bought a ticket for me, and said good-by, bursting in
tears.   O Mrs. Hardy, is it not wonderful that the
providence of God has fallen on me, a poor Japanese,
so much?

Last Monday M—— told me my trunk had come.
Mrs. Hardy! when I opened the trunk I said within
my heart: "What shall I do to you?" because
you give me so many things as your own boy.   Not
these things only, but my education, hoping that I
might do great good to my native land.   I think,
though you help me so much, you hope no reward
from me, because you know I am poor.   Therefore I
may say surely that your heavenly reward shall be
increased.   Please remember the words of the Lord
Jesus how He said: "It is more blessed to give than
to receive." . . . Last Monday evening Mrs. C——
died.   I think she is sitting now by the right hand of

Jesus. A few weeks ago Mrs. Shedd asked to you about my joining the Seminary Church, and she wrote to Mrs. Flint that you are approved of it. If you and Mr. Hardy approve it, I shall join it the next communion. Now I believe Jesus Christ is the Son of God who died for our sins, and we shall be saved through Him. I love Jesus more than anything else. I cast whole self to Him and try to do right before His sight. This is my vow. I will go back to Japan and persevere to turn the people to Jesus from Devil. I determined myself to Jesus so fast that nothing can separate my love from Him. But my flesh is weaker than my spirit, therefore I wish to join church and to unite in Christ, that I may grow more Christlike and I may do great good to my nation for his name's sake. If you approve it, please give me answer in the next week. Please care for yourself and give my love to Mr. Hardy and all your family. I would like to see you sometime. . . .

TO MRS. HARDY.

ANDOVER, *December 25, 1866.*

It is the beautiful morning of Christmas. I feel very bright and happy, and I am thankful to Heavenly Father for his remarkable care on me from the time of my landing on Boston till now, as you know yourself surely. . . . The communion of the church in the Seminary will be observed in the next Sunday. I shall join to it in that time and shall be baptized in the name of Father, Son, and Holy Ghost. Perhaps you will be very busy on the last day of this week, therefore I dare not say: "Please come up here and spend the next Sabbath with me." But I should be very happy to have you and Mr. Hardy present at the communion season. . . .

TO MRS. HARDY.

ANDOVER, *May* 18, 1867.

Since I departed from you I wanted to write a few lines to ask how you are, but I was just as busy as bees with my studies. . . . After the class got through the study of natural philosophy they took botany for the remainder of the term. I hesitated to take it because I thought I could not spend my time for flowers. My teacher was in favor of it and told me it was a very fine study, just as useful as natural philosophy; so I was obliged to take it, and borrowed his book, because it costs so much. I did not like to get it without consulting you. It is very hard to remember names of flowers, but I enjoy very much, being encouraged to it by that God would not forsake me, because He cares for the minutest flower. I would like to have a book of my own. If you please, send your word by M—— and let me know if I may buy it or not. Also my teacher and Mr. Flint advised me to commence geometry. . . . The class in the Academy was too far advanced for me to enter it, so Mr. Flint offered to hear me recite half an hour each day. . . . I like to see the Japanese Commissionary, but I think better for me to hide myself from them, because I am runaway boy and the law-breaker of the government. . . .

TO MRS. HARDY.

NORTH CHATHAM, *August* 8, 1867.

I left Andover on the 25th July to visit my friends who live in North Chatham. When I came to Boston I met showers many times, but I carried my trunk from the Maine depot to the Old Colony depot in the interval of many showers. . . . I took my seat unfortunately in the back part of the car, not knowing future occurrences. When we came to Tremont the conductor called out the changing of the cars, but I was reading a book in which I was much interested, and the same time a pretty heavy shower passed us, so that I could not hear his calling. When I thought that I had come to an halfway place where I changed cars when I came to Chatham the last time, not knowing the cars changed some time ago I asked a gentleman how far is the place where I may change cars to go to Chatham. He said, "Chatham!" much surprised, and told me "you have the wrong train now. You cannot go to Chatham to-night because this will go to New Bedford." I told the conductor about it and showed him my ticket to Chatham. He was a very good and kind man. He said: "You cannot help it now, and you must go to the next station, New Bedford;" and he said also he would not charge me at all. I came to Fair Haven about 7 o'clock P. M. Between it and New Bedford there lies a large river. I crossed it by a ferryboat and arrived at the city of New Bedford safely.

I knew not anybody there at all, therefore I thought it would be a safe way to find the right kind of people. When I found a church I asked a gentleman about its denomination and its minister's name. He answered me very kindly: "It is an Orthodox church, and the minister's name is Mr. C——." I asked him about his residence. He showed me his house very plainly. When I went to his house and rang the bell, a young lady came to the door. I asked her to see Rev. Mr. C—— a moment. She took me to the beautiful parlor and gave me a chair, saying she would call out Mr. C—— pretty soon, and she asked me my name. I told her my name very plainly, but she could not get hold of my last name hardly, and went away understanding only that my name is Joseph. After a while Mr. C—— came to the parlor and shook my hand. Then I told him: "I am a stranger. My name is Joseph Neesima. I left Boston this afternoon at four o'clock to go to Chatham, but I took the wrong train, not knowing the cars changed at the station of Tremont, and I arrived in this city unexpectedly. Be so kind as to direct me to a house where I may pass the night with the least expense." He asked me: "Have you money enough to pay for your lodging?" I answered him: "Yes, Sir, I have, but I hope to pass the night with the least expense, because I did not expect at all to come to this city to-night." He thought I was a poor traveler and gave half of a dollar saying: "This may help you to a half of your lodging." I did not take it from him, saying: "No, thank you, Sir, I do not wish to take this from you, but I hope you will direct me to a safe place."

It was quite dark inside of his house, because it was a cloudy evening and it was after seven o'clock. He took me out of his house and told me he would take me to a Seaman's Home, because he thought I was a poor Spanish fishman, seeing my dark complexion and knowing that many Spanish people are coming in the city for the whale business. When I was in his house I could not distinguish his appearance hardly, but I saw him very well out of the door. He is about fifty-six or seven years of age, and his stature is about middle size. He has dark hairs, and some of them are turned to gray. His manner is very simple, yet his appearance is very graceful. He did not talk much, but spoke very distinctly and eloquently. He asked me where I came from. I answered: "I came from Japan." "How long ago?" "About two years ago." "Where do you reside?" "I reside in Andover." Then he said he knew some people there. I asked him whom he knew there, and he said he knew Deacon A——. I told him I knew him and I resided a very short distance from his house. He said he knew Prof. E. A. Park, and told me Prof. Park came to the city a few weeks ago to ordain some minister. He asked me what I did there. I answered: "I am a member of Phillips Academy." He asked me how I liked American customs. I— "I like them better than our heathenish customs."— He asked how I like the religion... "I like the true God better than gods of wood and stone." He asked how I came over to this country. I gave him a short account of my leaving Japan—and how Providence guided me wonderfully to this enlightened country. Then he said he would take me to a different place from that which he mentioned before. He came with me to a large and beautiful Hotel called *Parker House*, which I supposed the best hotel of the city, and he paid also for my lodging. When I saw him take out money from his pocketbook, I took my money quickly and paid back to him. But he would not take it from me, saying: "When I go to your country and am a stranger, then please show me your kindness," and went away quickly, bidding me good-night. He wrote his name on a paper which I found in my pocket — Rev. Wheelock Craig. I took a nice supper there and slept in a splendid room. . . . The next morning I took breakfast early. I came back to the same place where I missed the cars to the Cape, and arrived in Chatham little after 3 o'clock P. M., taking a coach seven miles from the centre of Harwich. I was received cordially by my old acquaintances here, and I was very glad to see them. Before I arrived at the city of New Bedford I prayed to the Lord that he would take care of me and guide me to a safe place. So he answered my prayers and guided me to such a kind and godly man to help to pass that night safely. Perhaps some people, who trust in their own wisdom and do not believe in the providence of God, would say that I was lucky at that time, not thinking of his providence at all. But I can say surely the Providence guided me to a safe place, because I believe nothing can occur without the Providence of God.

TO MRS. HARDY.

North Chatham, *August* 26, 1867.

. . . I was received by Capt. Taylor's father's family kindly and welcomely. They are all pleasant and social people and they treat me as their own family. I am thankful to God for his perpetual care to me. Though I had nothing with me when I left Japan, yet I do not suffer at all for the destitute of the daily necessity. *He* gave me you and others as friends to care me. Therefore I do prove this precious verse: "Be strong and of good courage, be not afraid, neither be thou dismayed; for the Lord God is with thee whithersoever thou goest." When I read this verse my grateful feeling towards Him caused me many streams of tears. . . . I do not read much this vacation, but I read the Book and a few pages of geography every day. I hope my eyes will grow strong enough to enter into new study in the next term. I love study dearly, so that I cannot leave it entirely. . . . Now we have quite number in the family. The sum of them is twelve. We went to the seashore yesterday and dug out one bushel of clams, and we shall go to woods to-morrow to get blackberries if it be fine weather. . . . Though I do not write to you very often, I do feel grateful for your kindness always, and mention you in my prayers daily for your prosperity in this world and future blessing in the another. . . . I have communicated very often to Japanese who are in Monson Academy. I think a youngest of them is a fine scholar, and I hope he will become a good instrument for the future civilization of the benighted Japan.

EXTRACTS FROM JOURNAL WRITTEN AT CHATHAM.

"I study Latin every forenoon, and exercise myself every afternoon in elocution, walking by the sea. In the evening I read the memoirs of Rev. Henry Martyn. It kindles my cold heart, and lowers my pride into humiliation. My faith and love to God and my fellow-men seemed me so faint that I could hardly perceive them. I am comforted by the words, 'Be of good cheer. Thy sins are forgiven thee.' While I was walking by the side of that boundless ocean I recalled also, 'Deep calleth unto deep,' and I said within myself that though my sins are deep they would by no means exhaust the deep of God's love. Then I thanked God that my face was turned neither back nor to the sides, but forward. Afterwards I found myself very foolish and ignorant, saying: 'How could I promote his kingdom to my heathen friends, seeing I am so foolish and ignorant?' It seemed me the Lord answered: 'I will be thy master and teach thee my way.' It is very strange that with such desire I find also evil powers in me very forcible.

"This is hottest day of the year. But in my walkings I do not suffer much heat because of love of nature.

"I was very weary this morning. Evil powers in my heart tempted me to stay at home, saying it would not be sin if you kept your heart right; you can read and praise and pray just well as in the church. I said, 'No, no.' Evil powers came in afternoon in like manner, saying, 'You are most too tired; you would not get much benefit because your head is drowsy.' I replied also, 'No, no, I will not miss the service unless I be too sick.'"

FROM MISS HIDDEN TO MRS. HARDY.

ANDOVER, *July* 11, 1867.

. . . It has occurred to me since breakfast that it would afford me some pleasure to write you a few lines in reference to Joseph in connection with the list of his needs which you requested him to make known to you from day to day. He is very modest about these things and has not the least disposition to take any advantage of your charity, but is often troubled that his present position brings necessities for which he is entirely dependent upon you. He has been made very comfortable through you during his residence in Andover, and I know you must feel rewarded in your own soul as you observe the improvement he has made in his studies and also in his general appearance. There is no question but that he has uncommon abilities, and what gives them their greatest brilliancy is that he evidently does all that God may be honored.

From the first I have felt that it was a privilege to have his influence thrown in my way. It has been a talisman oftentimes to check my forgetful heart, and for this reason even I am very sorry to have him leave us. In him we are brought to see how truly we are one in Christ, — the whole family of man. My dear Mrs. Hardy, I feel that as God in his providence has given you the means and the heart to take this heaven-directed wanderer into your charge, you have found a diamond of which the world is not worthy, of which you may well be proud, and that there will come into your soul a wealth of satisfaction which is its own reward.

Joseph will shine anywhere. I hope the change to Amherst will be advantageous to him. At first he felt that he was hardly fit for college, but he is willing to acquiesce in all your plans, feeling they are made in his best interest. . . . He is careful to a fault, and shrinks from asking for *necessary* things, not because of your unwillingness, but from his high-born nature and manly character. We are sorry to lose his influence from our midst. May God prosper him and you. . . .

FROM EPHRAIM FLINT, JR., TO MR. HARDY.

ANDOVER, *August* 29, 1867.

. . . Please accept the thanks of Mrs. Flint and myself for your very kind reference to our instructions of Joseph, and for what you are pleased to term "our kind and valuable interest in him." We expect no higher pleasure in any work this side of heaven than we have experienced in instructing and in attempting to guide Joseph in the ways of virtue and knowledge. Though I have taught for years, I have never been so interested in the mental and moral development of any other pupil. Our labor for him has been one of love. We have felt ourselves blessed in being able to give our efforts, our quenchless interest, and our prayers. We part from him with regret, but rejoice that Professor Seelye is to direct his course at Amherst. . . .

FROM EPHRAIM FLINT, JR., TO PROF. J. H. SEELYE.

ANDOVER, *August* 31, 1867.

At the request of Mr. Alpheus Hardy I write you a few lines in regard to the bearer, Joseph Neesima. He has boarded in the same house in which I live, ever since I came to Andover, twenty-two months ago. Although he has attended Phillips Academy, Mrs. Flint and myself have given him much instruction in reading in the Bible, spelling, English grammar, arithmetic, algebra, geometry, etc. Joseph has *mastered* arithmetic, algebra, and the first two books in geometry. He is a very fine mathematician and is very desirous to study trigonometry and surveying. I think he would gain a good knowledge of these two branches in two terms. He wishes also to study physiology and supplement his present knowledge of natural philosophy with chemistry. I think he would be delighted with the experiments in optics.

He hopes very much to study mental and moral philosophy under your instructions.

His eyes have been very weak ever since he came to Andover, and in my judgment it would not be wise for him to commence at present the study of Greek, on account of the peculiar trial to his eyes in the use of the lexicon. His necessary use of the English dictionary has been of more injury to his eyes than all his other use of them.

We have noticed Joseph's mental and moral development with intense interest and the greatest pleasure. During the first eight months after reaching Andover, notwithstanding his very little knowledge of English, he mastered the whole of arithmetic. His progress in other branches has been hardly less marked. He has been a most faithful and diligent student of the Bible, and has feasted his soul upon it. I have never known a person more absorbed in a novel than he in the Word of God. He has apprehended its meaning more readily than that of any other book. As the meaning of some new passage has flashed upon his mind his soul has been most profoundly moved.

He is a gentleman in his manners. I have never, in a single instance, known him to be rude. His sense of propriety is most acute, and is often most beautiful. He fully appreciates all that is done for him. His gratitude to his instructors and benefactors seems to know no limit. His religious progress has been remarkable. I think he was converted before he reached Andover. As soon as truth reached his mind he seemed to be all ready to embrace it. He does his duty faithfully, fearlessly. Without doubt he would go to the stake rather than deny his Master. I have reason to believe he is most faithful in his secret devotions. He loves the society of the most devoted Christians. He is modest and retiring and his true worth does not immediately appear, but he is one of the noblest of men, and is worthy the fullest confidence. His word is truth. He will study all he is able to study without injury. Any funds in his hands will be most frugally spent; he needs no watching. His progress in speaking English has hardly kept pace with his progress in mastering the structure of the language and his facility in writing it. He is inclined to take too little rather than too much exercise.

Although I have taught for years, I have never been so interested in any other pupil. I rejoice that you are to direct his education for a season. I shall hope to hear from him occasionally.

It is not strange that those interested in educational and missionary work should feel drawn towards this young Japanese, whose hunger for light and truth was so intense, and whose flight from country and home was so dramatic in its incidents. But it is remarkable that this interest should everywhere and always develop into warm personal friendship. Wherever he went he found a home, — at Amherst, in the house of Professor Seelye, where he passed much of his vacation time, and where in illness he was received and cared for as a son. He often refers with pride in his journal to the fact that during Professor Seelye's absence he sat at the head of the table and led the family devotions, and, when ill in March, 1870, writes: "Professor and Mrs. Seelye are just kind and tender to me as my own parents." His health in Amherst was generally good, although he was at times troubled with rheumatism and weak eyes; but he was unfailingly cheerful, and bent upon improving to the utmost every opportunity. In 1868–69, Japan was passing through the stormy period of change, and Neesima was at this time very anxious concerning his friends, from whom he had not heard for nearly a year. Apprehensive for their safety and moved by that love of family which is so striking a trait of Japanese character, it was with the greatest joy that he heard at last of their welfare and that his aged grandfather was still alive and well. He possessed the elasticity of temperament characteristic of his race, but his deep faith in God, to whom he committed both himself and his dear ones, alone enabled him to maintain the serenity of his purpose not to turn back in the path which he had chosen.

His course of study in Amherst College was a special one, for he had no previous knowledge of Greek or Latin. China had been his Greece and Rome. He here, however, began the study of Latin, and in return for instruction in Japanese given to his roommate, Mr. Wm. J. Holland, received from the latter instruction in Greek. In 1869, Mr. Holland became the head-master of the Amherst High School, and Neesima was thus enabled to continue under his guidance his Greek studies. Of the natural sciences, chemistry, physics, botany, mineralogy, and geology, he was especially fond, and he retained his interest in these branches throughout his life. Mr. Holland, who subsequently visited Japan as naturalist of the expedition sent out by the United States government to observe the total eclipse of the sun, was at that time devoted to scientific study, and in his company Neesima enjoyed many pleasant excursions to the environs of Amherst in search of mineralogical and botanical specimens. His note-books contain very accurate and complete abstracts of the lectures on physics and chemistry, with drawings of all the apparatus employed. These drawings were made during the lecture with a rapidity and facility which astonished his classmates.

It is well known that the Japanese mind does not turn naturally to speculative inquiry. Confucianism, as a code of ceremonial usage concerned with practical, political, and social duties, has impressed itself far more strongly upon the national life than Buddhism, whose overshadowing content of philosophy has failed to awaken the national sympathies. An earnest student of history, Neesima was comparatively uninterested in the metaphysical abstractions of western philosophy. He pursued the subjects of mental and moral science with that fidelity which characterized his every effort to fit himself to be a teacher of his people, but the practical and ethical side was ever more attractive to him than the speculative and controversial, and western literature and poetry occupied his thought far less than western science, history, and ethics. His mind was alert, his perceptions quick, and his rank as a student high; but, while his mental ability was conspicuous, it was his character and life which left the deepest impression upon his teachers and associates. "You cannot gild gold," was the testimonial of Professor Seelye, when his pupil was about to return to Japan. His room-mate during 1868–69 says: "He was the soul of neatness, and entered lovingly upon the self-imposed task of keeping our rooms in perfect order. This scrupulous neatness and cleanliness was the first trait which impressed itself upon my mind. He was also uniformly cheerful and of a remarkably studious spirit. Not less striking was his religious faith. The broad study-table which we used in common was divided by an imaginary line upon which his Bible was laid, and night and morning this loved book was faithfully and carefully perused. He possessed a keen sense of the humorous, and even at times essayed a witticism in the English language. After a Leyden jar has been discharged, a feeble secondary discharge may often be evoked, known as the

'residual discharge.' The 4th of July, 1869, had
been characterized by an unusual degree of patriotic
hilarity in our quiet college town. On the morning
of the 5th, as Neesima and I were repairing to breakfast, we encountered a small boy who rushed out and
exploded a fire-cracker. Turning to me with a smile,
Neesima said: 'I suppose, Holland, that is the residual discharge.' As long as I shall live I shall deem
it one of the great privileges of the last year I spent
in college that I was permitted to be associated with
this man, and one of the greatest honors of my life
that I was enabled in some degree to help him forward in his education and partially fit him for the
great work which he accomplished." Another class-
mate writes: "He was always at the class prayer-
meetings and frequently took part. His English was
broken then and his vocabulary small, but his heart
was big and full of love. Through every word and
act transparent shone the man, winning the respect
of all. It is this characteristic which has fitted him
to 'stand before kings.' He was not one of those
good Sunday-school book boys, but bright, keen, and
full of fun; and it was always the great amusement of
the class to listen to his shrewd answers to the professors when we knew that these answers came from
his 'inner consciousness' rather than from the book.
No one ever saw anything mean in him: there was
nothing dishonorable in his make-up. He was modest, patient, brave, and the highest reach of his ambition was to lose himself in the consecration of his
life and thought to his Master." I quote from one
more witness to his college life: "Neesima possessed
that element of true worth which meets with recog-
nition, not because it is consciously revealed, but

because it is *not*. He was never obtrusive. I never knew him to speak of himself, or even of what he hoped to accomplish, unless questioned; then one discovered that his ambition was to do not only for Japan but for the world. It would not be easy for any one who knew him in college to forget him even if his life had ended there; for there was in him an uplifting influence which made one wish to be on the heights where he lived and walked. He seemed to be there and to belong there without any sign of struggle to get there or to stay there. The even quietness of his life did not exclude quickness of action and alertness of manner. He was a pleasant companion, a delightful member of the families fortunate enough to count him one of their number, a true Christian gentleman, always thoughtful of God and therefore always thoughtful of others."

From the letters written during his Amherst life constant allusions to his expenses have been omitted, only such references being retained as serve to show how exact he was in his accounts and with what scrupulous care he regulated his expenditures. On the other hand, he was entirely frank in making known his needs. The simplicity and truthfulness of his character shone in every reference to himself, and an air of self-possession compelled instant confidence in all he said; for this self-possession was seen to result, not from self-confidence, but from self-forgetfulness. In the recitation room he made known his ignorance with the same frankness with which he stated his wants, a frankness wholly devoid of self-seeking; and the same trait was conspicuous in sickness, when one felt that he described his pain in sober truthfulness, just as it was, making it neither more nor less because it was his.

TO MRS. HARDY.

AMHERST, *September* 23, 1807.

. . . I moved to the College (North College, No. 8) last Saturday. Prof. Seelye got for me all things which I need, and I paid up for them all, because he thought it is not best way to make little debts here and there. I send a list to you so that you may know how many things I bought and how much I paid for them. I wish you would send some money to me to get daily wants. I will make an oath to you that I will never spend money foolishly, but be very prudent, because my Heavenly Father provides all good things for me so that I can say: "I shall not want." When I buy anything I will write down each time and will show it to you sometime.

My room is quite large and very pleasant. My roommate is very quiet, nice, and Christian young man. I am thankful I have found such a young man to room with. We keep up our daily duty toward our Heavenly Father by faith and prayers. I enjoy to board in Club. We have a very nice table generally. I joined to the missionary band in the College. We have interesting meetings every Sabbath morning. It is very pleasant for us to meet together, sing, praise our Maker, and ask Him that he would help us to carry the glad tidings to poor heathens. I am thankful that God called me out of the darkness and made me know the place where I may rest the eternal rest. Therefore I am entirely willing to preach the Gospel to my countrymen so that they may also be happy as I am. When I proclaim the truth to them perhaps they will persecute me, but I am not afraid of it, having this confidence in Jesus that though I should die in the dark regions—*He would cause me to live in the bright heaven forever.*—I saw in some paper sixty-three Japanese native Christians were arrested at Yokohama. But I say, it will stand, it must stand, and the Gospel must be known to them.

I feel always grateful for your kind care and I pray in your behalf without ceasing. I would like to hear from you very much.

TO MRS. FLINT.

AMHERST, *October* 30, 1867.

. . . I am very happy to tell you about my father's letter which I have first received since I left home. He received my letter which I wrote him last spring from Andover. He says that some American gentleman in Yokohama sent my letter by his faithful Japanese friend to him so that no trouble might fall on it. He was waiting there to get his reply and carry it to Yokohama, therefore my father wrote it with great haste. I will not tell you all what he said, but a few particular points. He was very anxious of me since he heard the information of my escaping from Hakodate. But he was so glad to hear from me over the water and find out where I am and how I am successful. He did not complain much for my leaving Japan, but, seems me, he was very much contented of it, because I wrote to him about beautiful American customs, and told him also what I do, what I study, how I feel happy, and how *I believe in true God.* His family are all well. My grandfather is still living. He is eighty-two years old and his health is quite well. He wrote to me a Japanese short poem which means that he is expecting my return most every day. I hope he would live till my return, so that I may tell him the way where he may find Jesus. . . .

He did not reply about the religion which I explained to him quite plainly. I suppose he had not time to write many things. I also received letters from my friend who lives in my prince's house, my brother, and sister. My friend says he did always try to comfort my parents and grandfather so that they might not be too much anxious of me, and he will comfort them in future also. He told me he will take good care for my family as well as his family. My brother says when he read my letter that he was so excited that the tears ran over his face, and cold perspiration covered whole his body. He gave much thanks for my advice and instruction. He is studying Chinese in a high school. He feels quite ignorant and humble. He says he is like a flag which dwells in a small well and sees the heavens in little space. He wishes to see vast ocean and wide heaven. He comes in his prince's house every day and teaches Chinese to many children. My sister says she is praying for me to her vain gods every day — I am pity of her. . . .

TO MRS. HARDY.

AMHERST, *November* 16, 1867.

. . . My vacation will come pretty soon, but I know not where I may go. Will you tell me where I may go? I hope I would study some during the vacation, but if you find good chance I will work something to pay my expenses. I asked Prof. Seelye about my staying in the College room during vacation, but he told me the law of the college does not allow to keep any students in the rooms during the winter vacation lest the building should get fire. He invites me to spend the vacation with him. I don't know myself which way I should take. Please tell me which way I may take. I will follow your information.

Last Sunday morning Dr. Treat preached at the chapel. In the afternoon Rev. Mr. Wheeler gave full account of his work at Harpoot, and at the evening Dr. Clark made remarks to evangelize Chinese empire, and made a noble statement to send a thousand missionaries to North China within ten years. They were very good and encouraged me very much indeed. I was almost persuaded to go forth to fight against Babylon, and break down the great wall of Satan. Yet I must nourish up myself and must wait until I have full strength and knowledge of our Lord Jesus Christ. This thought keeps me always happy and encourages me to go on my daily studies. . . .

TO MRS. FLINT.

AMHERST. *December* 1, 1867.

. . . I had a letter from Mrs. Hardy last Monday. She invited me to spend the vacation with her and told me Capt. Taylor has arrived in Boston. So I must go up to Boston by all means. I proposed to go last Monday when I finish my sawing wood (O, hard wood! made my spinal column pain!), but the same morning two young men called on me unexpectedly. Do you think who they are? Two Japanese from Monson. They hindered my sawing wood but I was perfectly satisfied to spend a few days with my countrymen.

When I saw them I did not know whether should I speak English or Japanese, but they began to talk Japanese with me, so I was obliged to speak my own tongue. At first I found some confusion to talk to them, but I did speak better and faster than they did. They stayed in my room whole morning, and the afternoon I showed them all cabinets and Gymnasium. I called on them at Hotel in the evening and I stayed there after ten o'clock. We read together 28th chapter of St. Matthew. I think they understood the chapter quite well, but they found trouble to understand the Trinity; so I explained to them far as I know. They asked me to make prayers, but I could not make them in Japanese, so I made them in English. Though they cannot speak English freely, yet they understand English very well.

These two are best scholars among those Japanese in Monson. I hope they will become good instruments to their countrymen. I spoke with them about the religious matters during these hours. They found their sins ; they found also the way where they meet their Master. They have humble and beautiful spirits, just as little children. They thought first they would study some sciences to benefit their country, but God opened their blind eyes and took away thick veil between them and heaven. He made them know the grace through which they may have immortality. So they feel grateful for his tender care towards them (though they are sinners) and they hope also to do some good things to their people for the sake of Christ. I am thankful that God bless my countrymen so much, and I hope the time will soon come for Gospel to bear fruit in the barren and unmatured land.

The Japanese referred to in the above letter were two of six sent to this country, under assumed names and without the knowledge of the home government, by the prince of Satsuma. After the revolution of 1868, the Japanese government assumed their support and required them to resume their real names. They were all earnest students, and one of them was subsequently associated with President William S. Clark in the establishment of an agricultural college in Japan and was appointed governor of Yezo. In these fellow-countrymen Neesima took the deepest interest, visiting them at Monson on several occasions and corresponding with them for many years.

EXTRACTS FROM LETTERS TO MRS. HARDY.

January 10, 1868.

This is the beginning of the year, therefore I hope to renew my spirit to perform my Christian duty better, and to keep up my Christian light intenser and to be ready for His calling. I am praying and watching lest I should fall into sin. So I am praying for your family in same manner. Take good care for your health and enjoy yourself under the cross.

February 14, 1868.

I enjoy my college life very much, and I cannot express my great and deep joy in Jesus with my pen. He helps me to resist all evils, He comforts me with the Holy Spirit, He guides me in the path of righteous with his gentle hand, saying, "Come, take the water of life freely." Is it not kind invitation for a sinner like me? When I think of his grace I do not think about the world's things. I like to do something boldly for the advancement of his kingdom.

February 21, 1868.

I had a recent news from Japan which told me about war between Shogun and princes. Shogun's residence in Yedo was burned by a mob of Satsuma prince who educates the young men at Monson. It is very short walk from my home, but I do not feel anxious about my folks because I demand them under the protection of the Almighty Hand.

To-morrow will be holiday. We shall not have any recitations. I should like to have such a day once and a while. I salute you all for the day, for the gift of the hero to this nation, and for independence. I should like to see such freedom in my country.

March 25, 1868.

My coat sleeves and button holes almost wear out, and its color fades away some. If you have coat at hand I wish you would give me one so that I may wear it to the church. But if you have not any I will wait till the next fall, because it is not my privilege to wear new clothing. But it shall be my great desire to wear a pure and white robe in the future world.

March 30, 1868.

I have been quite nervous these four or five weeks. I was not able to sleep soundly. Dr. Hitchcock recommend me to take footbath every evening and eat some light things just before I go to bed to stupefy my brain. I did so faithfully sometime, but I stopped it last week because I can sleep better than used be — also I do not wish to spend money in such vain way. Does Mr. Hardy take much walk? I think the walking is essential and also desirable for business men and students. When I study long while in my

room I feel oppressive and tiresome, but when I go
out in field, open my lung and breathe abundant oxy-
gen, I feel always light, happy, and vigorous.   It is
only way for me to restore my health, so I wish Mr.
Hardy would take much exercise in open air.   Please
give my love to him and all.

In April of this year Neesima was confined to his
bed for several weeks by a sharp attack of inflammatory rheumatism, and was kindly cared for at the
house of Professor Seelye.

AMHERST, *April* 27, 1868.

I received your kind letter and check and an inclosure from Japan in due time.   I thank you for
your kind request for my illness.   I feel almost better, but Prof. Seelye still keeps me in his house.   I
do not know what I should do for his kindness but
thanks only.   He is very much afraid that I should
take cold again because the weather is so changeable
and unpleasant, and does not allow me to go to recitations.   So I am still staying in his house.   He pleases
to have me in his home very much because Mrs. Seelye
does not yet come back from Albany.   But I must go
back to my room soon as I can.   When I received
your check I thought it would be very hard work for
me to obtain so much with my own hand and felt
grateful for your gift.   When Prof. Seelye's man
brought me your letter he told me, "this is from your
home," not knowing truly where it came from.
When I looked at its direction I perceived it came
from you, but I felt some soft thing in it like Japan
paper, so I replied him "probably it may be."   Then
I opened it.   It was really a letter from home.   My fa-

ther told me he wrote me sometime ago before that, but I have not received it yet. He says his family is all well except my mother, she has been so anxious of me since I took my adventure. My sister wrote me also. They send their especial regards and much thanks to you. Beside that, there is great confusion among the people. | The people of Yedo have great fear that the enemy of Shogun should attack the city, so my father and all wish me come back. But I am not his own. How can I go back now, having a plow on my hands? I must prepare myself for my Master's work. \ Yet I think I can do great good for my mother here. I can pray fervently for her. God is present everywhere, so I trust He will take care of her. If I go back now I suppose I must go to war. / I do not wish at all to kill myself in such a barbarous war. But I devote myself to go to battle against Satan, taking the helmet of salvation and the sword of the Spirit, which is the word of God. \ Will you remember my mother in your prayers? I pray for her many times a day. I hope God will preserve her life till she may hear the *word of life.*

Amherst, *June* 15, 1868.

I began lately to collect minerals, because I thought it will be worth to me to know something about them. When I was home I thought Japan is a farming country, but I think now she is a mineral country. There are several mines of gold, silver, copper, iron, platinum (lately discovered), and many precious stones. But the people generally keep temples of gods on summits of mountains, and dare not touch them, even though they see veins of minerals very plainly, lest they should defile the temples of gods and gods would pour out wrath upon them. Perhaps I may not spend much time for minerals when I go home, but I hope I will teach them only wise Creator, remove their foolish ideas, and stir them up to take in Christian civilization.

Most of his vacation time Neesima spent in visiting his friends in Boston, the Flints at Hinsdale, the Hiddens at Andover, and the family of Captain Taylor at Chatham. He also made several extensive tours in Massachusetts, Connecticut, and Rhode Island, collecting minerals and geological specimens, and in the summer of 1868 planned with great anticipation an excursion for this purpose to the White Mountains, an account of which he gives in the following letter: —

TO MRS. HARDY.

AMHERST, *August* 22, 1868.

. . . I am very happy to write a few lines to you from my beloved Amherst. I returned here yesterday very safely. I was received kindly by Prof. Seelye, and I am now staying in his house because I cannot get in my room until next Monday. I can only say I have had a great grand time. I have been tramping more than five weeks and more than four hundred miles. Yet my feet are not sore at all. I understood very well how to manage them. I feel grateful to you for furnishing money to me for spending this vacation in such a profitable and pleasant manner. I met my companions at Worcester and began our tramp from there. We came through Boston, Andover, Lawrence, Salem, N. H., and we spent the first Sabbath on our way at Raymond, N. H. We were invited to make some remarks in evening prayer-meeting. We made remarks about mission work to awake up missionary spirit among that church. The meeting was very full and the people very attentive to our remarks. A gentleman made a motion to raise more money than the last time to help the mission cause. They gave us meals and lodging without charge.

We crossed Lake Winnipiseogee with a steamboat. It was mostly smoky weather to see distant view. I was unwell a little while at Jackson by taking bath in Diana Fall. I stopped in Jackson House about two days. It took my money off very badly. We went up Mt. Washington on 3d inst. from Glen side. We stopped there two days and one night on account of the smoky weather. We saw most glorious sunset. Then we came down Crawford side. We went up Cannon Mountain and went near to the rock which forms profile of Old Man. Then we visited Flume, and took photograph of our party. I suppose I can procure one for you. Our party was broken up from Flume, because I wanted to visit several mines in Franconia, Lisbon, and Warren, and they would not care about visiting them. They went down on Plymouth route, and I came up Ore Hill in Franconia, gold mine in Lisbon, and copper mine in Warren. So I obtained quite knowledge about minerals in vacation. Last Saturday I left Warren about half past four P. M. and traveled through a woods after 7 o'clock. It was quite dark, yet I could not find any house to pass that night, and when I came across a house, man would not receive me in his house, even in his barn, so I was obliged to come still farther. Finally I found a house some way beyond that and passed that night in a barn. Just after I got in barn it stormed furiously. It was rather old barn and leaked all over, but rubber blanket kept me dry. The next day was the Lord's day, but there was not any house where I may keep the day. Many folks round that way would not care about the day. Some of them worked in garden. So I was obliged to travel nine miles on that morning. I arrived at a meeting-house of O—— just before the morning commences. Out appearance of the house is very old and looks unpainted, but inside is very well furnished. They had not a regular preaching there on account of the absence of their pastor. The people of that place seem me very rich. Yes, rich enough to support several pastors. Yet they did not get any minister to supply the pulpit. The people dressed very nicely, but they appeared only cold in the worship. I can say surely that I never have been such a dry and cold meeting since I came to America. I went in some old gentleman's class in the Sabbath-school. It is most cold and uninviting school I ever been. I crossed the river and went in F—— meeting-house that afternoon. I heard an old and bright preacher there. I found out afterwards it was Miss McKeen's father, and I tried to see him, but he does not reside there. A gentleman received me cordially, and I was also invited to make some remarks in prayer-meeting. I told them our heathenish customs and manners. The night after I stopped in a part of Windsor, Vt. When I went near to a house I saw a young gentleman sitting on a chair. I asked him whether he would let me sleep in his barn over the night. He asked me who I was and whence I came. I told him my name and where I came from. He called up his mother to see me. When she understood I am a Japanese she told me she read something about me in a religious paper. She said very kindly, 'I would not let Christian man sleep in our barn.' After a few conversation she took me to a handsomely furnished bedroom and brought me all things which are necessary. I had very sweet rest and sleep more than eight hours. The next morning she gave me nice breakfast, also many tracts and small pocket hymn-book. I doubt not she is good Christian lady. Also that young man gave me ride to the village about a mile and half. Some people are so liberal and good to such a stranger.

On his way down the Connecticut valley Neesima passed through Hanover, and with his characteristic habit of seizing every opportunity attended a lecture at the medical school then in session. Professor Oliver P. Hubbard, on the way to his morning lecture, met the young pedestrian and mistook him for one of the St. Francis tribe of Indians from Canada. He was about to accost him when Neesima inquired for the professor of mineralogy. Professor Hubbard then introduced himself and invited Neesima to his laboratory, where the latter exhibited the minerals contained in his satchel and watched with interest the preparations of the assistant. After the lecture was concluded, he courteously took leave and resumed his journey.

TO MRS. HARDY.

September 19, 1868.

. . . Regard to $10. which I obtained from furniture, I do not know where it has gone. It disappeared very strangely. I kept it in my trunk, but it is lost somewhere. I am sure no one could steal it because I kept trunk locked always. So I think I have taken it out and paid it to a store in some evening, mistaking it as one dollar. I do not spend money foolishly, as you know well, and if I do I give you its account always. I am sorry to say I have lost it by my carelessness. I wish you would excuse my carelessness, but do not think I have deceived you, spending it by some foolish way. I am preparing myself to be good man and striving daily to walk with God. So I would not deceive you by all means.

October 1, 1868.

. . . I received a package a week ago Tuesday. I found in it a coat, a tail-coat, a vest, and a pair of pants. I hope you will excuse me that I do not take that tail-coat. I think I have not old enough or dignity enough to wear that coat. You must excuse me, because my chum laughed at me when I put on that tail-coat. I have three vests now, so I shall not take that vest too. I want clothings, but not more than necessary.

November 8, 1868.

. . . I asked Mr. Hardy to procure Dana's Mineralogy. I wanted it very much but durst not ask you so long on account of expense. But I made up my mind some time ago that I would save its expense by some way. I stopped my drinking tea. It does not amount to much in one term, but it will be considerable in the course of a year. I hope you will excuse me my asking you to procure such an expensive book. I inclose the list of my college expenses. I spent more than I did expect, but I hope you will not find any fault in me. . . . I hate indeed to trouble myself so often and so constantly in this carnal supply, and anticipate now I shall be exceedingly happy when I get rid of all troubles of this kind and reach to the place where I may wear one pure and white robe which shall not need any more mending, washing, or changing. Yet I think it is very reasonable to take care for my body while I am in this world.

TO MRS. HARDY.

AMHERST, *May* 21, 1869.

. . . I heard from my folks some time ago as you know. I have been longing their news more than one year, so it gave me great pleasure and consolation. My father wrote me very long and kind letter and informed me all about what wonderful change has taken place in Japan within a few years. Most of the people of high ranks cut their hairs short and dress in the American style.

My father find more satisfactory in my being in this country, seeing such a wonderful change is going on among the leading class of the people and knowing that the educational system of the western nations would soon be introduced into Japan. You may see in his letter which he has written to you how he was glad when he heard from me and understood that I have found good friends in this side of the world. He asked me to translate it into English so that you may know what he writes about. I have translated it nearly as he expressed his idea in his own way. My sister and brother have written to you too, but I have not translated them, because they contain nearly the same thing as my father said. I hope you will accept their thanks and best regards and appreciate how they have felt grateful for what you have done for me. I wish you would give him a reply, at least a few lines, and if you please, I will translate yours into Japanese. I think it will please him greatly.

TO MR. AND MRS. HARDY FROM NEESIMA'S FATHER.

YEDO, *February*, 1869.

Though I have not known you personally I will write to you a few lines. I suppose you are enjoying your good health, though the weather is still cold, and I am glad of it in your behalf.

When my son Shimeta came over to your country desiring to obtain some knowledge, you did sympathize with him and hearkened his request so kindly and sent him to a school, promising him that you would supply all his wants while he is in the school. So you have already supplied his wants without any lack during the past years. I could not express my joy and thanks neither by pen nor paper for what you have done for him. Though I myself and all my family have felt very grateful for your kindness, and talked over of you most every day, yet I have not written to you at all. It condemns my conscience greatly that I have neglected it thus far.

Though my son is not very bright yet I expect he will become a reputable man through your kindness and I rejoice greatly in his behalf. I humbly entreat you now that you would continue your mercy on him while he remains in your country. I have also the great obligation to your wife for what kindness she has shown to him. I have felt somewhat proud and spoken often of myself "what happy man I am!" for my son has fallen into such good hands as you are. I have been talking and wishing to come over to your

country to see you face to face and give you my
thanks, which is higher than the highest mountain
and deeper than the deepest ocean. Yet I am bound
in my duty and am not able to cross over the water,
so I will send you only my thanks which burst out
from my heart. My father is eighty-four years old
now and is always talking of your kindness and also
his grandson's fortune. He asked me to send his
thanks and best regards to you all. I hope I shall
write to you again. I write this with a fear and reverence.

Neesima Tamiharu.

TO MRS. HARDY.

Amherst, *September* 3, 1860.

. . . I enjoyed my trip through Connecticut and
Rhode Island very much and had also very enjoyable
time at Chatham. It is rather quiet place, but I
liked it more than a noisy city because the quietness
of nature led me to a quiet meditation. I think it
was the best part of my vacation to have my mind
free from the study and to have a quiet meditation on
the wonderful economy of nature or a sweet communion with Him who rules our whole universe and even
cares for a poor sinner such as I am.

I am getting along nicely in my study. I like my
new chum very much. He is very earnest Christian.
O, what charming place Amherst is! I shall never
be tired in studying here. I hope you will be charitable on me and not laugh at my hasting letter. I
am just busy as bees and cannot spend much time for
doing else but study. I hope God will sustain my
strength to prepare for my life work.

Though you should delay your reply for my letter

a month or a year I shall never have a slight doubt of your interest in me, because I hope you are my dearest friend. Yet I am always desiring to hear from you, and when I write to you I am anxiously waiting for your reply, because I always wish to know of your prosperity. If you are too busy, please write me a few lines, only a few lines. Let me know how you are.

TO MRS. HARDY.

AMHERST, *October* 24, 1869.

. . . A secretary of the American Missionary Society preached to us this morning, and stated to us very vividly in what fearful point the American people stands now. They have 8,000,000 Irish people and many Germans and French, 4,000,000 negroes in South, many thousands of Chinese, and a few Japanese on the Pacific coast. Unless the American people stretch out their hands to enlight, elevate, and educate them with the Christian truth they will ruin the free institution which is the pride of the nation. I was quite animated by his earnest discourse and felt indeed it is our best privilege to co-work with Christ and to promote his kingdom. When I came out from the chapel I heard great many say, "I don't like his sermon," and they did not manifest their sympathy with him at all. I felt so sorry for their coldness in their heart and disinterest for the Church of Christ and for the welfare of their own country. All heathens look at America as the centre of the Christian light. If the centre of the light has not much intenseness, how could it enlight those who are lying in the remote dark corners? My dear friend, let us pray earnestly for those Christians who live for themselves and not for Christ. Let us pray for the American church so that she may be more jealous for promoting the blessed gospel to all nations. . . . My folks are all well. My father is still staying in Yedo with his prince, but he says he will soon leave his office and go home for rest because he has found his duty rather tedious in his age. Sometime he was obliged to sit up till two or three o'clock toward the morning for his inexcusable duty. It would be better for him to take a rest in a quiet country town, but his leaving the city will cause me a sad thing. Perhaps I may not hear from him so often as used to be. When he writes to me he always carries it himself to Yokohama to be mailed to America. He is very careful for sending his letter to me. He never trusts it to a postman lest his secret communication to me should be revealed by some accidental way. When he gets home he could not carry his letter down to Yokohama any more, because it would be most too far for him to walk, — about 60 miles from Yedo. I demand my folks entirely on the providential care. Whatever thing may happen to them, I will say it is the Lord's doing.

In the summer of 1869 Neesima made another excursion, partly on foot and partly by rail, of which the following notes are taken from his diary: —

"July 15th. I left Amherst on 10.30 train for Hartford, where I stopped with my old acquaintance, Mr. D. E. Bartlett. I was very cordially received by him. He took me to the city library, and also to the top of the State House where we could look down the whole city. It was a most striking sight that the brick and sandstone edifices were interwoven with the green trees.

"16th. I left Hartford for Middletown. on the noon train. When I came to the town I was told that the commencement exercises of Wesleyan University are being held in Methodist church. But the house was filled up by the audience. While I was hesitating near the entrance somebody pulled my arm from behind, and when I look back I behold Mr. A. of '70 smiling with his large blue eyes. He had just come from Haddam and informed me whom I should see there, and where I may obtain my loving objects [minerals]. So I was very much encouraged to go forward to Haddam. But it was not quite time then for the steamer. To pass the time profitably I crossed the river by a ferryboat, and visited the sandstone quarry at Portland. Though I saw many specimens of bird-tracks, the man in the office would not part me any. I left Middletown on six o'clock boat after the dark. It thundered and rained furiously, and I admired the scene very much. Mr. W. B. accommodated me a room and meals, though his wife was not quite well. I think they love me some. I was very successful in obtaining tourmalines, but not very in getting columbites.

"21st. I left Haddam for New Haven on foot, walking about seventeen miles that afternoon, though I spent considerable time for trouting and berrying. I passed the night in a farmhouse in North Guilford. The lady in the house treated me very kindly and would not charge me positively for either lodging or breakfast.

"22d. It rained quite hard in the morning, but the weather was very beautiful and the sun was quite hot in the afternoon. I washed my undershirt and stockings at a small brook. When I reached New Haven I went to a hotel to pass the night.

"23d. The commencement exercise of Yale College is held at the Central Church. I saw there two Japanese, Yoshida and Ohara. I did not like the exercises quite well, not seeing much Christian element in them. I visited the Mineralogical cabinet and Art Gallery. I admired the picture of the prophet Jeremiah. Some careless fellows thought I was a society man and invited me to Δ. K. E. Society hall. The room used for the literary purpose is very well furnished. I saw there many glasses, and wine bottles on the stairs. So I am glad to find out what *secret* meant. While they were showing the rooms they asked me where did I join to the society. I replied: 'I have not joined to the society yet. Perhaps I shall if I find time enough.' I think they were no little surprised to hear my reply.

"24th. I visited limestone quarry at Smithfield, eight miles from Providence, and found nice specimens there. I came to Providence to pass the night."

Neesima was intensely interested in all mechanical processes and the industrial arts, most of what he saw being of course entirely new to him. On this excursion he visited the arsenal at Springfield, the factories and foundries of the cities through which he passed, his notebook containing over two hundred pages describing minutely the manufacture of iron, brass, small arms, cartridges, gas, paper, wire, cotton cloth, plated ware, confectionery, etc., with innumerable drawings of the machinery and tools employed.

The remainder of the summer vacation Neesima

passed at Chatham with the family of Captain Taylor.
On December 11th Captain Taylor was caught between the ferryboat and the dock while landing at
East Boston, and died almost immediately. Neesima's journal of this month contains the following
passages : —

"I write this to remember this sad event for myself,
and also to warn my friends to be ready always for
the Master's call. It was on Monday morning, Dec.
13th, 1869, that a little fellow brought me a yellow
letter, asking me quite briskly whether it belonged to
me. It was a dispatch informing me that Captain
Taylor was dead. It gave me a great surprise. I
did not know myself what to do. I was perfectly
silent and calm. I was still sitting in my chair, saying to myself 'I do not believe this, it is my dream.
It is not possible. It is not true.' I was without a
tear, without a word, but . . . Then I rose calmly,
and slowly went to a wall where hung his small likeness, and gazed upon it with wide opening eyes. He
looked very active, not like a dead person. So I hastily stepped to the telegraph office and asked an officer
whether there was no mistake in that dispatch. It
was true. So I gave up all my doubts and hastened
to the railroad. While I was in the cars I was
deeply affected. It was very heavy cross for me to
bear. When I walked it was like a lame man, helped
by my umbrella. I did not see Mrs. Taylor that evening lest my presence might excite her grief, but when
I saw the brothers and sisters I bursted out in a loud
cry. I cannot describe by my pen such sad scenes.
All his kind deeds of deep interest in me since I knew
him in China, and how I spent my vacation with him

about ten weeks ago, came to my memory. I could not possibly raise up my head, but only turn aside and weep bitterly. How can I tell why he was so dear to me. I fell into his kind hand at Shanghai; he gave me China jacket, showing me how to sew; he taught me navigation; he spoke patiently, forgave me always, and never spoke to me any unkind words; he introduced me to him who became my kind friend ever since. At our last good-by he kissed me. My captain, this is my last kiss. His forehead was cold as marble.

"Then I said good-by to Mrs. Taylor and her little infant boy. 'For the Lamb which is in the midst of the Throne shall feed them, and shall lead them unto living fountains of waters; and God shall wipe away all tears from their eyes.'"

TO MRS. HARDY.

Amherst, *April* 5, 1870.

Having found myself quite comfortable I will write you a few lines. Since I wrote you my last letter I have been improving gradually and gaining strength. I began to go out of doors last Friday and walked to and fro in the front yard of Prof. Seelye's house, but to-day is quite cold and stormy, so I am obliged to keep myself quiet in my warm room. Though I feel almost well as usual, yet it does seem me strange that I cannot endure long while in doing anything. Though I get over my cold I have not enjoyed my health ever since; partly I had headache and partly I was nervous. Yet I was so much pressed by my duty, and kept up my study just much as I could. I never liked to complain for it, and kept up cheerfully my studies and my prayers till I was taken down entirely by this rheumatism. I never had such an ill health since I have been in this country. I fear somewhat if I continue my study in the beginning of next term as I did this term I may entirely break down. So I think it well for me to rest for a while and to get a renewed health. But you must not understand that I am getting tired of study. I am longing it and strongly tempted to begin it, like a starving wolf goes after his prey. Though I have been ill more than four weeks, yet I have not entirely wasted my time.

You informed me that you should send me up to Andover next fall to study theology for two years. When I left Andover you told me I should study two years in Amherst and a year in Andover. But I have been in Amherst a year longer than your fixed time, though in my sorrow I have wasted nearly the latter half part of this year by being sick so much. Now you are willing to support me two years more in Andover. It is a great offering to me indeed. I do not know how I could get along without it in my study. I appreciate your kindness very deeply in my heart, and hope indeed that your offering for me would be very productive hereafter.

CHAPTER III.

SEMINARY COURSE AT ANDOVER.

DURING the latter half of his last year in Amherst Neesima was again attacked by inflammatory rheumatism, and this illness seriously interfered with his studies. His health returned with the warmer weather, and in April he resumed his work. He took the degree of B. S. with the class of 1870, and was selected by his comrades to deliver the oration in the grove on class-day. The question of his future course of study was not a difficult one; his desire to return to his people as the bearer of a heavenly message was supreme, and to this end it was decided that he should enter the Theological Seminary at Andover, a decision which gave him the greatest satisfaction. At this time the question was raised whether he should return to Japan as a Japanese or an American citizen. It was the opinion of those of whom advice was sought in Kōbe and Yokohama that he should be naturalized in the United States, that thus he might, in case of difficulties arising from his missionary work, secure the advantages of consular jurisdiction. On the other hand, while the treaties did not prohibit missionary effort, it was extremely doubtful whether they would afford any protection in case of complaint from the Japanese government; nor was it probable that, if naturalized and thus made a foreigner in the eyes of the law, this fact would protect him, a native-born

Japanese, from private malice. Events subsequently proved this question to be without importance; yet it is interesting to note the form it assumed at this time in Neesima's mind. With him it was not how to secure the amplest protection, but how to exert the greatest influence. That his influence would be seriously impaired by the surrender of his rights as a Japanese citizen was clear. He therefore decided against naturalization, and, in the fall of 1870, returned to Andover to begin his theological studies.

In the winter of 1871 he again suffered from rheumatism, and was for some weeks helpless. On January 10th he writes : —

" Through my sickness and pain I can have more sympathy with the suffering and dying Saviour, and by beholding Him on the cross I can bear all my pains and sufferings most cheerfully, rejoicingly; knowing that my Master has suffered a far greater pain than I do now for the salvation of the lost race. When I profoundly think of the plan of salvation I almost lose myself in its beauty and grandeur. Though I cannot use my body now, I can exercise my mind. I can think, pray, and glorify God through my suffering. Pray for me, not simply for my illness, but that I may be ever submissive to the will of my Heavenly Father."

TO MR. HARDY.

ANDOVER, January 29, 1871.

A letter which you forwarded to me last Friday is from my home. It brought me a sad news, that is, the death of my grandfather. The letter is dated on the 5th of last August, though his death occurred on the 14th of last July.

According to my brother's brief statement of his case I judge he died with cholera, which is a prevailing disease in the country. He was sick only four days, and died without much trouble, owing to his old age. He was then eighty-six years old. My brother says he was not sorry to go, for he lived long enough and has seen his grandsons grow up, and heard of what I am doing in America. But he would have more satisfactorily died if he could have seen me once more on his last day. For he has been talking of me so much in his late years and anticipating to see me with a great pleasure. Oh! he is no more with his friends. He has gone without hope in Christ. I dare say he was a most earnest and trustworthy man I ever saw among our neighbors. I trust God will judge him without law, for he lived without law. My prayers for him, and my translations of a few precious passages in the Scriptures, which I sent to him some time ago, have done some good to his soul. When he heard the news of my running away from Hakodate, he was sore afraid lest I should fall into a trouble, but when he heard that I am studying in one of the best American institutions he was overwhelmed with a great joy, and recognized that the people in the United States are far more liberal than his own people.

This news caused me a great grief. I would have broken down with a grief if I had not had my Saviour to sympathize with me in my affliction and help me to bear this cross. Pray for me that this affliction may be a means to bring me closer to Christ and to calmly repose myself upon his arms. I have a still more sad news to tell you, the death of our dear friend, Dr. Samuel Taylor. He died suddenly in the

Academy Hall when he went up to the morning prayer. May the Lord sanctify all these sad scenes to our souls. I suppose you and Mrs. Hardy will be present at Dr. Taylor's funeral, which will be on next Tuesday. Then let me have a pleasure of seeing both of you.

TO MRS. FLINT.

ANDOVER, March 21, 1871.

I saw Mori, Japanese minister sent to Washington from Mikado, at Boston a week ago last Wednesday. He told me if I write a letter to the Japanese government stating briefly who I am, what I have been studying in America, and also my intention for returning home, he will forward it to the government and get a passport for me. He told me also the present internal movement among the higher classes concerning Christianity. They begin to see a vast difference between Protestant and Catholic religions. Though the government forbids the people to embrace Christian truth, yet I trust it will open the country to Protestant missionaries within a few years. I am afraid that Mori, the Japanese minister, will pay up to Mrs. Hardy for what she has expended for me so far, because he asked Mr. Hardy to give him a list of all the expenses which have been spent for educating me. I fear Mr. Hardy will give him its list, and if he receives the payment from Mori I shall be bound up to the Japanese government by that sum of money. I would rather remain a free Japanese citizen and consecrate myself wholly to my Master's business. I hope to see Mr. Hardy very soon and talk over the matter with him. I hope the Lord will give us a wise and prudent thought for deciding this matter. [The proposition of Minister Mori was promptly declined.]

TO MRS. FLINT.

ANDOVER, *June* 7, 1871.

Three weeks ago yesterday I was invited to Amherst by the Japanese minister, who brought a young Japanese to Mass. Agricultural College to study the mode of American farming. I spent two days with him at Amherst and had very pleasant time. He treated me very gentlemanly and paid all my traveling expenses. The main idea of his inviting me is that he was intending to establish schools at home after the American system and desired me to take charge of it. I encouraged him to do so, though I did not give him any definite answer for my taking charge of it — for it is woe to me if I do not preach the gospel of my blessed Master.

TO MRS. HARDY.

AMHERST, *June* 13, 1871.

Since I returned here I attempted to rewrite my letter to the Japan government for obtaining a passport, for in my first letter I did not say that I have embraced Christian faith, but simply mentioned what I am studying at Andover. I did not even say that I am studying theology, but mentioned that I am studying the true secret of the progress of civilization. When I saw the Japan minister at Amherst I told him that I would not go home concealing my Christian faith like a trembling thief goes in the dark night under the fear of discovery, but go there as a Christian man walking in a Christian love and doing things according to the light of my conscience. I told him, furthermore, that if I write to him I would rather make known to government my new and healthier religion. But he said he did not know whether it would be safe for me to do so or not, but I might try that. But after a still more careful investigation I found it would not be desirable for me to make known my being here openly, for if I do so perhaps I will receive an order to do some service or to study a certain thing. In such a case I cannot conveniently refuse it, for if I do the government will no longer be friendly. While I am studying I do not wish to be hindered by the government's affairs. As I understand that you are willing to keep me still longer, I would rather receive the Christian's willing and cheerful gift than that of the government, which will bind me as a slave. Yet I will try to keep up a friendly relation to the minister at Washington, so that when I get ready to go home he might be some help to me. So I am decided not to write to the government till I am about ready to go home. I used sometimes to do things without much circumspection, though I was very successful in certain things. But with regard to the above case I shall be pretty careful, for my all future success may depend on this single action. I shall wait entirely on the providential guidance.

When I came out from the prayer-meeting recently I saw a grand display of northern lights. While I was watching the change of streams of light, and also gazing upon those innumerable bright stars twinkling in the blue dome, I thought of the hymn, " Nearer, my God, to thee," and thought that if, through the grace of God, I am permitted to fly on joyful wing onward and upward, leaving the sun, moon, and stars behind me, how grand my feeling might be.

The vacation will begin two weeks from next Thursday. I don't know what I should do this summer. I am partly tempted to read or study, and partly to take a trip somewhere to collect the mineralogical and geological specimens.

TO MR. HARDY.

ANDOVER, *June* 21, 1871.

I received yours of yesterday, and am very thankful for your kindest offering for my wants for the vacation. I am desiring to take a trip to Niagara Falls, Trenton Falls, Utica, and some other places to collect fossils and minerals. I had an invitation from one of my college chums who lives near Utica to come there and spend a few days with him. I feel rather delicate to ask you to furnish my wants for going so far, but I also believe I shall be benefited by it very much, and I also expect to study geology and mineralogy practically. Perhaps I may give lectures on Japan here and there and may get my expenses paid partly.

TO MRS. HARDY.

EVANS MILLS, N. Y., *August* 18, 1871.

I fear you may think I have forgotten to write to you. But if you read on you will know the reason why I have not written thus far. Since I began my journey I have had no fixed abode, and consequently I have scarcely found time to sit down to write letters or read. When I stopped with my friends I was a kind of novelty to them because they have never seen any Japanese. I was invited out to the dinners and tea, and was asked by them so many questions. At the same time I have kept myself busy geologizing.

When I went to any friendless places I was obliged to lodge at the hotels. It seemed me so painful to pay so much that it would not do to hang around too long in such places. I hastened myself to see what I could see, and did not stay more than necessary for geologizing. Thus my time has been fully occupied with visiting, tramping, geologizing, and occasionally discussing with spiritualists and infidels. I thank God for giving me strength to meet with all his enemies without surrendering myself to them.

I went through the heart of New York State, crossed over Lake Ontario by a steamer, and am stopping with one of Andover theological students at Evans Mills. Oh, I wish I could have eloquence enough to write out all my happy and rich experiences during my trip. Notwithstanding the broken English and imperfect grammar, I will attempt to write you a brief sketch with this unskillful hand.

After I bid a farewell to my dearest Boston friends, I set my face towards the west. My first stopping - place was Leominster, where I spent five days with the brother of Captain Taylor, including a Sabbath. I spoke for him in the afternoon service. It was my first attempt to address before a large audience in a regular service. I spoke on the history of Japan, and recent changes and progress of the people, and addressed to the Sabbath-school in the evening, showing a few articles of Japan. It pleased the children very much. I think I got through it better than I expected to. My second stopping-place was my beloved Amherst, where I spent only two days and a half with Professor Seelye. I attended the commencement exercises and enjoyed them very much. My third stopping-place was Hoosac Tunnel. I went in from east side. The inside of it was very dark, damp, and chilly. I wore a woolen coat, and an oil-coat, in order to keep myself comfortable. I did not make any long stay in the tunnel lest I might be injured by the dampness and low temperature. I met the instructor of schoolship in Boston harbor at the tunnel, and accompanied him to central shaft. The men could not work at all in the shaft on account of much water, and were simply dipping out water by the means of steam-engine. It will be 1,030 feet deep when it is completed. I suppose you know all about the tunnel, but please let me draw for you a section of the mountain to illustrate the tunnel. I passed the night on that wild romantic mountain. I rose very early the next morning, breakfasted hastily, and left at half past four o'clock. The morning air was so cool and the mountain breath so very gentle, yet invigorating, I might take a double quick to go over the mountain. But the scenery was so grand, splendid, and beautiful, it made me to stop my feet every five or ten minutes. The morning dawn awoke up those sleepy birds on the mountain tops to sing melody for a lonely traveler. The white and silvery fog arising from every valley appeared like the Mer de Glace on the Alps. Although I was alone I found many companions round about me, on my right, left, above, and beneath. Everything in nature seemed to welcome me, and joined me in praising the Maker of all things. I was alone, yet not alone.

I reached North Adams some time before six o'clock. I felt somewhat afraid to go to the place so early in the morning lest I might be taken for a " heathen Chinee." But I went in and came out from the place without any difficulty. I paid a visit to those

Chinese in the shoe-factory. They could not speak English at all, except their leader Ah Sing. When I went in there they took me for a Chinaman, but I could not understand them at all. So I took out a piece of paper and asked them to write down their questions. The first question was: What part of China did I come from? My reply on the paper was: " I am not from China, but from Japan. I came from Yedo, the capital of Japan, and am studying now the words of God, intending to preach the crucified Saviour to my countrymen." This reply surprised them in no less degree. I wrote down still further about the love of Christ. They seemed quite intelligent, and one of them said Jesus Christ was the Son of God. I wished to converse with them still longer, but they could not stop their work very conveniently. I went through their working shop, dining-room, and sleeping-room. They still keep up their own way of living and use the chopstick to eat rice with. They are very economical. They wash and mend their own clothes and cultivate the vegetables for their own use. I think they shall not be able to make money so fast as some Yankees can, but will accumulate it by steady and gradual process. They have neither so much aspiration or patriotic feeling as some of our young Japanese have, but they are simply contented with a few accumulations of the almighty dollar. On the other hand, the Japanese are not very anxious of making money, but are always craving after the knowledge and ideas of the western civilization. They don't do it simply for themselves, but it is their intention to elevate and enlighten their native friends. They love their own country and are willing even to give up their own lives for her. So if they love *truth* they would stand up for it as they would for their country. O, may our merciful Father give us power and grace to bear the blessed standard of Christ on that benighted shore, and proclaim the glad news of salvation to their despondent souls.

My fourth stopping-place was Troy, N. Y. I found there three Japanese students, and spent two days with them, including one Sabbath. They are not yet Christians, though they study the Bible and respect it as the word of God. I hope the free grace will cause them to be born in Christ. I had quite a talk with them and enjoyed it exceedingly. I stopped at Albany only four hours, visiting State Street, the Medical College, State Geological Room, State House, etc.

My fifth stopping-place was Kirkland, where I spent two weeks with my college chum, Mr. George Sutherland. Kirkland is a great centre of geological formation, and I made it a headquarters, spending many days in Clinton, Dansville, Oriskany Falls, Waterville, New Hartford, and Trenton Falls. Trenton Falls is a grand place to visit. Some people say it is not so sublime as Niagara Falls, but it is far prettier. The second fall is the best one. When I was ready to leave it began to rain quite hard. I stood in the rain and sketched the falls hastily.

I am requested to speak to-morrow evening, so I must stop my writing and plan out what I shall speak.

EXTRACT FROM JOURNAL WRITTEN ON HOOSAC MOUNTAIN.

July 15, 1871. If I stayed on this hilltop several mornings I should be inspired by the revelation of wonderful nature and write at least one or two verses of poetry which might make my name immortal. But, alas, un-genious man! I cannot compose even one verse on this single morning. I have no skill to describe the grand scene with a figurative language. I am like a practical Yankee and my remark is wonderfully plain. I have no inspired mind or pen, as see the following : —

> Arise, O sleepy sun.   Do not tarry, O lazy sun !
> For on a top of Berkshire hills I am standing,
> Standing alone, and for thee I am waiting.

TO MRS. HARDY.

ANDOVER, *September* 17, 1871.

Since I returned here I was intending to write you again, but I have been unusually busy these past two weeks and unable to describe to you my journey still farther. I had very rich experiences on my journey, and would be glad to narrate to you some of them, but I will not undertake to do it just now. On my return here I found a letter from my old teacher, and was informed by him my brother's death. He did not describe how he died, but simply informed me his death. He advised me to come home, for my father would be very lonely without me. Having been informed by a Japanese student who entered into Phillips Academy this term that there is a Japanese at Boston Highlands who came from Yedo very recently, and was once a pupil of my old teacher, accordingly I went to Boston about two weeks ago to see him, in order to ascertain by what manner or by what disease my brother did die. But he could not give me any information about his death. I stopped with that Japanese friend two days, and had very enjoyable Sabbath with him and Mrs. Captain Taylor. I called on Mr. Hardy, Jr., in State Street on Monday to get a letter from home which he spoke of a few days previously.

The letter was from my father. He informed me more minutely about my brother's death. He was ill about three months and died last March. It is almost too painful to think of, how he died in his early age. It is still more painful to read my father's letter accompanied with his great grief and disappointment. It is a most shocking news to me and caused me great sorrow. Yet I can bear it wonderfully, for I do not bear it alone. I can say cheerfully and willingly, "Let thy will be done." I submit all my affairs to his hand, for He knows best and does all things for my good. But when I sympathize with my disappointed and comfortless parents I could hardly refrain myself from dropping tears. I wrote to him last week and sent him your own likeness. I hope it might be some comfort to him. It would please my father exceedingly if I go home immediately, but I feel I am no longer a property of my father. I have consecrated myself to my Lord, and also give myself up to the service of my country. If the Lord calls me to labor for Him in his vineyard, it is the highest and most honorable calling we could ever obtain on the earth. If the Lord desires to promote his glorious kingdom to Japan through me, a least and weakest vessel in his household, I will most cheerfully and hopefully submit myself to his will. I have a plow on my hands ; I must work for my Lord. It is my earnest prayer for my parents that God should spare their lives until the light of truth and life will be preached to them. I thank God for what He has done for me always. Though I heard a sad news from home, yet He never does leave me comfortless.

I received a passport from the Japanese government, together with a letter from my old teacher. I hope you will rejoice with me, because it does seem me that the Lord is going to make my path plain.

I brought back quite a number of geological specimens from New York and Canada. They are my property. I feel quite rich now.

TO MR. HARDY.

ANDOVER, *September* 27, 1871.

You have asked me to give you a translation of the passport sent from the Japanese government. I think I will take the passport with me to Salem next week where I may expect to see you. I have several other papers sent to me with the passport; I will explain them all to you when I see you. I heard from my father again this morning. His letters have been sent to me by a private conveyance thus far, but his last letter came to me through the hands of the Japanese minister of foreign affairs. He says in his letter that, in the first part of last May, the government did send an officer to his prince to inquire whether there was such a man by the name of Neesima in his home who disappeared in such a time. He went away having ascertained everything. A few days after that a paper was sent to him and its contents was as follows: " It is permitted by the government to Neesima Shimeta to remain and study in the United States of America." I am sure it must have given my poor father a great gratification. He did not know thus far how I should get home safely, knowing that I broke the law of the country by running away, and was expecting me to come home secretly as I did run away. Now he knows that I can go home safely and at any time, and desires me to come as soon as I can. He thinks I am ordered by the Japanese government to stay in America several years longer, and says it is to his highest honor that his son's name was made known to the court. But, says he : "Come home as soon as you can, and let me look at your face, once more, and then I shall be satisfied. For I am getting old and my stay on the earth may not be many years. If I can see you once more it is enough. I shall let you go back to America hence to stay as long as you might. If your stay in America can be of some benefit to my country, I am willing to let you stay there until you can complete your study ; but please remember your *poor father*, and let him look at your face once more before he dies." Dear sir, it is pretty hard plead to me. But as you know I have a plow on my hands; I cannot look back just yet. I think I will let my poor father wait till I will finish my study here. I will send to Mrs. Hardy one of my father's letters in which he expresses his greatest obligations to both of you. He says : "My language utterly fails to express my grateful feeling towards you. I have told my friends, neighbors, and even strangers, that how you " (myself) " have fallen into the good hands in America, and how you are supported and educated by your American friends these long years. Every one of them who heard of your fortune, and the kindness of your friends, says there is no such thing in their own country." Although I krow that Mrs. Hardy has shown her kindness to me for her highest motive and worthiness, yet I hope that she will feel that she is somewhat rewarded by seeing my father's letter and receiving his greatest obligations expressed in it.

TO MRS. HARDY.

ANDOVER, *November* 7, 1871.

I believe I have not written to you since I saw you at Salem. I suppose you know what some old-school men say in regard to their trying to be perfect. They say we shall be perfect to-morrow or some future time. When to-morrow comes they will say the same and will never be perfect. So I have been deferring my writing to you thus far, saying, "I will do it to-morrow." When the next day comes I said, "I must read up Edwards on the Will, and also write an essay for our discussion," and deferred my writing to some future time. I have been attending Professor Park's lectures, and have got theory enough to be a new-school man, and have made up my mind to do or to be as I believe, that is to say: "I will do it now, *this moment;* I will no longer defer it till to-morrow." Though I have nothing particular to say, yet I should like to inform you something about my study. I am attending Professor Park's lectures and reading along with them. It may be the hardest year in the seminary, because it requires so much close attention and thinking. My study reminds me my trip to White Mountains. It was rather hard for me to climb up the mountains, but the grandeur of surrounding scene excited my ambition and aspiration to go up still higher so that I might get better view of wondrous nature. So I have just begun to take my most delightful trip in the intellectual and spiritual fields. It is not my question how far my destiny may be, but simply go as far as I can and do as much my strength permits, leaving all my future in the hand of Him who sees all the affairs of the universe from the endless to the endless.

BOSTON, *February* 16, 1872.

I am requested by the Japanese minister to come to Washington to inform the Japanese Embassy about the system of American education. So I have been studying it since last week. It gives me plenty to do. I will go to Washington as soon as the Japanese Embassy arrive there. I expect to *stand up for Christ* before the heathen embassy; I think it is a good opportunity for me to speak Christ. I wish you would make special prayer for me, and also for the embassy.

In 1872 the most important embassy that had ever left the shores of Japan visited America and Europe. Men of inferior rank had at various times been sent by the shogunate on missions of inquiry to other countries, but this was the first great embassy representing the imperial government of the Mikado. It was composed of four cabinet ministers, of commissioners in the several administrative departments, and was under the conduct of one of the most distinguished of Japanese nobles and statesmen, Iwakura Tomomi. Accredited to the fifteen nations then in treaty relation with Japan, its objects were thus stated in the letter of credence presented at Washington: "The period for revising the treaties now existing between ourselves and the United States is less than one year distant. We expect and intend to reform and improve the same so as to stand upon a similar footing with the most enlightened nations. . . . It is our purpose to select from the various institutions prevailing among enlightened nations such as are best suited to our present condition, and adopt them, in gradual reforms and improvements of our policy and customs, so as to be upon an equality with them." In its diplomatic character the embassy was a failure. The Treaty Powers were unwilling to abandon their extraterritorial rights, and to commit the sole administration of justice to a people without a civil code, tc whom trial by jury and the writ of habeas corpus were unknown, and whose criminal procedure was still characterized by cruelty and contempt for personal rights. In its subsidiary quest for information on the political and social institutions of Christendom, the embassy was, however, eminently successful, and its return was signalized by a very remarkable series of reforms.

Its leading members were Iwakura Tomomi, Okubo Toshimichi, Kido Takayoshi, Ito Hirobumi, Terashima Munenori, and Tanaka Fujimaro. Iwakura, the chief ambassador, was a Kugé or court noble, and had been a chamberlain of the imperial household of the father of the present Mikado. On the overthrow of the shogunate he had entered the cabinet as Minister of Foreign Affairs. With Kido, Ito, and Okubo, he was active in the movement which led to the restoration of the supreme authority of the Mikado. The memorable address to the Emperor, signed by the powerful daimios of the southwest, in which these princes resigned to the crown their feudal rights, was drawn up by Kido, who was the head, as Saigo was the arm, of the imperial cause in the revolution of 1868–69. On their return home these men occupied important posts in the government and took a prominent part in the reconstruction of the empire. Mori Arinori, at this time representing Japan in Washington, and the first Japanese to be appointed under the restoration to a foreign mission, had previously met Mr. Neesima at Amherst, and now summoned him to Washington to assist Mr. Tanaka, the Commissioner of Education. This summons was an exceedingly fortunate one for Mr. Neesima, for it brought him to the knowledge of men who were to control in large measure the future policy of the government, and whose friendship in later years, when beset with difficulties and enemies, proved of the greatest value to him. He received it, however, with apprehension, and obeyed it with reluctance. He had previously feared that the government would assume his support, as it had already done in the case of students sent abroad by the daimio before the restoration, and that in so doing would also assume the direction of his studies and subsequently claim his services. Anything which threatened his cherished plan to return to his native land as the free emissary of Christ alarmed him. He was therefore careful to stipulate that Mr. Mori should explain to the embassy that he was pursuing his studies under private auspices, and that any service desired of him must be based upon a contract acknowledging his freedom from all obligation to the government. His meeting with the embassy, as described in the following letters, the dignity and modesty with which he asserted the distinction between his own position and that of his fellow-students under government patronage, and the zeal which, having gained his point, he displayed in the furtherance of Mr. Tanaka's mission, were eminently characteristic of him. Of Kido he made a personal friend, and he soon proved so valuable to Mr. Tanaka that the latter insisted upon his accompanying the embassy to Europe. This proposition was in many respects very attractive. The change would doubtless be beneficial to his health ; the opportunities for meeting men, for studying western institutions, for seeing the world and enlarging his horizon under exceptionally favorable circumstances, and, above all, for impressing upon the future educational system of Japan his own views of the relations between education and religion, civilization and Christianity, were unique, and would surely never recur. He was the channel of communication between the commissioner and the world, for Mr. Tanaka then spoke no foreign language ; he had been requested to write a report on a general system of education for Japan ; his friends unanimously advised him to accept the commissioner's offer. Yet he hesitated to commit himself to a course which might end in his becoming the servant of the Mikado rather than the servant of Christ, and referred the question to his " American father " for final decision. This decision was favorable to his acceptance of the commissioner's offer, and he was thus brought into daily contact with some of the most influential and progressive men of New Japan. Trained in the Confucian philosophy, familiar from experience with the social and family life to which it leads, yet always condemning the Confucian doctrine of filial duty as tyrannous, he was particularly anxious that Mr. Tanaka should become acquainted with the life he had known in the Christian homes of New England, and during the three months passed in visiting the schools and colleges of the Eastern States the commissioner was the guest of many leading educators and philanthropists in New York, Boston, New Haven, and Amherst.

In his journal and letters Mr. Neesima alludes with modesty to his services to the embassy ; yet it would be difficult to overestimate the influence he exerted through it upon the educational progress of Japan. In Europe, as in America, he gave all his time and strength to the study of the best methods of instruction then prevailing, the organization and conduct of schools and institutions of learning of all grades, and it was on the basis of his reports that Mr. Tanaka, appointed on his return Vice-Minister of Education, laid the foundation of the present educational system of Japan. His personal influence also was felt by all associated with him; for his character marked him off from all others connected with the embassy in a like capacity, and won for him that sympathetic esteem and respect which was so valuable to him in later life. Traveling in close companionship with others, he never failed in his private devotions, in his conscientious resolve to rest on the Sabbath, in his effort to speak for Christ.

TO MR. AND MRS. HARDY.

GEORGETOWN, D. C., *March* 8, 1872.

I arrived at the capital safely yesterday morning and was cordially received by Mr. Mori. I found myself very tired when I arrived, therefore I did not go to the hotel where the embassy are, but went directly to the Japanese Legation and asked the minister to put me in some quiet private family. He was very kind to me and told me to lie down in his house, but I could not sleep at all for there was so much confusion. In the afternoon the American private secretary of the minister secured a good place for me in Georgetown only two miles from the capital, not far from his own house. Mr. Mori requested me to come to Arlington House this morning. I went there at the settled time and saw the Minister of Educational Bureau of Japan. Twelve Japanese students in the States were summoned to meet him to give him some advice. The power was granted them to make any motions or give any advice to him, and the motions would be carried by the vote of the majority. When they went in the parlor to meet him, they made the Japanese bow to him; but I was behind them, standing *erect* at a corner of the room. Some time before this meeting I handed a brief note to Mr. Mori stating my present relation to you, and asking him to distinguish me from the rest. Mr. Mori stood for me very favorably, and told the Commissioner that he must not rank me among the other Japanese; for I have been supported and educated by my Boston friends and have not yet received a single cent from the Japanese government. So he had no right to treat me as a slave of the Japanese government. "At my request," Mr. Mori said, "Mr. Neesima came here, not as a bondman, but with his kindness to give you some advice concerning education. So you must appreciate his kindness and willingness to do such a favor for you. As Mr. Neesima has such a relation to his Boston friends, he cannot commit himself to the Japanese government without their consent, neither has the government any right to lay claim on him, or to command to do this or that, but the things ought to be done by a contract between him and you. Fortunately he has three weeks' vacation, and will do some good service to you if you treat him as a friend. He is a lover of Japan, but not a slave." This speech pleased the commissioner exceedingly and made every one in the room to look at me. When he noticed me standing erect he asked Mr. Mori whether the corner-stander was Mr. Neesima. When he ascertained that it was he stepped forward from his seat, shook my hand, and made a most graceful yet most dignified bow to me, asking me to be a kind friend to him. He bowed himself 60° from the perpendicular. So I made like bow in return. I could not help laughing within my heart that a behind or corner-stander was so honored by him in the room. He gave me an order to be an interpreter to him when he goes around the country to examine the schools, and to tell him all about your school system. I told him if I am ordered to do this I would rather refuse it, because he should distinguish me from the others who received aid from the government; but if I am requested to do this for a certain compensation, I would gladly do any favor for him. The commissioner told Mr. Mori to treat and receive me exactly as I requested of him.

It was voted to meet to-morrow morning at 11 o'clock. During the meeting the students made several motions, but I did not vote or say anything, in order not to place myself on the same platform of the rest. When the meeting was dismissed the others made 30° bow from the perpendicular to the commissioner, without shaking his hand. But he came to me and asked where I reside and requested me to call on him privately. He then shook my hand and made 70° bow to me, wishing me for the improvement of my health. I could not help laughing at my being distinguished so much among the Japanese, for I have never thought myself that I was something, and have always desired to keep myself unknown from the public. So when I went to the parlor I stood at a corner keeping myself behind the rest, standing erect and not bowing, desiring to keep my right. I am glad to say I kept my right and my right was granted to me. I wish you would rejoice with me at this triumphant hour, for I am a free man, a free man in Christ. I could not help thanking you through whose aid and means I have attained this liberty. I know your prayers have been answered now, but pray on still. I do not care for the esteem of men, but only wish to remain a humble child of God.

I suppose you would not object of my spending this vacation with the embassy, if I take a good care for my health. I have not seen Iwakura, the chief ambassador, but had a pleasant interview with his secretary, who was a friend of two of my best Japanese friends at home, and found out all about them.

My boarding-house is very near where some Japanese girls are staying for the present. I saw two of them yesterday. One of them is about fifteen years of age, and another is only eight years old, the second daughter of my old schoolmate, who is now a prominent officer in the country. She is a little cunning and acute thing I ever saw. I had very pleasant conversation with them and dined with them too. They don't understand what the ladies in the families speak to them; so when I go there to see them they are delighted to see me, and ask me ever so many questions. They feel so friendly to me, and are not afraid to ask me questions, for I told them I shall be very sorry if they do hesitate to ask me anything. Though I do not preach to them, yet I am teaching them some moral principle in a pleasant way. So I think they would not take me as a lover of girls, though I call on them so often, but a kind instructor, because they make such graceful Japanese bow each time when I speak to them. I am so thankful that I can do some service to them.

TO MR. AND MRS. HARDY.

GEORGETOWN, March 10, 1872.

Yesterday morning I went to the legation to attend the meeting of the Japanese students. I found there the twelve who were summoned to Washington. They are divided into two parties. One half of them is called the upper party, and another half the lower party. As I had obtained, or rather kept up my right, to remain a free Japanese citizen, the Commissioner of Education and Mr. Mori agreed to hire me during my vacation and pay me so much for my service to them. I at once accepted it, because I thought you would not find any objection to my doing so. The object of our meeting is to make statutes for the Japanese students who are supported by the government in the foreign countries. I am a member of the upper party. You must know I am a free member, and can withdraw myself from it at any time. Several topics for discussion were given out by Mr. Mori. The parties divided the topics and met in different rooms to discuss their own topics. This morning we met together and brought our separately discussed topics into the general assembly. The commissioner was appointed our chairman, but he did not appear this morning. I rather suspect that he is somewhat afraid of us, because we, the students in this country, are the true democratic. We do not hesitate to say anything. Last Saturday we made a petition to the chief ambassador to grant us a power to make a statute by the vote of majority, and when it is passed we may order it even to the Commissioner of the Educational Department. So we have more power of making statutes pertaining to

students in the foreign countries than the minister
himself.' The topics discussed to-day may not interest you much, therefore I will not write you about
them. My principal mission is to write an essay on
" The Universal Education of Japan." I think it is
a most important mission. It will be handed to the
embassy and probably may be some service for opening the country to the light of *truth* and *life*. Pray
for this untiring soldier of the blessed cross, for I feel
my active battlefield has come within my sight. I
am ready to march forward, not asking whether my
powder is dried or not, but trusting simply and believing only that the Lord of Hosts will help me to
do my duty.

Mr. Mori is ever friendly to me.

TO MR. AND MRS. HARDY.

GEORGETOWN, D. C., *March* 15, 1872.

This is the very first time here I see the clear blue
sky and bright sunshine. I am feeling quite cheerful
and stronger than ever before since my arrival here.

I went to the Legation this morning, to attend the
meeting of the Japanese students. I stayed there
some time to hear them speak, but their view was
entirely impracticable, and I was not interested in
such child's play at all. I excused myself before the
meeting was dismissed and called on Mr. Eaton, the
Commissioner of Education, who promised the Japanese commissioner to take him to a private female
school only a short distance from his office. Then
Mr. Eaton accompanied us, the Japanese commissioner, his two under-officers, and myself, to the
school. Mr. Eaton introduced us to the lady teacher
and then gave us seats. Very soon the exercises be-

gan. One young lady was called up to read poetry, not only for us but as one of the exercises in the examination. She stood very gracefully and read it wonderfully well. Then they were examined on algebra. I do not think they were remarkably bright on algebra. After this was done another young lady was called up and read prose. She read it very well too. After the examination was over Mr. Eaton gave our cards to those young ladies. The names amused them very much.

After I had taken the noon lunch I called on General Babcock. He told me he had an American interpreter, and also finds several English-speaking individuals among the embassy, and as I have a hand full of work for the Japanese Commissioner of Education he would not call upon me for any service. He said also he would be very glad to introduce me to the President, but unfortunately he is out to-day. He asked me to call again, and sent an order to the usher to show me all the rooms and conservatory of the White House. I called on Rev. Mr. Rankin and had very pleasant conversation. He is an old Andover graduate and was glad to see one who came from the same seminary. He invited me to attend his service to-morrow. Thence I went to the Patent Office. I was perfectly bewildered by the grand sight of the collection. I did not take much pains to examine it, but simply went around and got some idea of wonderful Yankee ingenuity. I went to the office and obtained the last report.

I am thinking now to invite the Commissioner of Education to Mr. Rankin's Sunday-school. I suppose he will go there because he is so anxious of seeing the American institutions. The commissioner

is very well educated man in our way and well acquainted with my old teacher. He feels very friendly
to me and wished me to go to Europe with him to
examine their school system. He knows my health
is rather poor and advises me to take a short trip to
Europe. He says if I should go there with him he
would pay all my expenses and give me certain compensation for services. He would treat me as his
friend, not as his under-officer, and would give me
leave to return to America at any time. He says he
would go to Europe as soon as he gets through visiting the schools in the North, and would start before
the embassy proper, and take pains to examine the
systems of England, France, and Germany. I told
him plainly all my history, what poor fellow I was
when I arrived at Boston; to what kind hands I have
fallen; how I have been supported. I told him especially my great obligation to you, and that I am your
minor and cannot decide on the matter without consulting with you. He was much pleased with my
narration and wished me to write you soon as possible
to get your advice, or rather permission. Mr. Mori
told me the same thing some time ago. He says it
is my choice; I can either accept or refuse. The embassy will respect me as a free Japanese citizen. He
thinks it is a rare opportunity. I spoke it to several
individuals here; they say it is my golden opportunity.
I am much perplexed with this free and rare offering,
and almost inclined to go to spend this spring and
summer in Europe for my health, and also for widen-
ing my information. As I said before, I am your
minor. I would not do anything unless I get your
approval or consent. Please make consideration with
your wisdom and sagacity and tell me what I shall do.

Sunday. The snowstorm has prevented me to go to Washington to attend Rev. Mr. Rankin's church this morning, so I went a nearest meeting-house I could find here, which was Methodist church. The service was very quiet and impressive. I was much pleased with the sermon. It was an extempore and simple sermon, yet very persuasive. It is very much different from the reading some cold and philosophical discourse which is spun out from some intellectual head, but not from warm pious heart.

Mr. Tanaka, the Commissioner of Education, requests me to move to Washington so that he might see me oftener. I think I will do so some time this week.

TO MR. AND MRS. HARDY.

GEORGETOWN, D. C., March 10, 1872.

I visited the Patent Office and Smithsonian Institution with the Japanese Commissioner of Education to-day. Very kind attention was given us by the officers of the buildings, so we had better opportunity to see them than common visitors. After we got through visiting those places the under-officers returned to their boarding-places, but Mr. Tanaka invited me to dine with him. It was some time beyond my lunch hour, so I gladly accepted his invitation and dined with him at Arlington House. After the dinner I went to his room and spent nearly three hours in conversation on the subject of national education. I did not speak to him on the subject of religion thus far, but I could no longer keep down my burning zeal. I gradually poured out my humble opinion on the national education. It is impossible to write and give you all the idea that I spoke to him, but only in a condensed form.   A nation or an individual shall need to be intelligent in order to be a good citizen. An intelligent citizen can be governed much better than an ignorant.   But his intellect is not sufficient to control himself morally.   If he has intellect only, and has not the moral principles, he will do more harm to his neighbor and society, than do them good. His sharpened intellect will be very much like a sharp knife. He may ruin his fellow creatures and also destroy himself.   If such a ruinous person exert such a bad influence among his society, the hundreds and thousands of such will surely cause the ruin of a nation.   Therefore there must be a moral principle to keep down such a ruinous intellect, for if a person has moral principle he can make right use of his intellect.   Therefore the Japanese government must provide some means, or allow some person, to teach moral principles to the people.   Education only is not sufficient to make men virtuous ; neither intellectual nor moral philosophy is enough for it.   I never knew any persons become virtuous by studying the philosophy of Plato or books of Confucius.   But on the other hand there is a power in the Christian religion to make men free, vigorous, and virtuous.   If a man loves virtue he indeed is a true man and does know how to take care of himself.   If each Japanese knows how to take care of himself, the government shall not need setting detectives here and there throughout the country.   If the whole nation love truth and virtue they will govern themselves, nor give or cause much trouble to the government.   The strength of a nation is the strength of their virtue and piety..   Some people make use of the Christian religion as a mere instrumentality, but if so his religion is not a true one.

There is truth in the Christian religion. We ought to take truth *because it is truth*, and not as a mere instrumentality.

Then the commissioner told me that what I said concerning the education and religion agrees with his view very much except one point. He said he knew something of Christianity, and has begun to appreciate its goodness and value more and more since he came to this country, seeing so plainly what the Christian people are doing here. He is almost awe-struck with the schools, churches, and some charitable institutions supported by the Christian people or societies. Then he thought Christianity one of the best instrumentalities to govern a people or elevate a nation; but he said, " I do not know enough to say that we ought to love truth because it is truth, and not use it as a mere instrumentality."

As he said, he does not know truth enough. He is anxious to know of it to a fuller extent. He says the government has no right to interfere in any form of religion, for belief in any religion is in the heart and not in outward deeds. The duty of the government is to keep the people in good order, and it ought to let the religion be free to the people. Let them worship true God or heathen gods according to their consciences. If there is truth or goodness in one religion more than the others it will prevail after all.

I was exceedingly pleased with broad view on this subject, and felt so thankful for this new opening way to speak so freely. The commissioner is going to visit a deaf and dumb school to-morrow, but he gave me leave to rest myself, because he has one more Japanese interpreter beside me. He is very anxious to know whether you will permit me to go to Europe

with him or not.   I did not say much on the matter,
only that I must depend on the decision of my
patrons in Boston.   If this is only opportunity for
me to go I would rather do so and with Mr. Tanaka,
for he is such a man of broad view.   I may possibly
do him some good, especially for promoting Christ's
kingdom in Japan.   If I do show him some favor,
he might become a great help for my further labor.
Please let me hear from you as soon as you can.

TO MR. HARDY.

GEORGETOWN, D. C., *March* 20, 1872.

I wrote you this evening asking for your decision
on my visiting Europe with the Commissioner of Education of Japan.   Some time after mailing it I was
carefully thinking of the subject, looking not simply on
one side, but the other.   I may be of some use to Mr.
Tanaka, but if I become useful to him he may possibly lay a snare to catch and take me back to Japan,
and make use of me for the educational purposes.   If
I once connect myself with the government I shall be
its slave.   Though I may do some good in doing so,
yet it is not my predominant choice to commit myself
to the hand of the government.   I have already recognized the Sovereign King, the Saviour, as my lord and
government, and shall not need any other government.
Therefore it would be my best policy to keep myself
free from the snares of the Japanese government.
They may keep good terms with me; they may invite
me with a word like honey, and treat me as a hired
servant at first, and then they may gradually lay hold
of me.   I believe the commissioner is a perfect gentleman and would not treat me treacherously.   Yet what
I have said above is my Yankee speculation.   There

is some danger and tendency of my trusting in other persons too soon, not thinking deep enough. But in regard to my future steps I must be pretty cautious. I must do what is noble, right, and true. As I have consecrated myself to the work of my Master, I must try to seek opportunity to discharge my duty to Him and my benighted fellow-creatures. I would rather preach or teach truth which is in Christ Jesus with the bread of affliction than to do any other things with the earthly luxuries, pleasures, and honors. Then the question is, What would be most advisable for me to do? It is a grand opportunity for me to visit Europe now. It is rather a sacrifice for me not to go. But though I may not go there yet I shall not lose very much, because I shall study theology at Andover. It is very hard matter to decide. Please give me your advice and guidance. If you say *no,* I will cheerfully obey your advice; and if you say *go,* I shall not decide it at once.

The Commissioner of Education of Japan will be in Boston within two or three weeks to visit the famous schools in the city. Will you be kind enough to notify his coming to the city, and to those schools which you may think worth while for him to visit. If you do me this favor it will also be much gratifying to Mr. Tanaka.

TO MR. AND MRS. HARDY.

GEORGETOWN, D. C., *March* 22, 1872.

I am greatly obliged to you for your kind consent to my request for my accompanying the Japanese Embassy to Europe. Since I wrote you on this subject I have been carefully and prayerfully considering on the question, but I could hardly know what should be the guidance of Providence. Your last letter gave me a clear decision, and made me feel and think that it may be a voice, not human, but from on high, to open the way to my active life or Christian labor. Though I do expect only to accompany him for a short time, yet I may possibly do some service for promoting Christ's kingdom in his heart, hence to Japan. So I would no longer doubt or hesitate, but say I will go wherever the Lord will direct me and do what I can for honoring and glorifying Him. When I wrote you my last letter I was almost inclined to refuse the Commissioner's offer and resume my study at Andover. But all my Japanese friends have encouraged me to go; Mr. Mori advised me to go, and Mr. Lanman, his American Secretary, told me not to lose such a golden opportunity. Professor Seelye told me " better go," and lastly you, whom I regard more than my own parents, gave me a consent to go. I will simply say " Thy will be done."

I am sure it will be gratifying to Mr. Tanaka, for he has been anxiously waiting for your reply since I wrote you my first letter on this subject. When I see him I will ask him to give me a note of stipulation to send me back to the United States before next September, or whenever I get tired of traveling, and will keep it as the sign of agreement.

I accompanied Mr. Kido, vice-ambassador, Mr. Tanaka, and General Eaton, and four other Japanese, to Columbia College yesterday morning, and had very enjoyable time, though it was busiest day I ever have had since I came here. I kept up talking partly in Japanese, partly in English, from 9 A. M. till 5 P. M. It was long eight hours' pulling. We returned to Arlington House at half past eight. Mr. Kido

invited General Eaton, my fellow - interpreter, and
myself to dine with him in the room reserved for the
chief ambassadors.   I was sorry no blessing was
asked when we commenced our dinner.

Mr. Kido is one of the strongest men in Japan, and
has taken most prominent part in the last revolution
of Japan in overthrowing despotic government of the
Shogun, and establishing the new, healthier, and liberal government of the Mikado.   His manner is very
gentlemanly and agreeable.   I had quite a chat with
him at the table and behaved myself just as if I was
talking with my fellow-students at the club of Andover.   I have been resting to-day for preparing myself
for the coming Lord's day ; for if I overdo to-day I
shall not be able to enjoy the service of the Sabbath.

We are going to leave Washington next week to
visit the schools of Philadelphia and New York, and
we may possibly reach the *Hub* of the universe within
three weeks.

TO MR. AND MRS. HARDY.

WASHINGTON, D. C., *March* 28, 1872.

Since I wrote you my two last letters I have made up
my mind to accompany Mr. Tanaka to the Old World.
I am so grateful for your kind consent and best wishes
for my success.   I would not go abroad unless I feel
it may be good opportunity to promote Christ's Kingdom to the heart of heathen nobleman and Japan.
Mr. Tanaka is trying to finish visiting the schools and
institutions so as to leave Washington within five days.
He is quite anxious of seeing and knowing the good
American family life and wished me to inquire you
whether you could find some private family at Boston
where he could see and learn the true American life.

He has thus far stopped at the hotels.   He told me also he does not care for seeing the grand style of American living, but the true national character.   It is too much to ask you to accommodate Mr. Tanaka and your humble servant during our stay in Boston. If you could do it without causing you much inconvenience I am sure it will do him a great good.   I have been telling him what you have done for me these seven years, since I began to room with him at the hotel.   He is quite anxious to see you.   I will leave the matter in your hands entirely.   Please do it as you please and think the best to satisfy his wants.   I think Mr. Tanaka is sharp enough to see the true pride and glory of America.

I believe that I have forgotten to inform you that I was requested by Mr. Mori to be present when Mr. Northrop had his first interview with the embassy.   Mr. Mori asked many questions to Mr. Northrop concerning the national and universal education, for the embassy, and I took notes of Mr. Northrop's plain and practical talking.   Although I have not had much interview with the whole embassy, yet I am very well acquainted with Mr. Kido, who is the ablest man among them and the great friend of the universal education.   I have seen him very often and told him my humble opinion concerning the national education. I told him it ought to be based on virtue. I am now at the hotel with Mr. Tanaka and have splendid opportunity to talk with him on the subject of true elution, *i. e.,* the education of Soul.   He was deeply impressed with my humble opinion a few nights ago and told me that all religions should be free, and the Bible should be studied by each student, not as a text-book, but a virtuous food.   He could not yet see or say spiritual food.

March 29th. Yesterday Mr. Northrop, his daughter, and her friend Miss Page, accompanied us to Mt. Vernon. The weather was quite smoky in the morning, but the report of the weather said " fair," so we had much courage to start on our pilgrimage to American Mecca. While we were approaching the sacred spot the smoke was getting gradually cleared off and the sky was bluer and fairer. The breeze on the river was quite agreeable and charming. Finally we landed with hundred or more of our fellow-visitors. It was some time after one o'clock, so we sat on the front piazza of the general's home and took our lunches, which Mrs. Dr. Parker furnished for us. It tasted much better than splendid dinner which I had with embassy at Arlington House. After the lunch we went round the house and all the rooms. I saved a few leaves of that famous magnolia tree. Now I can proudly say that I have visited the Capital of the great republic and the tomb of the Father of Liberty.

We shall leave Washington next Monday. Will you be kind enough to drop a line to Professor Taylor to inform him what I am doing here and get excuse from him for my not coming back to the Seminary. May the Lord help me to keep myself very humble.

TO MR. AND MRS. FLINT.

BOSTON AND ALBANY TRAIN, *April* 10, 1872.

Since we left Washington I am rooming with Mr. Tanaka. I have kept up my morning and evening devotions in his presence. I become Sunday-school teacher to him. Of course he cannot read English Scriptures, but he has a copy of Chinese New Testament ; he reads it in Chinese and I read it in English, and explain to him what he could not understand.

Though he is not a professor of religion, yet he is almost Christian in his heart. I trust God will bless my humble labor in a near while. Grace of God may save him from heathen darkness and make him a great instrumentality to promote his kingdom to Japan.

TO MR. AND MRS. HARDY.

NEW HAVEN, *April* 30, 1872.

Since we left Boston we have been just busy as we were in Boston. When we reached Amherst we tried to stay in Amherst Hotel, but Professor Seelye came after us and would not suffer us to stay there. He welcomed us to his home and gave us very kind attentions. Professor Seelye and President Clark took us to Holyoke Seminary in his carriage last Wednesday, and Mr. Tanaka enjoyed our visit there exceedingly. President Clark also took us to the Agricultural College and showed us what he has there. On Thursday we spent most of our time in Amherst College. On Friday we attended experiments on optical instruments, and on the same afternoon we were invited by Professor Seelye and Dr. Hitchcock to visit the Northampton Institute. The new method of teaching deaf and dumb was most marvelous thing I ever saw. *The dumb can speak.* We bid farewell to Amherst last Saturday and arrived in the City of Elms on the same afternoon. We went to the New Haven House and had a long rest until the evening. I called on Mr. Northrop, but he removed somewhere, and his new house could not easily be found. So I gave it up and thought I should wait until next morning. But he came after us with carriage the same evening and took us to President Porter's house. We did not expect to find

such kind hospitable friends everywhere. Mr. Tanaka sends his kindest regards to all, and also much
thanks for your hospitality.

May 2d. I am in a great hurry and can scarcely
think of what I am writing you, being so tired of
visiting so many schools, and also horrified with the
idea of my going to visit so, many more places. Mr.
Northrop is a most hasty gentlemen I very seldom
meet. He crowd up a great deal within a short space
of time. You may be interested to know how much
we have seen during our brief stay in New Haven.
Monday we visited Yale College, Cabinets, History
and Art Gallery, and Sheffield Scientific School.
Tuesday we visited Deaf and Dumb Asylum, one
high school, Brown School, Insane Asylum in Hartford, one normal school in New Britain and State
Reform School, and silver and gold plating factory in
Meriden. Wednesday we were guests to the inaugu-
ration ceremony of the new governor of the State,
riding in an open carriage nearly four hours. To-day
we visited three public schools in this city. It has
been pretty hard pull since we came here. Mr.
Northrop is such a busy man and would not give us
time to think. Though we have planned to leave
New Haven for New York this afternoon, we are still
detained by Mrs. Porter. She has been so anxious
that we should take some rest before we go, and has
persuaded us to remain here one day more. So I can
have this afternoon for myself quietly and feel thankful to her for detaining us one day longer. President
Porter is making a list of books for me which may
be useful for my future labor, and has given us letters
of introduction on prominent English gentlemen.

Since we were invited to your house we have found

friends here and there, and feel so thankful to you for your first opening the pleasant home for us.   It is so pleasant for me to be in such a Christian family as President Porter's.   I am glad Mr. Tanaka had a good opportunity to see so many Christian families, and the ways and modes of Christian living.

When I left your home I was thinking to speak to you a great many things, and to express my innumerable thanks for your parental care and unceasing love to this poor and helpless runaway boy.   After I was sitting at the dinner-table that afternoon, all my past life, my leaving home, my works during the voyage, my finding Mr. Hardy, and your *unceasing* kindness ever since, was reviewed in my mind just as the dishes and plates on the table were set before me.   I felt so thankful for the kind providence of God as to lead me to you, the spiritual mother, and also I was so affected by the sense of gratitude I became entirely speechless.   It may be the unfailing decrees of the Infinite Father that I should be sent to you, be cared for and educated by you for a special purpose, though I shrink with the idea of my littleness and unworthiness.   So it is my constant cry to Him to guide, guard, and strengthen this untiring soldier.

New York, May 6th.   Through Professor Seelye's effort we are received at Mr. William Booth's house. His father, Mr. W. A. Booth, took us yesterday morning to Mr. Stewart's store, Bible House, and Cooper Institute, and in the afternoon to Five Points, Newsboys' Lodging House, and the Times Office.

Dr. Booth, a brother of W. A. Booth, dined with us last evening, and we had a very interesting conversation with him.

I am glad to say that Mr. Tanaka is impressed with

the result of Christian education by his visiting so
many charitable institutions since we were in Boston.
He does kneel now at the morning prayer with Mr.
Booth's family, though I said nothing to him about
his position of worship. I think he has an instinctive
reverence to the Infinite Father. He is always re-
membering your kindness and wishes me to send you
his kindest regards. Please let me hear from you before you sail for Europe, and I will try to write you
once more before next Saturday.

I have been working just hard as my strength
permits, for I dislike to leave things in a half way.
I have written many letters for Mr. Tanaka.

Good-by and also good-night to you all.

CHAPTER IV.

FIRST VISIT TO EUROPE.

TO MR. HARDY.

Steamship Algeria, May 20, 1872.

I received your very last letter on the steamer just before we left Jersey City. Through Providential care we are still permitted to enjoy the running cup of blessing on the great deep, and are hoping to reach Queenstown at midnight. During the 12th, 13th, 14th inst., we met dense fogs more or less, but after we passed by the banks of Newfoundland we have been free from fogs, although we met frequent rains. During last three days we are facing to head wind all the way, though she is sailing twelve or thirteen miles per hour. This hard struggling against head wind gives very unpleasant motions to the steamer, confining Mr. Tanaka to his berth. As for me I am like an old Jack, so called among seamen. I have been enjoying good appetite and sleeping well every night; I have also been enjoying good company on deck; for instance, Rev. Mr. Porter of Lexington, his friends Mr. and Mrs. Goodwin, Prof. Charles Elliot of Chicago, and some other English gentlemen. During the voyage I have noticed a strange thing, *i. e.*, that everybody on board drink something, some sort of liquors, which I abhor with all my soul. Gentlemen, ladies, even D. D.'s, have something before them. As for me I shall not take it as long as the water is wholesome and drinkable.

I write this brief note to you hoping simply to inform you our safe voyage thus far. I think we shall remain in Glasgow and Edinburgh only a few days, and will try to meet you in London within a fortnight.

TO MR. HARDY.

EDINBURGH, *June* 3, 1872.

Supposing that you have just reached London, I will write you this brief note to inform you how we are getting along in Scotland. As you may have understood by my last letter we touched at Queenstown two weeks ago to-day and to-morrow will be our third Tuesday since we arrived at Liverpool. We did not find any trouble in landing at Liverpool, for the Custom House Officers were very civil to us. They did not inspect our luggage at all, and moreover one of them accompanied us to our hotel. Staying there only one day and a half, we took our first trip in England to an awful smoky city, Manchester, where we had very pleasant interview with the Bishop of Manchester and obtained a great deal of information on the English education. We were very much pleased with his politeness to the Orientals and also very sound advice on our future steps.

We left Manchester a week ago last Friday for Glasgow, but finding the journey rather wearisome we stopped at Carlisle for the night. On the following morning Mr. Tanaka had not courage to get up, finding himself very tired; so I did leave him alone and took a walk on a little busy street, a long street. Fortunately I discovered an old castle standing on an abrupt hill at the outskirt of the city. What inviting view it was to a lonely walker. I went up there and was kindly received by the guardmen. On top of rampart I had the whole view of city. If your little grandson Sherburne was with me he might undoubtedly have said, "It is splendid."

We stopped at Glasgow only a few days. Mr. Tanaka works hard as ever and we are getting along nicely in our business. We start for London to-morrow, and are hoping to see you with a great pleasure.

TO MR. HARDY.

LONDON, *June* 8, 1872.

Yours of the 3d inst. was received yesterday at Barings. I have been very anxious to know of your arrival for some time, and am so glad that you have arrived safely at Cork. We had a very pleasant time at Edinburgh, and get along splendidly in visiting schools. We were very much pleased with the Scotch character, especially the people of Edinburgh. They are truly the Bostonians of the British Empire.

We had very serious time procuring our hotel in London, riding around the city from 8.30 P. M. till 11 P. M. Finally we got in Golden Hotel, Charing Cross. There was only one single room, so they emptied a drinking room for us, and its bedstead consisted of one sofa and three chairs. The day before yesterday we called on Mr. Donald Matherson, who is a great friend of Rev. Charles Douglas, a missionary in China some time ago, and whom we met at the great Assembly in Edinburgh. He was very attentive to us and procured us lodging in a private family for our temporary abode until we may find a still better place. I am getting quite tired for visiting schools so constantly since we arrived at Liverpool. Everything comes upon my shoulder, even for keeping up accounts. Mr. Tanaka is perfectly a gentleman, but does not know how to count English money. We expect to remain in London three or four weeks, and I hope to shake your hand once more on this side of water.

I made a loudest Macedonian cry to Dr. Mullens to send a few missionaries to Hakodate where no Protestant missionaries are, but only a Russian Greek priest to whom I used to teach the Japanese language just before I ran away from that port. I told Dr. Mullens this cry does not come to him in his dream, but with a living voice and personal appeal of a representative of that benighted nation. I left my photograph to him, writing a portion of Romans 16: 9. Pray for us.

TO MR. AND MRS. HARDY.

Macon, July 21, 1872.

It does seem a long while since our separation. though it was only a week and six days ago. We arrived in Paris safely last Wednesday via Dover. It was rather trying to Mr. Tanaka. He was very sick notwithstanding a calm weather. When we came to Paris we were very much struck with the fine streets and beautiful buildings, but felt pity with the people who take so much pain for the outward show and vain glory, but are neglecting the soul's culture.

We left Paris for Geneva yesterday. Finding the journey rather tiresome, we stopped in this place last night, intending to take the early express train for Geneva this morning. When I started from Paris I thought it was Friday instead of the last day of week. But finding this Sunday I refused to travel to-day, though Mr. Tanaka was wishing me to go to Geneva with him this morning. I told him I cannot conscientiously travel on the Sabbath. Wherever I may be I must halt on the Sabbath to rest my soul on the Lord, except some unavoidable case. So Mr. T. could not urge me to travel with him to-day and went to Geneva with his French-speaking Japanese, asking me very politely to excuse him for his not staying with me here. So I am left alone in this strange place, although I do not feel lonesome at all. I went to the French Protestant church this morning, but I did not understand the preaching. I knew only that the preacher was earnest by hearing his exciting voice and noticing his constant gesture. The congregation was very small, about twenty ladies, five gentlemen, and a few boys and girls. Although the ladies dressed not very neatly and the gentlemen dressed with frocks like butchers, they appeared very attentive during the service; I trust that they were rich in the inward person, though poor in their apparel.

There is no single cloud in the sky, and the sun is shining brightly on the blue and tranquil stream of the Saône. I am so thankful for God's giving me such a privilege and freedom as to worship Him according to my conscience amongst strangers, without any fear or disturbance. I find the French keeping of Sabbath very different from New Englanders. The men and boys are fishing along the banks of the Saône, and the women wash the clothes here and there. All the drinking saloons are opened as it were some week day. So I can at once discriminate the Roman Catholic people from the Protestant nations.

BERLIN, *August* 6, 1872.

Since writing you from Macon I have been to Geneva, Berne, and Zurich, and arrived here last night via Augsburg and Leipzic. We leave for St. Petersburg this evening and may possibly remain in Russia for a week. Then we will return and begin to study the Prussian system of education. As yet we have only called on our Japanese friends here. We unexpectedly met Mr. Sears in the street. I was very glad to find him and learn something of you. Thus far I have been moving from one place to another, but after I get back from Russia I shall engage to a hard study. Another Japanese who speaks German is added to our party and will go with us to St. Petersburg. Mr. Tanaka feels quite proud for having three Japanese with him who would individually speak English, French, and German. He remarked to-day that he can go round the world without any difficulty with three of us. I think I am of little use to him on the Continent, for the English is very little spoken here, but why he desires to have me go with him is that I should study the European systems of education and see the operations in the schools myself. The three of us have been getting along without slightest difficulty among ourselves. The others say nothing against my religious faith and observances. Although they pay some respect to Christian institutions, yet they have not drank in the rich cream of truth which we can obtain only by coming to the tender and forgiving Saviour. As Mr. Tanaka is somewhat hasty person, he does very often travel on the Sabbath when it is convenient to him, especially to save time. I

have not said anything to him against it, but always
I halt on the Sabbath whether in the city or country.
I have already explained to him the reason. I have
attended the English services at Berne and Zurich,
but I am sorry to say that the preachings did not satisfy me at all. They spend over an hour for services,
and about fifteen minutes for sermons. Their dis-
courses are somewhat cold and lifeless.

Since I left France water does not agree with me at
all. So I have made a new resolution, to take some
diluted wines or beer until I may be accustomed to
water in any new place. As I have been long ab-
staining from any sort of liquors, I am very easily affected by a few swallows, which is rather trying to my
old Puritan principle.

St. Petersburg, *August* 10.

Two of our party who are influenced by French
infidels and German rationalists went out for sight-
seeing on the Sabbath morning and hired one guide
without consulting me. In the first place they asked
Mr. Tanaka and myself to visit a Russian church.
When I saw a guide coming with us I objected their
hiring him simply for going to a church. I went to
the finest Russian church in the city with them, falling into their net, but soon after I inquired of that
guide for an English or American church and asked
him leave to let me do my way. When I came back
from church I found they did not accomplish very
much; they went to some garden, but were very much
disappointed and disgusted with it. I found Mr.
Tanaka reading some Christian books whole afternoon. I am glad to inform you he has found some
difference between the motives of my own and the

other Japanese. I feel more and more a heavy responsibility is resting upon my shoulder.

TO MR. AND MRS. HARDY.

COPENHAGEN, *September 3,* 1872.

We did not stay long in St. Petersburg, only five days; visiting there the University, a training-school, the Foundling Hospital, Museum, Hermitage, etc. The Foundling Hospital is very large building and can accommodate nearly 6,000 persons. There were 800 babies under care, and all of them are only a few weeks old. What struck me most among the large collections of the Hermitage was the painting of the Holy Family by Raphael. St. Petersburg is very striking city. It is built on a grand scale. The palaces and government buildings are very extensive and beautiful at a distance, though some of them may be hardly called beautiful in the architectural view. The churches are also large, and the interiors of the cathedral and Isaac's Church are exquisitely wrought. They very much resemble Roman Catholic church. The pictures of Holy Family and relics of old saints are numerous and are kissed and bowed before by the ignorant people. The devoted Russians make regular Japanese bow before them and also make a double cross before their chests when they pray. I have a great sympathy with those devoted Russians, for they appear very earnest in their devotion, but am sorry that they are led away by a false method of worship or a false notion of doctrine.

I must not forget to mention to you that famous mammoth in Museum, which was discovered in an ice-bank in Siberia in 1799. It is proved that it is non-existing creature in the present age by two main points; namely, in the first place it is hairy, and secondly its teeth are growing too close together.   I saw its hair, kept in a glass case; it is quite long and has sandy complexion.

The people of high rank look very intelligent, and most of them speak at least one or two foreign languages; whilst the lower class of the people are very ignorant, very inferior in appearance, and cannot read even their own language.   I never saw any cabmen reading newspapers as I used to see in the other European cities, but I found them always sleeping while they are waiting.   The cabs are very heavy and small.   The driver's dressing is also peculiar, as you may see in my sketch.   The accommodations in the Russian hotel are not good at all, and the waiters are very slow and lazy.   They never get up before nine o'clock in the morning, and when we want to get anything at that time we are obliged to touch our bell half a dozen times before we awake them.   The chief business of the city seems me in the hands of the Germans.

We came back to Berlin on the 16th ult.   Finding all schools unopened there, we thought time may be better spent visiting other parts of Europe.   Accordingly we started for Holland via Frankfort-on-the-Main.   We came down the Rhine by steamer as far as Rotterdam.   Without stopping in that busy city we proceeded to The Hague, where we were kindly received by the Minister of Public Instruction, and a fine opportunity was given us to visit all schools in the capital.   I was much pleased with the cleanliness of the school-rooms and neatness of children.   The school system is excellent in Holland.   It is open to all classes of the people.   But the other schools are still better than the free ones. The American system is far superior to the Hollanders. In their public schools the Bible is entirely kept out. I rather suspect the Hollanders are not so devotedly religious as they used to be in the time of Republic. We visited the Royal Palace and also the "House in the Woods," the Queen's private residence, and had there a fine opportunity to see the Queen. While we were in the ball-room she came there without giving any previous notice. She looked at first as if she was quite amazed at our appearance in that room; then cast her eyes down on the floor slowly, as if nothing happened to her. She must be over fifty years of age, though I could not see her face very distinctly on account of her black veil.

We stopped at Leyden a couple of days on our way to Amsterdam, and visited the University, Botanical Garden, a fine ladies' school, — that is, a fine school for ladies, — and museums, where we saw a large collection of Chinese and Japanese curiosities.

At Amsterdam we were accompanied by a member of the Department of Public Instruction to visit all different grades of schools. One school is a peculiar one, in which youths of the working class are theoretically and practically taught particular branches of industry. The most striking thing in Amsterdam is the numerous canals and bridges. We could not help seeing them everywhere. We spent last Sabbath at Hamburg. My two companions went out to take walk along the harbor. Of course I could not spend the Sabbath as they did. I went alone to English Reformed Church, and listened to a very fine discourse by Rev. Mr. Edward, an English clergyman.

We came to Copenhagen yesterday and called on

the Minister of Public Instruction this morning. In the afternoon we went to the exposition held presently in the city and have spent there the whole afternoon. I felt very much wearied after my return, but I could not forget my best American friends, so I began to write these lines to express my greatest affection and respect to both of you. Allow me to assure you that I ever appreciate your kindness shown to me more and more by visiting the institutions of learning in Europe and finding the great value of education. I never can feel that I can repay to you for what you have done for me, but will try with my utmost power to conform my whole future to your chief object, that is to say, that I should preach the crucified Saviour in whatever condition I may be. I begin to see a great obstacle before me in the way of my preaching, for the most of our educated men in Japan are falling into the infidelity. But I am happy in a meditation on the marvelous growth of Christianity in the world, and believe that if it finds any obstacles it will advance still faster and swifter, as stream does run faster when it does find any hindrances on the course. Oh, what pleasant thing it is that we can rely on the hand of the living God. He will make a great use of us humble vessels in his household if we simply remain faithful to Him.

I wish you would render my compliments to all my American friends. My health is improving very much. I shall be *always* happy to hear from you.

On the return of the commissioner to Berlin Mr. Neesima had again to meet under another form the question which had perplexed him at Washington. It had been his intention to resume his studies at Andover in the early fall. Mr. Tanaka now announced his speedy departure for Japan by way of Suez and his earnest desire that Mr. Neesima should accompany him. Decision was not easy. Mr. Neesima had become an indispensable assistant, and from the nature of the case was of all persons most fitted to aid the commissioner in the important work which awaited his return, and to which all that had yet been accomplished was but preliminary. To leave him at this stage of affairs would, he felt, be almost a desertion. Moreover, his old enemy, rheumatism, had again attacked him, and he dreaded another winter in the cold climate of Andover. Health is dear to all, but to none more so than to him who feels the burden of a great responsibility, to whose purposes and plans for work is added the conviction that he only can best accomplish it. It is noticeable, however, that as the years passed this solicitude for his health diminished. Always ready for self-sacrifice, the discharge of duty became less and less a sacrifice, till, like the soldier when the battle is at its height, with an enthusiasm and devotion which the bystander may characterize as rashness, he forgot himself entirely and literally gave his life away. The real question before him was one of ways and means, not of end. It appears from his journal that even at this early date the germ of that idea which led to the foundation of a Christian university in Japan was in his mind. Feeling deeply the importance of Christian elements in education, should he go back to New England, complete his theological course, and return to Japan as an evangelist, or embrace this rare opportunity to influence at its very inception the educational movement about to be inaugurated there? It was, however, by no means certain that Mr. Tanaka's plans, either in general or for him specifically, would be approved by the home government; and this uncertainty, together with the fear of becoming permanently committed to an official career, decided him to hold to his original intent.

Some months intervened after Mr. Tanaka's departure and the opening of the seminary year at Andover. These Mr. Neesima passed in continuing his investigation of German schools, in acquiring the language, and in the attempt to improve his general health by treatment at Wiesbaden. The persistent return of his rheumatism depressed him, and he was especially restive under the necessity of spending so much time in this pleasure-loving city. Intent always, however, upon his Master's service, he here made the acquaintance of a young Japanese officer in charge of the manufacture of paper currency for the government, at Frankfort, and persuaded him to study the Bible. Two years later, on the eve of his return to Japan, Mr. Neesima received a letter informing him that his fellow-countryman had embraced Christianity, and in his journal writes: "While at Wiesbaden I was disheartened on account of my long illness. I now begin to see that my being there was not entirely in vain. It is a great comfort for us to know that the Lord does sooner or later turn our bitter waters into sweet, and I am thankful to Him for my illness."

TO MRS. HARDY.

BERLIN, October 2, 1872.

I found yours of the 25th of August from Berchtesgaden on my return to Berlin. I was very much pleased for your kind and interesting letter, and trust your health and Mr. Hardy's was very much benefited by breathing in that invigorating mountain air. I have had a difficult matter for my consideration for these past few weeks. As you know well I was quite undecided whether I should go home with Mr. Tanaka, or come back to America to finish my study in Andover. I have been deliberating on the question these long whiles. But since I came back here I am requested by Mr. Tanaka to go home with him. He says he could not get along without me, for he has some intention to print some Christian books besides his own reports. Another thing has arisen to hasten me to go home for a while. That is to say, I began to feel cold weather sensibly here in Berlin within a few days. So I fear my old trouble may come back to me if I expose myself to a very cold weather. This thought does discourage me to go back to Andover to resume my study this year. So I thought that I might go home for a year or two to get rid of this rheumatic trouble in that milder climate, and then I may possibly be prepared to meet the cold New England winter again. It causes me a great regret for my not resuming the study at present, but I am obliged to look after my health. If you have no objection I would rather decide to go home with Mr. Tanaka. I wish you would tell me what I should do. As you know, it was an understanding between you and me that I should come back to America by all means before I go home. Mr. Tanaka is talking to go home via Suez, for it would be a great deal warmer than by the American continent. But I would rather go via Boston; and if the cold weather might be very unsafe for my rheumatism, I might tarry in warmer part of Europe until the next spring. But I fear Mr. Tanaka would not wait for me until the next spring, for he has detached himself entirely from the embassy. If I forsake him he will be alone. Shall I satisfy my own ardent desire to see my American friends and cause an inconveniency to Mr. Tanaka, or accommodate Mr. Tanaka and deny my own appetite? I am determined to come back to the United States to resume and complete my theological study in order to fit myself wholly for the missionary labor. I have no desire after the worldly wealth or fame, for I believe I have firmly fixed my eyes to the glory and excellence of Christ. Since I came to Europe and saw so many ungodly people I can clearly see the necessity of the gospel truth to human souls.

We have now about eighty Japanese students in Berlin, but all of them have fallen in the habit of ridiculing Christian people without knowing what Christian truth is. One of them asked Mr. Tanaka's intimate friend whether Mr. Tanaka has become a priest, because that irreligious Japanese has heard of his being with me and reading Christian books with an intense interest. When Mr. Tanaka heard about that contemptuous remark he did not mind of it, but was only smiling. I think if these men go home they will cause a great hindrance to the cause of Christ's church, which has just begun to exist in Japan. I am thinking it may be a good season now for me to open a way to the missionaries and shade the national education with the Christian and moral principles before they attempt to do great mischief to the country. O that God may direct all my thoughts and affairs. I pray you to advise me what steps I should take. I trust you will throw a better light upon me.

I am working pretty hard now, spending nearly six hours a day for translating the school laws and reports of different European countries.

TO MR. AND MRS. HARDY.

BERLIN, *October* 20, 1872.

Your fatherly kindness and deepest sympathy with me did move me to many tears. I have been prayerfully and more deeply thinking upon the question I did propose to you in my last letter, and am earnestly seeking for a better light not to plan my future affairs worldly, but to yield myself to the whispering voice "follow me."

Yes, I may possibly render some good service to our people by going home with Mr. Tanaka and assisting him in establishing a new school system in Japan. If I do engage to such a work I would not. give it up in a half way, and if I do wish to accomplish it, it could not be done at least within two or three years. Mr. Tanaka does not think that the work would take much time, and as soon as an educational system is established in the country he would send me back to resume my theological study. He does think our work no less easy than his traveling through a large part of Europe within four months. But I must not take what he says without careful consideration. It is well for me to exercise the Bible teaching: "Be wise as serpent and harmless as dove." If I go home now without looking afar off I may probably be fallen into a snare and find a considerable difficulty to get out again. If I am fastened by such a way, what shall I do with the voice "follow me"? As our lives are too brief I must not take too much of my time for the worldly affairs. In order to work for my Master it is necessary for me to make a due preparation; in order to qualify myself to the work it is also necessary to breathe once more in the pious atmosphere of New England. Would you pray for me that Providence may bring me once more to Andover Seminary? Please let all my things be in Andover as they now are.

TO MRS. HARDY.

BERLIN, *December* 16, 1872.

In regard to my future steps, not hearing from you any further advice, I made a decision not to go home with Mr. Tanaka. Please allow me to give you a reason for my decision. 1st. Mr. Tanaka does not know exactly what position he could get for me, only that he should make use of me by some way. His invitation is not authoritative, but his private opinion. The Japanese government is still unsettled; and if he is replaced in his position, who will be responsible for me? Therefore I will not accept his invitation, for it seems me too much like a child's play. 2d. If I go home now, while I may possibly render some service for our government, I fear my time will be taken up too much for that purpose and cause me delay to commence my service to my spiritual sovereign. I feel more and more that I am captured by my Saviour, and shall not be happy if I do not work for my Master. As my theological course is not yet half finished, I would like to resume it until I should be ordained to preach the gospel to my benighted countrymen. It was my first choice that I should ever take my cross and follow my Master. It is my happiest choice, and I believe it is the best choice. As you have been my spiritual mother and kind patron thus far, I trust you will still continue your kindness and allow me to promote my study still further. I have been intending to send you some money, which I have saved for my educational purposes, to be kept by you. I should like to tell you some of my experiences in Germany, but time does not allow me to do so. I called on Mr. Sears a few days ago; he is much interested in music. Since I wrote you my health has been very poor, — nervousness, sleeplessness, and dizzy headache. I once almost concluded to discontinue my work, but I am slowly gaining now. I was perfectly awestruck when I heard the news that the charming city, the Queen of New England, was devoured with the tongues of consuming fire. I do not know how large share you have in the calamity, but I trust it would not be very heavy upon you.

TO MR. AND MRS. HARDY.

Berlin, *January* 6, 1873.

Allow me to shake your hands at a great distance and congratulate you from this side of Atlantic for your entering into another year with ever increasing happiness and prosperity, as I trust. As for me I can simply say as Apostle Paul said, I am what I am. Though my health has been rather poor I am still permitted to keep up my engagements for our government. How good God has been with me during the past years. As our future is entirely unknown to us, I simply trust He will lead you and me step by step, as it was in past, into eternal future.

Now allow me to inform you what a pleasant time I had last Christmas Eve with Mr. Sears. It was the first for me to see the real German Christmas festival. It is customary with the Germans to sing on every occasion. It was opened with singing and reading the New Testament. Then we were shut up in a room without light, and after a while were led into another room where we found many piles of the presents on the tables. He gave me a pretty traveling valise. I was much pleased with the festival, not simply that it was rather a new and strange thing to me, but that every one in the room was smiling with the intense admiration.

Since that time I have been very busy for getting Mr. Tanaka ready to leave Berlin. He left three days ago for Vienna and Rome, and will start from Paris for Japan this month; so I shall be obliged to finish my report for him before he starts. Besides the educational affairs I was requested by him to write a brief report on the Christian churches in England and America.

Perhaps you have already noticed in your paper that our government has given up our old calendar, and adopted the European one. All our eighty Japanese students in Berlin gathered at one of the restaurants and drank beer to celebrate our new epoch. I went there also, but did not enjoy it very much. There was the uncle of our emperor in that gathering. He appeared very humble and gentlemanly. I am also glad to inform you that one of the Japanese students in Berlin came to me the first Sabbath of this year and requested me to explain the Bible to him, and also take him to the Methodist church, where I generally go. I was quite surprised by his request; it is entirely voluntary. We took the Gospel of St. John for our first exercise. He had the Chinese and German Bibles and I the English and German. Of course we used our native tongue for the conversation. We were very much interested, and two hours of hard study seemed to us very short. He went away quite satisfied and promising to continue his study every

Sabbath. He told me that none of the Japanese students in Berlin study the Bible. How sad it is that so many know nothing of Christianity. I wish you would offer special prayer for that one who has just begun to study with me, that the thick unbelieving scales may fall from his eyes and he may see the gentle Saviour standing by him.

TO MR. AND MRS. HARDY.

BERLIN, *January* 15, 1873.

I have just received your kind letters. It does seem to me a gentle and refreshing rain to a dry and parching land. I am so glad you passed the last Christmas with your friends so pleasantly and were ready to enter into the new year.

Through your description of the present state of Boston I could almost see the ruin before my eyes.

With regard to Japan, she is getting brighter and brighter, although the progress is somewhat superficial. I am so rejoiced to know that my aged father had an opportunity to see my teacher and friend, Professor Seelye.

I have not felt well at all since my return to Berlin, probably owing to my extensive trip and continued labor. I have been unable to go out for three days on account of rheumatism. Dr. Keep and my physician advise me to go to Wiesbaden. I could not reconcile to the idea of going there, for I thought it is not the place for a poor fellow like myself; but after an investigation I found it not so expensive as I thought, so I made up my mind to go there. If you have no objection I should like to remain in Europe until next summer, partly for my health and partly for my further investigation on the educational system of Ger-

many. But as I am your minor you must tell me
what you think the best and I will follow your guide.

I have sent you a check for $480 gold. I calculate
it will be sufficient to support me for another year's
study in Andover.

TO MRS. HARDY.

WIESBADEN, March 5, 1873.

I have been here just three weeks and taken nine-
teen baths. My health has been improving pretty
steadily, and I hope as soon as the weather is settled
to be well again. I think this bath is an excellent
thing for rheumatism, but it does rather excite my
nerves. Hence my nervous headache is no better than
it was three weeks ago. My physician advises me to
continue the bath a week or two longer and also drink
the mineral water. When I started from Berlin I
was much disheartened, for I thought it too bad for a
young man like myself to be unable to do much bodily
or mentally, and to go to a bathing place for cure.
But since I came here and saw many suffering young
people in much worse condition than myself, I began
to feel very much encouraged and also to be thankful
for God's gentle dealing with me.

I suppose you are well acquainted with this place,
so I shall not make you any description of it. It is a
very pretty place, but a large part of the people are
pleasure worshipers. The theatre, dancing party,
and masked ball are very well attended, but the
churches are empty. Yet I have found here a few
real Christians and made several acquaintances among
them. They were so glad to see me who was brought
to light from darkness. Although I am living here
amidst strangers, I begin to feel quite at home by

knowing these few Christian people. Taking the whole it seems me that Protestantism in Germany is a matter of policy and does differ vastly from what it is on the free shore of New England.

April 6, 1873.

My thought daily flies towards you, but, alas, my bodily infirmities! Although my rheumatism is entirely over, I am still troubled by heavy, dizzy, and constant headache. I left bath house two weeks ago and came to Pastor H——'s house. He is a very pious Lutheran preacher. Although his dogmatic view is somewhat different from mine, there is no slightest unpleasantness between us. He wishes that I should study the Lutheran theology and tries to convince me it is purest among all others. But I cannot quite agree to some points.

Mr. Sears informs me that he is decided to start for home on the steamer Germania, June 14th, from Hamburg. I thought at once I should accompany him. While I was reflecting upon this subject in my sleepless bed a thought came upon me which you may possibly call an ambitious one. As you know, I have been in Germany over seven months, five of which I spent entirely for Mr. Tanaka; so I have not had great opportunity to learn the language. If I return to America or Japan without knowing the language sufficiently I shall be very much laughed at by my countrymen who are now making such a progress at home in sciences and European languages under foreign instructors. I also think it very necessary for me to keep myself a little ahead of them in modern thoughts, sciences, and language, in order to be a public man religiously. If I return to America in

June it would be just vacation time, and I may not accomplish a great deal there. So I am rather persuaded to remain in Germany until the first of August.

I received a good news from home about two weeks ago. My father and sister wrote me very pleasantly. He says in his letter how pleased he was with the news of my accompanying Mr. Tanaka, and says also his long anxiety for me is well paid by it. He went to Yokohama and received the money which I sent him from Boston. Since the Japanese feudal system is abolished and he is deprived of his possession in his prince's house, he has been living on what he has saved during his service. A missionary in Yokohama told him the story of Joseph, comparing him to this unworthy Joseph. He says he came to Yokohama on a little carriage driven by man instead of horse. It is the present fashion of our conveyance.

TO MRS. HARDY.

ELSINGEN, GERMANY, *August 6, 1873.*

I finished the second course of mineral baths at Wiesbaden two weeks ago and took my departure from that fashionable city for Friedrichsdorf, a small town not far from Homburg, to pay a visit to my old Berlin acquaintances. Most of the inhabitants are descendants of Huguenots and are still speaking their mother tongue. They read the French Bible and sing the French hymns. To my great surprise some of them could not speak German at all. Through my friends I was introduced to several Huguenot families, and was invited by them to dinner or supper every day of my stay. I was so pleased to see some of them clinging to the old faith, and keeping the Sabbath as their poor suffering fathers did, while the large part of

Germany is taking the Sabbath as holiday instead of holy-day. I could not help shedding out my tears when I heard three little girls of the family where I stopped offering sweet French prayers in their morning devotion. I attended the French service with them in the morning and went to a Methodist chapel in the evening. Most of the Huguenots go there in the evening, although they are still Calvinists. I visited two famous institutions in the town, one for boys' and another for girls' education. They were much pleased to see a converted Japanese, and the girls brought me 5 thalers 13 groschen for the Japan mission, expressing their best wishes. Each one gave about 8 cents, which I consider a great sacrifice for these young girls.

I came to this place to find out the management and regulations of the teachers' seminary. I have been here just one week, visiting the seminary and elementary schools attached to it every day. I will not write you my observations, because it will require a considerable time; but suffice me to say that German system is excellent, slow but sure. I am intending to leave Germany next week and go to my beloved America by the way of Paris and London. My friends and physician in Wiesbaden advised me to return to Japan on account of rheumatism. But I feel a plow is on my hands. On the other hand I fear my health would not allow me to work enough to satisfy my craving appetite for knowledge. I am now entirely free from rheumatic pain, and also from headache from which I have been suffering for nearly five months, but my nervous system is not quite strong yet. I get tired easily when I try to use my brains. I have saved money enough to carry on my study one year longer.

TO MR. HARDY.

LONDON, *August* 27, 1873.

I found your letter at Barings' yesterday. I had some thought to go home before next winter, fearing to spend it on that windy hill of Andover. But your kind advice gives me a new courage to take up again the plow in my hand. Then I shall go home. The Lord has preserved me thus far so wonderfully, though I have been often troubled by my body, that I will put my confidence boldly into his hand and try to do my best to prepare myself for my future labor among my countrymen. Pray for me that I may give bold and faithful service in his ever-conquering battle-field.

Mr. Neesima returned to Andover in September, 1873. During his absence he had laid aside from the salary received from the embassy a sum which he proposed to devote to the completion of his theological course, but he was persuaded to invest it and to allow his friends to continue their aid. Anxious to begin at once his active life, he resolved to remain at Andover but one year and to accomplish as far as possible in that year the seminary work allotted to twice that time. Fortunately his health continued good. His letters of this year are the simple record of persistent study. In February, 1874, he writes: "The young ladies in the Academy have invited our students to their private levee this evening. All good-looking men are invited. A few stupid fellows are exempted. I am one of them. I could not help laughing at it." He adds: "I have received a letter from Mr. Gordon, a missionary in Ōsaka. He is very anxious to have—

me come there. He finds it quite hard to preach in Japanese. If I did not know him to be a careful man I would not believe that his statement is true, it seems so graphic and highly colored concerning the rapid growth of my country. I do not yet know my future destiny in Japan. I have not yet an idea where I shall be settled or how I shall be supported."

In March he writes: "Dr. Clark, Secretary of the American Board, sent me word to call on him as soon as possible, in order to talk over with me my future plans. Accordingly I did so. He showed me a letter from Mr. Green, a missionary at Kôbe, and asked me whether I was willing to offer myself to the missionary work in Japan. Of course I made an unconditional surrender to this call."

At the same time an urgent appeal for his presence and coöperation was received from the missionaries at Kôbe, several of whom were his personal friends and had been associated with him as fellow-students. Even a perfect morality must suffer from lame exposition, and the need was felt of one who could speak in the Japanese tongue, who could interpret much that was harsh and forbidding, because foreign, to the Japanese mind, and who should add to intellectual power that of winning confidence and giving sympathy, a power which a native only could effectively exert.

As a result of his conversation with Dr. Clark, Mr. Neesima definitely offered himself as a missionary under the auspices of the American Board, to whose secretaries he addressed the following letter: —

To the Secretaries of the American Board of Commissioners for Foreign Missions.

Andover, April 30, 1874.

Dear Sirs, — Allow me to state to you a brief history of my early education, my later Christian experience, and especially my motive in offering myself to the missionary work in Japan.

I was brought up in the faith of Buddhism, and was also instructed in the moral precepts of Confucius. Afterwards the former became offensive to me and the latter were unsatisfactory. Under these influences I became somewhat skeptical, notwithstanding at times I had some desire for something higher and better.

In that state of mind I came across a Chinese translation of the Bible history by an American missionary in China. Its expressive view of God led me to inquire still further after Him. With this purpose I was led to leave my home, and took passage for America. The Providence which ordered my way so far provided friends at Boston who have thus far supported me in my education. I date my conversion some time after my arrival in this country, but I was seeking God and his light from the hour I read his word.

With my new experience was born a desire to preach the gospel among my people. The motive in offering myself to this work is my sympathy with the need of my country, and love for perishing souls and above all the love of Christ has constrained me to this work. I expect to complete my study this summer. I am not in debt at all. My health was quite good while in Japan, but since my arrival in this country it has been somewhat poor; still it is improving now. I expect to remain unmarried some time.

Respectfully yours,

JOSEPH NEESIMA.

In reply to the questions propounded in the manua. of the Board for missionary candidates, he wrote: —

"In my view the leading doctrines of the Scriptures are: the existence of one true God, inspiration of the Scriptures; the Trinity; the decrees of God; the freedom of the will; the total depravity of man; the atonement; regeneration; justification by faith; the resurrection of the dead; the final judgment. I have not the least doubts respecting any of the doctrines commonly held by the churches sustaining the missions under the care of the Board. My confidence in the reality of my conversion is in my growing trust in Christ and increasing sympathy with truth. My views of ministerial duty are to preach the gospel to the salvation of men. My desire to enter the ministerial work is due to the need of it in Japan, and my hope that I may be of some service in supplying that need. I expect to meet with some difficulties and trials; yet I shall count all joy, not only to believe in Christ, but also to suffer for his name. It is my purpose to give my life to this work."

Mr. Neesima was thereupon appointed corresponding member of the Japan mission. He preached his first sermon from the pulpit in the church of Rev. E. G. Porter in Lexington, Mass., on May 10, 1874, choosing for his text the verse he so dearly loved (John iii. 16). On July 2d he graduated as a special student from the Andover Theological Seminary, in a class of twenty-one, and was one of nine speakers in—

the graduating exercises. The subject of his address, delivered in Japanese, was "The Preaching of Christ in Japan." The summer of 1874 was devoted to preparations for his homeward journey and to farewell visits to his many friends. The latter part of August he passed with Mr. and Mrs. Hardy at their summer home in Bar Harbor, Maine, returning to Boston for his ordination, which took place on Thursday, September 24th, at the Mount Vernon Church in that city. Delegates were invited from twenty leading churches in the vicinity, and there were also present as delegates at large, Prof. J. H. Seelye of Amherst, Drs. Anderson, Treat, and Clark, of the American Board, Dr. J. L. Taylor of Andover, and Dr. G. W. Blagden of Boston. The ordination sermon was preached by Dr. Seelye from the text: "And I, if I be lifted up from the earth, will draw all men unto me." The right hand of fellowship was extended by Rev. Ephraim Flint of Hinsdale, and the charge was delivered by Rev. A. C. Thompson of the Prudential Committee of the Board.

On Friday, October 9th, the sixty-fifth annual meeting of the American Board of Commissioners for Foreign Missions was held at Rutland, Vermont. At this meeting Mr. Neesima was present, and was asked, with others who, like himself, were about to leave for foreign stations, to make some remarks at the farewell session in the evening. The subject of his brief address, which was an earnest appeal for the establishment of a Christian college in Japan, had long been in his thought. He had had some conversation with Secretary Clark and Mr. Hardy upon this plan of his, but received little encouragement. Just before his death, when this long-cherished scheme had become a reality, he referred to it as at this time only a day-dream. The importance of education as the hand-maid of religion, and the advantages to be derived by the Board in its special evangelistic work from an institution whose courses of study should be pursued under Christian influences, were fully recognized. Still, education in itself was not the primary object of the Board, and its officers were reluctant to encourage appeals for special purposes, however praise-worthy, at a time when the expansion of its regular work rendered increased contributions imperative. But it is evidence of Mr. Neesima's breadth of view and persistence of purpose that he should have conceived this project at this early stage, and in the face of fifteen years of difficulties and opposition carried it to a successful issue. Mr. Neesima was a true evangelist. In every circumstance, at every stopping-place in the journey of life, he spoke for his Master. His life is a record of personal endeavor. But he took no narrow view of duty or opportunity, was wedded to no single line of effort. He had pondered deeply upon the future needs of his countrymen. He knew their thirst for knowledge. He foresaw the advancing tide of education; he wished it also to bear the seeds of a Christian faith. He belonged himself to a class whose intelligence and patriotism destined them to the control of their country's future. This class he wished to win over, and to accomplish this he foresaw the necessity of an educated native ministry. In a communication addressed to the Prudential Committee ten years later he said: —

"Though the feudal system was abolished by the late revolution, still the men of that (samurai) class are leading the nation. Their young generation, catching the chivalrous spirit from their fathers, will also be our leaders in the immediate future.

"It is a curious class. Perhaps you could nowhere else find such in the whole Asiatic continent. It is neither like the exclusive Brahmins of India nor the warrior robbers of Arabia. So far as my own observation is concerned, they are the most haughty and ambitious race you could possibly find in the country. They have been trained to be faithful to their feudal masters even unto death. The spirit of patriotism has been handed down among them from generation to generation. To them honor is everything; life and property are of no account. *Harakiri,* an act of self-destruction, was only practiced among this class because they deemed it a shame to be killed by others. They are indeed the oriental knights, the spirit of Japan and flower of the nation. Though their rank seemed rather servile, in truth they have been ruling the nation from behind the screen of nominal potentates these past six centuries. It was truly they who started the late revolution. It was they who crushed the Shogun's despotic government and restored the reigning power to the sacred personage of the long-secluded Mikado. It was they who cast off the old worn-out Asiatic system and adopted the vigorous form of European civilization. It was they who started schools, pushed the press, cried out for personal rights, and are now working out the way for a free constitution. I am happy to affirm here that they also are destined to carry the glad tidings of human salvation to their fellow-countrymen. They are far better educated than any other class. They are no longer ignorant, or worshipers of dumb idols. Modern science is a whetstone to their intellect. European politics are but juicy beefsteak to their desperate appetites. If we let them take their own course, what will be the future destiny of Japan? If they fall down Japan will go down with them. And if they rise they will certainly raise up the whole nation. If you take them away from the people, nothing but old-fashioned plodders will be left behind. National prosperity or misery hangs upon the pivot of this particular class. I believe it is just the time to reach, rescue, and win them to Christ. If we let them swim away from the gospel net, they will certainly be caught by the Devil's hand. Remember that he is far wiser than the children of light. If we fail to reach them now, we fear we shall find the process of evangelization an uphill work. But if we win them we shall certainly win the whole Sunrise Empire. Being far better educated than any other class, they are more susceptible to Christian truth. Being strictly trained to faithfulness to their feudal masters, they will be more faithful to the Master of masters, if He is made clearly known to them. Being middle in rank, they can reach both the higher and the lower. This may be the very class where you may expect to find a Saul of Tarsus. Yea, this may be the people whom God has chosen from the beginning to be the foremost cross-bearers, to lead their fellow-countrymen to the Eternal City.

"Your question will naturally arise: how to reach this class? to which my reply will be very simple. *Provide for us the highest and best possible downright Christian institution.* It is the only way to both satisfy and win them. My ten years' experience in Japan has induced me to affirm that the highest possible Christian education will be a *power* to save the nation."

On the evening of the day previous to the farewell meeting Mr. Neesima consulted Mr. Hardy upon the advisability of laying this plan before the Board. Referring to this incident in a letter written in 1889, he says: "Mr. Hardy was doubtful about my attaining any success; however, I was rather insisting to do it because it was my last chance to bring out such a subject to such a grand Christian audience. Then he spoke to me half-smiling, and in a most tender fatherly manner said, 'Joseph, the matter looks rather dubious, but you might try it.' Receiving that consent, I went back to the place where I was entertained and tried to make a preparation for the speech. I found my heart throbbing, and found myself utterly unable to make a careful preparation. I was then like that poor Jacob, wrestling with God in my prayers. On the following day, when I appeared on the stage, I could hardly remember my prepared piece —a poor untried speaker; but after a minute I recovered myself, and my trembling knees became firm and strong; a new thought flashed into my mind, and I spoke something quite different from my prepared speech. My whole speech must have lasted less than fifteen minutes. While I was speaking I was moved with the most intense feeling over my fellow-countrymen, and I shed much tears instead of speaking in their behalf. But before I closed my poor speech about five thousand dollars were subscribed on the spot to found a Christian college in Japan."

No record of Mr. Neesima's address has been preserved. The movement was unpremeditated and unexpected, and the action which followed was not that of the Board as such and consequently found no place in the secretary's minutes. But all present felt the intense earnestness of the speaker, and refer to the scene as one never to be forgotten. Swept away by his feelings, refusing to resume his seat until his appeal was answered, declaring that he would not return to Japan without the money he asked for and that he should stand on that platform until he got it, the young Japanese carried his audience with him. Hon. Peter Parker of Washington rose and subscribed one thousand dollars; Ex-Governor Page of Vermont and Hon. William E. Dodge of New York, followed with like sums, and before Mr. Neesima had finished, his day-dream had become a reality.

Towards the end of October, after an absence of nearly ten years, he left New York for Japan, via San Francisco, the first ordained evangelist of his race.

TO MR. AND MRS. HARDY.

Green River, Wyoming. *October 25, 1874.*

I must explain to you why I am stopping here to spend the Sabbath on this lonely mountain top. When I left Chicago I made a miscalculation about spending the Sabbath. I thought I could reach Salt Lake City Saturday evening. But it was not so. Then I thought I must not travel on the Sabbath. I might have stopped at Cheyenne or Laramie, but I found it not best to lose time, so I traveled last night and got out from the train at this breakfast station. Soon after breakfast I engaged a room in a small and miserable inn, — a pretty rough-looking one. The people in this place are rough-looking workmen. I found a half-dozen Chinese in the dining-room of the station. I talked with them through my pen and found most of them agreeable and polite. One of them wrote good Chinese, asking me why I stopped in this place.　My reply was, to spend the Sabbath.　I asked him whether he does believe in Jesus Christ, and his reply was, "I belong to."　It was indeed a pleasant answer.　I told him when he was through his work I should like a few minutes in conversation with him and his countrymen.　Here is no church, but many drinking houses, and I do not know what kind of Sabbath I shall have in this lonely mountain town. If I could not wisely reach these rough settlers I will try to talk with the Chinese on the subject of religion. I told a few fellow-travelers on the train of my view of stopping in these wild regions, but none did encourage me, because it may not be safe or pleasant. Some told me there is no Sabbath west of Mississippi River.　I did not listen to them at all.　I must mind my own business.　My keeping the Sabbath does not depend on anybody else.

TO MR. HARDY.

SAN FRANCISCO, *October* 20, 1874.

I am just arrived in this city where our missionary party is (five for Japan and two for China).　I spent last Sabbath quietly at Green River, Wyoming.　It is a strange place.　I called on the Chinese and had pleasant conversation with them.　I found two out of sixteen somewhat acquainted with the Christian truth. The rest of them are unable to talk English, and are low, ignorant, and degraded.　They keep their gods in their house.　They live together like pigs.　It is a pretty rough place.　More than a half of the settlers are young and unmarried men.　I tried to reach them by some way but found it almost impossible. They are bound to be wicked.　I went to Salt Lake City Monday evening and tried to see Brigham Young, but was unsuccessful on account of his illness. I saw his secretary, and through him I was introduced to Orson Pratt, the ablest preacher and writer among them and also one of their twelve apostles. He was very gentlemanly, and answered very patiently all my questions about Mormonism. He desired me to preach the gospel which he preaches, but I thanked him and answered him I should preach the gospel which I find in the New Testament and nothing else. He was not offended by my reply, and willingly assisted me in visiting objects of interest, — the Tabernacle, City Hall, Mormon University, etc.

I enjoyed the trip exceedingly, especially the scenery on this side of Green River. My bag is almost filled with geological specimens. Snow at the summit was nearly eight inches deep, but within a few hours we found the climate mild and nature looking quite genial and inviting. I am invited to Oakland to speak to friends of missions.

October 30.

Your coming to New Haven to see me off made my leaving Boston easier than I expected. You seemed to know exactly what I felt about leaving your home. It was a great treat to me that both of you came, and gave me the opportunity of bidding you farewell the second time. I am also greatly indebted to you for your parting present. My father is in debt now, and this will help me to pay off his debt and also get a few things for my parents and sisters. I trust you know how grateful I am to you, although I utterly lack in words to express it.

TO MRS. HARDY.

LAT. 30° 6′ N., LONG. 158° 25′ E.
November 21, 1874.

Hoping to meet a homeward mail steamer before we reach Japan, I undertake to write a few lines to let you know how far we are advancing on this wide ocean. We embarked on the Colorado on the 31st ult. Just an hour before she left San Francisco the steward handed me Mr. Hardy's kind letter for my father. When we sailed out from the Golden Gate the day was remarkably bright, and the sea wonderfully quiet. We found the breeze so mild and agreeable that we could stay on deck quite late in the evening without overcoat. A few days after we left we began to seek for our congenial companions. I found the Sabbath the best time to find or rather read the moral and religious character of the passengers. By combining my observations on the Sabbath and week days I can get an approximate opinion of their chief aim for this life. We have forty-five cabin passengers and 230 steerage. The former consist of eleven different nationalities, *i. e.*, American, English, Belgian, French, Austrian, Prussian, Polish, Italian, Irish, Chinese, and Japanese, and the latter chiefly of Chinese. There are quite a number of opium smokers among the Chinese, and six of them died since we left San Francisco. Is it not a dreadful thing? It is a great curse to the Chinese. Woe unto them who first introduced it to that empire. These opium smokers are not allowed to smoke anywhere, but are compelled to smoke in a large box, the inside of which is lined with tin, once used for keeping ice in. Those who died were mostly aged men. I saw there a man who has not been out of that box since we left San Fran-

cisco. He is lying there day and night, and has
scarcely taken anything except that deadly poison. I
have not formed any special acquaintances among the
passengers beside our missionary friends except a
German doctor who is going to be a professor in the
Imperial Medical School at Yedo, and to whom I give
Japanese lessons every day. Our missionaries are
obliged to suspend its study on account of seasickness.
The sea has lately been very rough; even I who professed to be a good sailor have been ill this week on
account of the unceasing up and down motions. I
have read through Eitel's Lectures on Buddhism and
some other books, and am intending to write a Japanese sermon. I have observed among the passengers
that they form different societies. The smokers go
together as they were real and congenial friends, and
so do the drinkers. The Germans get up a beer
party every evening, and so do the English their rum
party. Here is one gentleman, who leans on an umbrella wherever he goes, who is intending simply to
go round the world before he dies. This is his ambition. He was in Egypt, Palestine, Austria, and
Switzerland last year, but has not much idea of these
countries. I asked him of Cairo and Alexandria.
He replied, "O, they are very large cities." A Cali-
fornia lady who is going to China and Japan with her
little (but very obstinate) girl, on account of consump-
tive tendency, looks pretty vain. She walks on deck
like a queen, and her little daughter goes likewise
with a royal atmosphere. A fat English gentleman
appears always smoking; he is perfectly satisfied with
his pipe. Here are two young unmarried ladies.
They are not afraid to speak with any one. A
number of young fellows are anxious to wait on them,

especially some Frenchmen. I often sat by the group
of these pleasure-seeking people, and to my great surprise I find them talking nonsense and laughing over
something which is not laughable at all. There are
two very hard workers among us; one German doctor,
my pupil, and one English gentleman. The former
studies seven hours a day, and the latter reads day
and night. As I said before, I have not formed
many acquaintances because I cannot enjoy their company. Their chief enjoyments are only eating, drinking, and indulging all sensual pleasures; they excuse
themselves by saying that their natures demand it.
In so giving themselves up, how do they distinguish
themselves from a mere brute?

I had a real hot argument with two Germans the
other day. I do not know whether I have done any
good for them, but at any rate I put them into a corner. They afterwards confessed to me that my argument is from the spiritual and ideal side, but theirs
is from observation among the common mass of the
human race. They told me, also, that I learned my
argument from priests.

The sea is getting more quiet, and we may possibly
celebrate Thanksgiving at Yokohama. It was very
hard for me to bid you farewell, and I am still feeling that I am taking some vacation trip and cannot
fully realize that I am so soon to enter ministerial life.
Certainly I shall realize it when I see a multitude of
benighted people before my eyes. I shall omit here
my deep reflection upon my past life. With regard
to my present feeling, you may think it very strange.
Only explanation I can give you is as follows: —

In my past experience I have always found myself
cold, self-possessing, and also somewhat indifferent,

whenever I have some view of great undertaking before me. But I cannot understand myself why I am so cold now when I have a view of going home. I suppose I shall not realize it until I come to Yokohama and see my father face to face. He may not kill a calf for me, but he will certainly welcome, embrace, and kiss me. I shall start for Yedo at once; and thence for Annaka where my parents live now. Dr. Treat gave me a permission to stay with my father at least two weeks. They will be very busy weeks in telling all my experiences in America, the land of my exiled adoption, and also visiting and receiving my old acquaintances. Although the distance between us is increasing more and more, my affection towards you is increasing. Whenever I think of you I feel like a crying child. I dreamed of you and Mr. Hardy another night. Although I do not believe in any dream sign, still I think it very pleasant. In it I welcomed both of you in my Japanese home, which was furnished in a real Japanese style. The pleasant smile of both of you seemed so real to me. So I take it as a good omen of your paying me a visit in Japan. Please remember my dream, and let me rejoice in welcoming your real persons in some future day.

CHAPTER V.

THE changes which had taken place in Japan during the comparatively brief interval of Mr. Neesima's absence have no parallel in the history of nations. Politically, Japanese history may be divided into three periods. The first begins in mythological times and closes with the twelfth century. The national records of this period are unbroken, describing in one continuous story the exploits of the divine ·generations whence, after countless ages, in 660 B. C., sprung the first human sovereign, Jimmu Tenno. But a thousand years must be added to the alleged date of Jimmu Tenno's accession before we reach, in the seventh century A. D., any solid foundation of historical fact. The central figure of this period is the Mikado, an absolute, heaven-descended sovereign, lord paramount of the soil and of all its inhabitants, governing through the kuge, or court nobles, themselves allied to the imperial family, being chiefly descendants of the Mikado's younger sons.

The second period, beginning in the twelfth century, and extending to 1868–69, is the feudal period of Japanese history, in which the political constitution of the empire assumes a more complicated phase. The Mikado, still the divine ruler and source of all authority, remains theoretically the head of the state, and the kuge nominally retain their offices and dignities.

But, practically, the governing power was gradually
usurped by the great military barons, and in 1603
passed definitely into the hands of the Tokugawa
family. Thereafter, for over 250 years, the succes-
sive heads of this house, like the Mayors of the palace
of the Merovingian dynasty, ruled the country under
the title of Shogun. The Shogun was but one of a
number of military chieftains or barons, equal in
rank but of unequal possessions and power, called
daimio, who had acquired their lands by the sword,
and whose vassals, the samurai, constituted the military class. Prior to 1603 the country had been devas-
tated by the struggles of these great feudal lords for
supremacy; but with the accession to power of the
Tokugawa family began an era of peace, which lasted
till the restoration of the Mikado in 1868–69. In
this second period, then, we have a nominal sovereign,
the secluded Mikado; an impoverished nobility, the
kuge, of about one hundred and fifty families; the
military barons or daimio, two hundred and sixty-
eight in number, enjoying independent authority
within their own dominions, but acknowledging by
certain acts the supremacy of the Shogun, in whose
government they shared; the samurai, four hundred
thousand families of military retainers, devoted to the
chiefs from whom they received their pensions; and
finally the heimin, a vast population without social
or political rank, the laboring classes of the empire.
Towards the close of this period the power of the
shogunate began to wane, not through any effort of
the Mikado to resume the direction of public affairs,
but through jealousy of the Shogun on the part of the
daimio and the irritation caused by his interference
in the internal affairs of their respective principali-

ties. This feeling was most intense among the great clans of the southwest, and especially in the province of Satsuma, whose lord was the hereditary foe of the Tokugawas and whose samurai were renowned for their independence and military spirit. It is probable that the desire of the disaffected daimio of the southwest either to reduce the Shogun to their own level as vassals of the Mikado, or to perpetuate the shogunate in the person of one of their own number, would have led to some political change independent of all foreign intervention.

However this may be, the assumption of treaty relations by the Shogun in 1858 with foreign powers, relations repudiated by the Mikado and opposed to the traditional policy of national seclusion, intensified the prevailing discontent and brought matters to a crisis. It is a notable fact that while the avowed purpose of the revolution was the overthrow of the shogunate and the restoration of the Mikado to supreme authority, in order that the country, thus presenting a united front to the foreign barbarians, might expel them from its borders, no sooner was the revolution effected than its leaders began to take steps towards the adoption of western civilization and the entrance of Japan into the comity of nations. These leaders had utilized the feeling of hatred against foreigners to destroy the shogunate and establish a centralized government, and while the intent of a majority of their supporters had been the expulsion of foreigners and a return to the old days of national isolation, the real directors of the movement were ready to reconstruct the national policy on the basis of European civilization. They had been convinced by the bombardments of Kagoshima and Shimonoseki of the futil-

ity of any attempt to exclude the west by force.
Many of them, moreover, were students of western
history, philosophy, and science, and with the characteristic readiness of the Japanese to appropriate from
any source what they believe to be for the benefit of
the country, after the fall of the Shogun they not only
repudiated that portion of the original programme of
the malcontents which related to foreign intercourse,
but openly advocated the Europeanization of Japan.
From this policy, in the face of formidable difficulties,
and of an opposition which did not hesitate at rebellion and assassination, they have never swerved. The
principal obstacle to centralization lay in the feudal
system, and the first requisite was the disappearance
of the clans as separate units in the political system
and the abolition of the hereditary fiefs and privileges
of the daimio. In 1869 the four great princes of
Satsuma, Chōshū, Tosa, and Hizen addressed a memorial to the Mikado in which they acknowledged
his ownership of the soil and formally surrendered
their possessions and territorial rights. Their example was followed by the lesser clans, the titles of court
prince (kuge) and feudal noble (daimio) were abolished, and steps were taken for the establishment of
uniform laws throughout the empire. One after another, in rapid succession, the props of feudalism were
cut away. The country was divided into prefectures,
and a centralized bureaucracy replaced the local administration of the clans. Officials were appointed
irrespective of their clans or residence. The social
disabilities of the lower classes were removed. A
general law, providing for the organization of a national army by conscription, destroyed the samurai as
a military class. The Mikado emerged from his se-

clusion, transferred the capital from Kyōto to Tōkyō, and solemnly promised a deliberative assembly and representative institutions.

When Mr. Neesima landed at Yokohama, December 6, 1874, the railway connecting Tōkyō and Kyōto had been commenced and was in operation between Yokohama and the capital; a national line of steamships plied between the principal ports, and the important points of the coast were provided with lighthouses; a general telegraphic system had been inaugurated, and a postal service modeled on that of the United States had been extended over the entire empire, excepting only the island of Yezo; the imperial mint had been opened at Ōsaka; the navy had been reorganized under English guidance, and the creation of an army on European models had been begun; the dockyards and machine shops of the naval station at Yokosuka had been established, and the arsenal founded at Tōkyō: European dress had been adopted by government officials, the European calendar introduced; Japanese journalism was already a factor in the formation of public opinion, and the foundations of a comprehensive educational system had been laid.

The rate at which these changes were effected is astonishing, but the fact of this wholesale adoption of western institutions is not in itself inconsistent with the Japanese character. Their experience with foreigners had not, it is true, been a happy one. Early contact with the Jesuits, who brought the spirit of the Inquisition, with the Dutch and Portuguese traders, who introduced the slave-trade, new forms of disease, gunpowder, and tobacco, was the beginning of an aggressive policy dictated by commercial and selfish interests whose results were fatal to the peace of society.

The deep-seated hatred of foreigners to which this
intercourse led, and the persecutions which followed,
can occasion no surprise to the student of Japanese
history during this period. On the other hand, the
Japanese have always shown a readiness to adopt
what is good from without, and the genius to adapt
what they borrow to their own peculiar needs. In
art, religion, and literature, the influence of their
neighbors so predominates that examination of their
civilization leaves little that can be called indigenous
save those changes wrought in the transplanted elements of Chinese and Indian civilization by the envi-
roning conditions of their new home.

Mr. Neesima returned to Japan at a time when the
elements of conservatism were gathering in the storm
which burst upon the country three years later in the
Satsuma rebellion. It was in fact impossible for a
feudal society to undergo a transformation so radical
and so rapid without the throes incidental to the birth
of a new order of things. The great majority of the
people were unprepared for so sudden a change and
too ignorant to appreciate the reasons which dictated
the policy of the liberal statesmen. Certain of the
daimio found that the movement they themselves had
inaugurated involved consequences unforeseen. The
restoration of the Mikado was now perceived to mean
a centralization in which all local dignity and authority was lost. Customs of dress, habits of life, social
privileges, all that was consecrated by the past and
associated with the national greatness were passing
away. The recruitment of an army by subscription
from all ranks was the degradation of a class long
accustomed only to military and ceremonial duties,
and a life of comparative ease and pleasure, secure in

the possession of fixed revenues, but never forced to occupation, which had always been despised. Resolute as was the government in its policy of regeneration, it had been obliged to exercise caution, and this to such an extent that, seven years after the restoration, the province of Satsuma was practically an *imperium in imperio*, where everything possible was being done to resist the unification of the empire and where independent military preparations were going on upon a large scale.

The prevailing political discontent was accompanied by a feeling of irritation against Christianity, in regard to which the government had adopted a temporizing policy. There can be no question that the more enlightened of the Japanese leaders had been impressed by the fact that the civilization which they admired was a Christian civilization. On the other hand they were more anxious to be strong than to be Christian, and in dealing with the anti-foreign element were forced to conciliate the fanatical spirit of popular religious belief. Long after the engine had disturbed the quiet of Japanese valleys, the edicts against the corrupt sect of Jesus remained posted in the public thoroughfares. The popular feeling of opposition to Christianity was, however, an inheritance from a remote past, and was far more a matter of sentiment than of conviction. Shintoism, the national religion, possessed none of the elements of aggressive strength, hardly even the power of resistance. Without dogmas or moral code or sacred books, a vague worship, of nature and one's ancestors, rather than a religion, it had offered no real resistance to the introduction of Buddhism from China, and its influence upon the conduct of life was, as compared with that of Buddhism and Confucianism, a mere shadow.

The year 1700 had seen a literary revival of pure Shintoism. This movement was purely patriotic and political in its nature, and in its condemnation of Buddhism, Confucianism, and all foreign influences generally, fostered in the public mind the desire for the fall of the shogunate and a return to the golden age lying back of feudalism. The disestablishment of Buddhism, therefore, and the installation of Shintoism as the state religion at the time of the Mikado's restoration, were natural results of causes long in action; but with the accomplishment of this its political mission Shintoism itself as a religion practically expired. The opposition to Christianity made by Buddhism was, however, far more energetic. Received from China in the sixth century, it offered to the religious nature of the people all of which Shintoism was destitute, — motives, penalties, functions, a profound philosophy, an ethical code, and an imposing ritual. Diplomatically admitting the Shinto gods into its Pantheon, in conjunction with Confucianism, whose practical rules for the guidance of conduct in the social relations of life were so eminently adapted to a feudal society, it gradually formed the basis of education and recast the political constitution of the empire. If the resistance of this aggressive faith has proved less stubborn than expected, it is because of the eminently practical character of the Japanese mind. It cares little for speculative inquiry and lacks interest in questions apart from their practical bearings. Buddhistic philosophy made no deep impression upon the Japanese mind and failed to rouse the national sympathies, and such opposition as Christianity has encountered has been that of the priesthood rather than that of the people.

On his arrival at Yokohama, Mr. Neesima's first

desire was, naturally, to visit his aged parents, from whom he had now been separated for nearly eleven years, and who had removed from Tōkyō to the castle town of Annaka.   He accordingly set out at once by jinrikisha, a light two-wheeled vehicle drawn by a man, a conveyance which had been introduced during his absence.

TO MR. AND MRS. HARDY.

ANNAKA, JAPAN, *December* 22, 1874.

I have informed you of my safe arrival in Yokohama, where I stopped only one night and half a day, going to Tōkyō on the 27th.   I left Tōkyō on the same afternoon for home, where I arrived on the midnight of the 28th.   I traveled in a jinrikisha (cart drawn by men) twenty hours without taking a least rest except for meals.   I hired three men for the purpose, one for myself and two for my baggage.   They ate five times in twenty hours, spending nearly an hour for each meal.   They ran sixty miles within fifteen hours, four miles for an hour.   It was my intention to remain in Yokohama three days.   But when I once stepped on the dry land, my dear native soil, I could not wait even three days.   Hence I hurried towards home.   When I came here it was midnight. Therefore I disliked to disturb my parents' sleep, and slept in an inn in this town.   The following morning I sent word to my father.   Then I came home and was welcomed by my aged parents, sisters, neighbors, and old acquaintances.   My father was ill for three days and could not move himself on account of rheumatism.   But when he heard of my safe arrival he rose up and welcomed me with the fatherly tenderness.   When I hailed him he stooped down without a word. I noticed his tears dropping on the floor. My old acquaintances gathered at home and requested me to tell them all my experiences in the United States. Since I came here callers come, not simply from this town, but also from the neighboring towns and villages lying within seven or eight miles from here. They have kept me busy all times. They come here by hearing of my humble name, hoping to see me even for a few minutes. They looked as sheep without a shepherd. I find it almost impossible to send them back without some spiritual food.

Soon after my arrival I presented your kind letter to my father, but for a long time I could not translate it for him, because when I tried to read it I could not help thinking of the scene of my last departure from you, and the very thought prevented me to speak freely. Another day I gathered my parents and sisters and succeeded in reading your letter to them. Before I got half through all of them began to weep, being much affected by your parental kindness shown to me. My father told me you were our saviour and our gods. Then I told him he must not make his American friends gods. If he feels grateful for their kind deeds he must worship that one God, Creator of Universe, and Saviour of mankind, who is the God of his American friends. I mentioned still further to him that you became so good and kind even to a wandering stranger because you are the worshipers of true God and the humble followers of Christ; that you saved me from a miserable condition and gave me necessary education that I might become a teacher of glad tidings to our benighted people; that you loved our people as much as your own American people. Since that time my father discontinued to worship the

Japanese gods and his ancestors. By his consent I took down all the paper, wooden, earthen, and brass gods from shelves where they were kept, and burned them up. I send a few paper gods to you which my mother threw over in the fireplace. There are no gods nor images in this house now. I trust they will be worshipers of true God hereafter. How thankful I am that our lives have been spared these past ten years and we are permitted to meet once more before we depart from this world. I hope you will pray for me that I may keep myself nearer and closer to my Saviour and make an entire consecration for his cause.

Beside my own friends my humble labor within three weeks in this place has been wonderfully blessed. You will doubtless be surprised at my success when I give you its account. On the 2d inst. I took a trip to a town where iron mines were recently discovered with eight of my acquaintances. We stopped in an inn near the place and on the following morning we awoke very early and began to talk some nonsense. Then I began to preach without any forms. There was one miserable drunkard among them. During my discourse he listened to me very attentively and kept himself perfectly quiet. Since that time he began to reform himself entirely. He called on me another day and told me that since he stopped drinking he can arise early in the morning and work better than ever before. I have heard of another case of reform, and quite a number of others are seriously thinking of it. I preached several times in the school-house. and also to small audiences in different families. A week before last Sabbath I preached to a large audience in a Buddhist Temple. All the priests in that community came to listen to the preaching of the new religion, and also the whole body of the magistrates of Takasaki, a neighboring city of 15,000 inhabitants. Day before yesterday I was invited by an official in the next village to spend the night with him. After the supper he gathered the whole family in the parlor and requested me to tell them about Jesus Christ. I began to talk at 8 o'clock and continued till half past ten that night. Thirty men in this town and a few men from outside took up a collection for purchasing some Christian books for themselves. They are hungry and thirsty for the Christian truth. I wrote Rev. D. C. Greene a week ago for permission to remain here still longer, but he persuaded me to go to Ōsaka next Sabbath. I find here everything ready for the gospel. If I continued to labor here two or three months I have no doubt that most of the above will become followers of Christ. It is very painful to leave this hungry flock. This community is entirely free from bad foreign influences, and it may be a more desirable place for me to establish a Christian society than Kōbe or Ōsaka.

TO MR. AND MRS. HARDY FROM MR. NEESIMA'S FATHER.

ANNAKA, *December 24, 1874.*

Dear Friends, — Yours of the 20th of last October was received through my son. I congratulate you for your good health and prosperity.

When my son went to your country as a helpless wanderer, you did save him from falling into misery, treated him as your own son, and gave him all necessary wants. I am greatly indebted to you for your kind letter with which you have sent my son back to me once more, acquainted with the knowledge of God. When I saw him after a long separation my heart was filled with joy and I could scarcely speak with him. [Following the practice so universally resorted to in Japanese society to prevent the extinction of families, after Mr. Neesima's escape and before the news of his safety was received, his father had adopted a young man of the province as the heir of the house and future head of the family.] Although he is my own son, I would no longer call him my son, but treat him as if he is sent from God. I daily listen to his instructions, and we have just begun to worship the true God.

Please rejoice with my son and also with us that the people in this place who have been living in midnight darkness have just awakened and opened their eyes to see the true path which they should follow. We hope and trust that a glorious time will soon come by the means of the gospel truth. Although I desire to say many things, my pen and paper do fail to do so. I wish this brief note to give you reply for your kind letter, and also to express my hearty thanks for your kindness shown to my son.

Please take good care for your health. My family unite with me in sending you their warmest regards and love.

With hundred bows,

NEESIMA TAMIHARU.

This is partly direct translation and partly ideal. I find it exceedingly hard to translate twisted oriental writing into straightforward American idea. My father wrote it without any suggestion. I came home just in a right time, for I found him getting quite poor. He has no special income now. I gave him the money you gave me, and also some of my own for fixing up his old house. I was hoping to take my parents to Kōbe, but I found it best to leave them, as the living is much cheaper here.

J. H. N.

At its meeting at Pittsburgh in 1869 the American Board had decided to establish a mission in Japan, and as Tōkyō in the north and Nagasaki in the south were already occupied by other societies, its first missionary, Mr. Greene, was stationed in the central portion of the empire at Kōbe. He was soon after followed by Mr. O. H. Gulick, who was located at Ōsaka, and in 1873 eighteen missionaries of the Board were on the ground. The translation of the Bible into the vernacular had been vigorously begun in 1872, but the version of the New Testament was not finished until 1880, while that of the Old Testament was completed only in 1887. The existence of Chinese versions had, however, rendered the Bible accessible to the educated class. The first Protestant church had been organized at Yokohama in 1872, and there were also small churches at Kōbe, Ōsaka, and Tōkyō, at the time of Mr. Neesima's arrival; but nothing had been accomplished outside of the treaty ports, and in his visit to Annaka Mr. Neesima was the first to carry the gospel to the interior. His bold utterances and open violation of the edicts still in force against Christianity led the governor of the province to visit Tōkyō to consult the authorities. Fortunately, through his connection with the Iwakura Embassy, Mr. Neesima was well known to those in power, his work was not interfered with, and he was thus left free to originate a movement which resulted in the foundation of one of the most thoroughly Christian communities in Japan, — a community which within a few years contained several self-supporting churches, and two thirds of whose delegation to the Imperial Diet in 1890 were Christians. It was with great reluctance that he left Annaka for his station. But in reality he had accomplished far more than he realized, for when he set out for Ōsaka he had planted the spirit of Christianity in the heart of Japan.

On his way through Tōkyō he interested several friends in his plans for a Christian college, and in Yokohama preached in a union meeting, the first Japanese to address a foreign audience in the English language. The same evening he spoke to native hearers, and writes: "I find it a great delight to tell of Christ to my own people."

Arriving in Ōsaka January 22d, he was welcomed by Mr. Gordon. The Mission had already been informed by the Foreign Secretary of the Board of the fund subscribed towards a training-school for Christian workers, but the opposition to Christianity was so strong that such a school seemed to all a thing of the distant future. In order to escape injurious foreign influences it was Mr. Neesima's plan to establish the school in Ōsaka outside the treaty limits, and with this in view he conferred at once with the governor of the city, a man bitterly opposed to Christianity, and who, a short time before, had been concerned in the persecution of the survivors of the Jesuit mission at Nagasaki. These Christians, numbering over four thousand, had preserved for two hundred years the rite of baptism, certain forms of prayers, and a few religious books, and, refusing to abandon their faith, had been forcibly removed from their native villages. Scattered as exiles over the empire for six years, they had, in

1873, been set at liberty and allowed to return to their homes. At Osaka, Mr. Neesima obtained the promise of 6,000 yen from a native merchant, but the governor, while sanctioning the establishment of a school, would not permit the employment of missionaries as teachers. Discouraged by the result of his efforts in Ōsaka, Mr. Neesima's eyes turned towards the sacred city of Kyōto, and the Mission reluctantly consented to the location of the school at that place, provided the necessary authority should be granted. Mr. Neesima was at this time contending not only with the opposition of the authorities, but also with that of the Mission itself. It was of course impossible for its members to conform to the condition of the government which required them to abandon their distinctive work as preachers of the gospel in becoming teachers in a Japanese school. Their thought, too, was naturally centred on a theological training-school for the education of native evangelists, while Mr. Neesima was convinced that nothing less than a broad collegiate course would win the sympathy of the class he wished to reach. In March, 1875, he writes: — "I fully believe we shall not prosper in our work unless we have a collegiate institution in addition to a training-school. I begged for this at the last meeting of the Board. But the Mission wishes to use the fund for a training-school only. I am willing to agree to this if only they will teach anything to satisfy the craving desire of our youth for knowledge. If we simply teach theology and the Bible I fear the best Japanese youth will not stay with us. They want modern science also."

Moreover, Mr. Neesima's plan for the occupation of Kyōto was judged premature and chimerical by many of his associates. Until the removal of the capital to Tōkyō in 1868, this city had been the residence of the Mikado for nearly eleven centuries, and was still the literary and spiritual centre of the empire. Situated in the heart of the main island, in a fertile valley circled by mountains, it was also the centre of the best tea-producing district, and had long been preëminent for its silk and pottery industries. As the home of the Mikado it had been the scene of many important political events. Here had been quartered the great officials of the land with their retinues, and as the dwelling-place of a heaven-descended sovereign the city had been for generations the resort of pilgrims, pleasure-seekers, and amateurs of antique lore and mysteries. Its material prosperity had suffered by the removal of the government, and several exhibitions of products from the various provinces of the empire had been held in the grounds and buildings of its temples to promote industrial activity and to offer some substitute for the vanished attractions of the court. These expositions had been of great service in breaking down the barriers imposed by the feudal system, — a system which had checked the industrial growth of the nation by artificial constraints, and interfered with any general comparison or examination of the products of widely separated districts. The conversion of the sanctuary of the imperial residence, where the exhibition of 1872 was held, into a repository of trade and commerce, brought old and new Japan, the Past and the Present, face to face. The reverence attached to the person of the Mikado had been fundamental in the thought of the people, to whom their sovereign was literally a god. His name could not be uttered nor his countenance seen even by those of the most exalted rank. During his journeys the silence of death preceded him, for the highways were deserted and the houses closed. Even his dwelling had become associated with his personality, and only its outer official apartments were accessible to his courtiers, those in which he resided being visible only to members of the imperial family. The opening of its doors to the populace, the abandonment of its secluded gardens to the crowd, was the surrender of the most sacred spot in the empire.

Permission to visit Kyōto had been rarely granted to foreigners, but the opening of the city for one hundred days at the time of these exhibitions had prepared the way for the accomplishment of Mr. Neesima's plans.

There was then living in Kyōto Yamamoto Kakuma, counselor of the Kyōto-Fu, a highly educated man, but blind, and unable to walk by reason of paralysis. Several members of the Mission had become acquainted with him when the city was opened to visitors, and one of them had presented him with a Chinese translation of the Evidences of Christianity. Of this work he said to Mr. Neesima: "It has done me great good. It has cleared away many of my doubts regarding Christianity, and has also solved a difficult problem which has for years oppressed me. In my younger days I sought to render some service to my country, and to this end devoted myself to military tactics. But feeling this too small a matter, turned my attention to jurisprudence, hoping to secure better justice to the people. But after long study and observation I found law had its limitations. It could indeed set up barriers, but it could not renew the heart. If its restrictions are removed, men will steal, lie, and murder. Law cannot prevent evil thinking. But day has dawned for me, and I now see the path, utterly unknown before, which I have long been unconsciously seeking." When, therefore, in April, Mr. Neesima laid his plans before the governor of Kyōto, Mr. Yamamoto gave them his warm support, and through his influence the governor was subsequently led to sanction the establishment of a school in which science and Christianity should be taught. In June, 1875, Mr. Neesima visited Kyōto again with Dr. Davis, and bought of Mr. Yamamoto a lot of five and one half acres, the site of the future Doshisha. It was admirably situated for the purpose, in a quiet and healthy district of the city between a large temple grove and the vacant palace of the Mikado, having formerly been the site of the residence of the Prince of Satsuma. Although the approval of the local authorities had been obtained, that of the central government was still necessary, as also permission for a missionary to teach in the school and reside in the city.

Accordingly in August Mr. Neesima set out for Tōkyō to present his petition in person. He had already written to Mr. Tanaka, now minister of education, and had received the promise of his influence in behalf of the school. On reaching the capital he conferred at once with the minister, as also with his old friends Mori and Kido, urging the general cause of religious freedom, and it is safe to say that the success of his effort to penetrate this stronghold of Buddhism was due to the esteem and confidence in which he was held by these liberal statesmen. After many interviews and a summer of much anxiety the petition was finally granted, with the caution that nothing should be done to arouse popular prejudice, and on October 19th Dr. Davis entered Kyōto with his family. Foreigners not being entitled to hold property beyond the treaty limits, a company consisting of Mr. Neesima and Mr. Yamamoto was formed, and the name Doshisha, meaning One Purpose, or One Endeavor Company, was adopted. The school of eight pupils was opened with prayer November 29, 1875, in Mr. Neesima's house. "I never shall forget," says Dr. Davis, "Mr. Neesima's earnest, tender, tearful words that morning." The regular exercises of the school were held in a building hired for the purpose. On December 4th the number of scholars was twelve, and during the winter increased to forty.

This was a winter of trial and discouragement. The year was one of political disquietude and apprehension, and the government was desirous of avoiding in every way whatever was calculated to rouse the ultraconservative spirit. The Hizen revolt, the agrarian disturbances growing out of the law requiring the payment of the land tax in money instead of in kind, the discontent caused by the pension commutation act, and the conspiracies of Chōshū, Akidzuki, and Kumamoto, foreshadowed the coming struggle with expiring feudalism, a struggle for which the authorities were preparing, but which they were anxious not to precipitate. The followers of Shimadzu Saburō, the haughty and powerful chief of the Satsuma clan, were at this time gathering in Kyōto, and a spark might fire the mine which had long been in preparation by the Satsuma leaders. On taking up their residence in Kyōto both Mr. Neesima and Mr. Davis had begun Sunday services in their house, preaching and teaching the Bible to audiences which within a few weeks numbered sixty persons. These services provoked the opposition of the Buddhist priests, who in November forwarded a strong protest to the central government. The owner of the building rented for school purposes gave notice that he required it for his own use. On several occasions Mr. Neesima was refused an audience by the governor, whose friendly attitude had become one of open hostility, and Mr. Neesima was finally summoned to explain the meaning of *Seisho* (Bible) which occurred in the programme of study. The result of this opposition was a request from Mr. Tanaka that Bible exegesis should be omitted from the list of studies. Compliance with this request allayed the excitement, and by permission of the governor Christianity continued to be taught under the name of Moral Science.

During all this time Mr. Neesima was also busily engaged in evangelistic work. July 7, 1875, he writes: "I preached in Ōsaka last Sabbath and received two interesting men into our church. One of them is an influential native physician residing in the suburb of Fushimi, who has fifty pupils to whom he lectures on Physiology, Chemistry, Anatomy, etc., and who daily gathers his neighbors into his house for Bible study."

This gentleman, with those who frequented their gatherings, were at once summoned before the Kyōto magistrates, and future meetings of this nature were forbidden. The conversation of the physician with the official, as taken down at the time by Mr. Davis, was as follows: —

"This Davis came up here to teach an English school, did he not?"

"Yes."

"Then he is like a man who has a license to sell deer meat, but who sells dog meat."

"Well, is it dog meat? I used to think so, but on tasting of it I find it is a great deal better than deer meat; and I would like to ask you one question. This religion is allowed to be taught publicly in Kōbe, in Ōsaka, and in twenty or thirty places in Tōkyō. How is it that here in Kyōto a man is not allowed to hear it in his own house? Are we not all under the same government? I do not understand it."

"Well, I do not say that this religion is either good or bad, and I do not say that you and your friends cannot hear it in your house; but you let in the common people, the lower classes, who cannot understand it. This we cannot allow. We have good and sufficient religions here in Japan; we do not want any more. We have Confucianism for scholars like you, and Buddhism for the masses."

"I would like to ask you one thing. If Confucianism is an all-sufficient religion, why is it, since its founder lived hundreds of years before Christ and taught during a long life, that it has not spread beyond China and Japan? And if Buddhism is an all-sufficient religion, started by Buddha hundreds of years before Christ, and taught by him through a long life, how is it that it has not spread beyond India, China, and Japan? And if Christianity is a bad religion, how is it, since its founder only taught three years and was put to death when he was thirty-three years old, that it has spread all over Europe and America, and is spreading all over Africa and Asia, and all the islands of the sea?"

"We do not say that it is either good or bad. But you must not allow people to meet at your house, and you are discharged."

Owing to this action of the authorities work in Fushimi was suspended; but in February Mr. Neesima was invited to Ōtsu, a city of considerable commercial importance east of Kyōto, where, by permission of the vice-governor, he began a series of Sunday services.

During the summer of 1875 Mr. Neesima had become engaged to Yamamoto Yaye, the sister of the counselor to the Kyōto-Fu, and a teacher in a government school for girls in the city. Her engagement to a Christian led to her immediate discharge. In announcing this attachment to his friends in America, Mr. Neesima said: —

"She is somewhat like her own blind brother, afraid of no one when convinced of her duty. She has often appeared before the governor in behalf of her school when its other officers were afraid to do so. Since becoming a Christian she has often spoken of the truth to her pupils, and she is now discharged by the governor because of his fear that they will learn of Christianity through her and be removed from the school by their parents. I do not know when our marriage will take place. I will let our missionary brethren decide for us. I have been living in hotels and private houses, but have recently hired a house near which, separated only by a garden, is another small one which I am going to rent for my aged parents."

On January 2, 1876, the ordinances of baptism and the Lord's Supper were celebrated for the first time in Kyōto, and the marriage took place on the 3d at Dr. Davis's house. Mr. Neesima writes January 6th: —

"After the ceremony refreshments were brought in, and every one seemed happy. It was the first marriage of a native Christian in this place. I ought to have informed you of this event before it took place, but I have been busy beyond my strength. I hope you who are always kind and tender to me as my parents are, will pardon me for this delay."

In March, 1876, the passes authorizing Drs. Taylor and Learned to reside and teach in Kyōto — passes which Mr. Neesima had for five months been striving to obtain — were received; but the Bible was still excluded from the course of study, and some members of the Mission questioned the wisdom of permanently occupying Kyōto under such conditions. At a special meeting held at Ōsaka in March, a vote to remain was passed with much misgiving, and in June the erection of two buildings was also voted, but reluctantly, for the approval of the government was considered more than doubtful. Even after the buildings were completed and dedicated, the Mission was inclined to force the issue of Bible teaching, and, if unsuccessful, to abandon the station and leave the city. In view of the hostile attitude of the authorities, and the fact that an institution from which the Bible was excluded could not properly be called a training-school for the education of a native ministry, the hesitancy to appropriate money given for this purpose and to commit the Board to an experiment whose success was so doubtful, was entirely natural. The location of the school beyond the foreign concession required that its proprietorship should remain in Japanese hands, and this also caused dissatisfaction. But Mr. Neesima was content to hold the ground already gained, firm in his faith of ultimate success. June 6th he writes to Mr. Hardy: —

"We are hated by the magistrates and priests, but

we have planted the standard of truth here and *will never more retreat.* To no one else but you will I say that this Christian school could have no existence here if God had not brought this poor runaway boy to your kind hands. The only way to get along in this country is to work courageously, even under many difficulties."

What these difficulties were may be inferred from the following extract from the "Sketch of the Life of Reverend J. H. Neesima," written by Dr. Davis and published in Kyōto:—

"This state of things led to continued criticism of the school and of Mr. Neesima as its virtual Japanese head. He felt these most keenly. He loved the members of the Mission, and he was ever loyal to the Mission, anything which seemed to imply the contrary paining him beyond measure. So great did the trial become that in September, 1876, the members of the station sent a letter to the Mission in order to remove some of these misunderstandings."

In this letter they stated that while Mr. Neesima and Mr. Yamamoto were the nominal proprietors of the school, its management had been left entirely in the hands of the resident missionaries; that none of the details relating to the course of study or the conduct of the exercises had been referred to Mr. Yamamoto; that Mr. Neesima had invariably followed the suggestions of his foreign associates and had consulted them even in the expenditure of funds subscribed through private channels, whose use was wholly at his own discretion; that in the organization and conduct of the school they had been as free as if there had been no Japanese proprietors, and that Mr. Neesima's whole effort was to conform to their advice and suggestions.

The estimation in which Mr. Neesima was held by his immediate associates of the station is seen from these extracts from their letters to Mr. Hardy written in 1875-76: —

"Your contribution of Mr. Neesima to our Mission and the cause of Christ in Japan is one whose value we feel no multiple of the sum you have contributed or invested in his education can represent. We are charmed by his thoroughly Christian spirit. . . . I cannot say a tithe of what is in my heart. . . . There seems no doubt but that his whole life, being, and purpose are consecrated to the Master for the redemption of his people. . . . He is profoundly grateful to you and to the American Board for what you and it have done for him and his land; and he accepts the will of the Board and of our Mission as God's will, no matter how it differs from his own. . . . If he is guided aright by God's Spirit and kept firm to his purpose and work, if his health is spared, I feel that he is destined to accomplish as much perhaps as all our Mission put together. . . . We need him for a larger place than a pastorate. We need him as a teacher in the training-school. He is better fitted for some department of teaching there than any foreigner can ever be. We also need him as an evangelist, not to use his influence always in the same place, but to go about awakening interest. . . . For a long time after his return we feared he would break entirely down. He was able to sleep but very little. He told me several times during those first few months that when he thought about these millions of his people passing into eternity without a knowledge of Christ it seemed as if he would go crazy. Since the opening of the year he has gradually improved and is sleeping better.

This is partly due to the successful starting of the school and his steady work there, but largely also to his marriage and settlement in a happy home of his own."

The house above referred to was provided through the generosity of Mr. J. M. Sears of Boston, who also sent money for the erection of a chapel. It was for several years impossible to secure preaching places in the city, and during this time services were held in Mr. Neesima's house and in the adjoining chapel, where two hundred people often assembled to hear the gospel.

On September 18, 1876, the new buildings were dedicated. Of this event Mr. Neesima writes to Mr. and Mrs. Hardy: —

"I must express my heartfelt thanks to you for your having led and educated me in such a way that I might found a Christian institution on my dearly beloved soil. As you know, we started our school in a hired house, but having found this very inconvenient, we began the process of building two months ago. The buildings are three in number, two of which contain recitation rooms and twenty-four rooms for students; while the other is a small structure and is used for a kitchen and dining-room. They are simple, but solid, and look very pretty in the large open space about them. We were permitted to dedicate them to the Lord the day before yesterday. The exercises consisted of a prayer of invocation in English and a prayer of dedication in Japanese; a sketch of the history of the school, and the singing of hymns in both languages. Addresses in English were made by Mr. Doane and Mr. Learned, and in Japanese by Mr. Yamamoto and myself. All but two of our Kyōto

Mission were present, and about seventy students, besides others from outside. Mr. Yamamoto's remarks were brief but wonderfully appropriate. He is regarded as one of our best thinkers, although bodily feeble and helpless. The existence of the Kyōto Mission is largely due to him. He was convinced that an immoral country like Japan could not be purified by any other means than Christianity, and by his influence and labor the proud and dignified governor listened to us and at last smiled upon our efforts. In the dark and trying hours of last winter he stood up for us and did his best to persuade the governor. The latter made no interference with our dedication exercises.

"You will be glad to know that of our forty-seven boarding students more than half are Christians. They have come to us with the purpose of studying the Bible and fitting themselves for the ministry. We are very fortunate to get such pupils at the outset. I pray that this school may be the nucleus of a future college and university for Japan. Our mission work has also bright prospects, the work being chiefly carried on by our students. A third church will soon be formed. My aged parents now worship God instead of idols, and my invalid sister, who grasps spiritual things faster than these aged ones, takes part in the prayer-meetings for women held at my house. My wife attends the Biblical exercises in the school. We are perfectly happy together and I am trying to make my home like the Christian home I found in America."

In September, 1876, the number in the school was increased by the arrival of thirty students from the province of Higo in the island of Kyūshū. Their accession was an important event in the early history of

the school.   The circumstances under which they came
were remarkable, and, in the light of the influence
which those young men subsequently exerted upon the
general educational and religious movement then in
progress, acquire an additional interest.   In the year
1871 Captain L. L. Janes, formerly an officer in the
United States army, had taken charge of a school in
the castle town of Kumamoto.   This school belonged
to the class known as private schools, many of which
were established at this time, especially in the southwest provinces, by the anti-foreign party.   While offering instruction in English and modern science, this
movement was a distinctly national one, the sole object of these schools being the formation of a body of
young men who by reason of their superior training
and intelligence might the more effectively resist foreign influences and oppose the spread of western ideas.
Kumamoto was an inland town in the centre of a province where the feudal spirit was still strong.   Isolated
from the influences prevailing in the treaty ports, Captain Janes had found the hatred against Christianity
so strong that for several months he did not dare to
allow his faith to be known.   As soon, however, as he
deemed it prudent he began to speak of Christianity,
and thereafter, for five years, his work in the school
was accompanied by constant and direct religious instruction.   About two years after his arrival he proposed to the members of the advanced class a system-
atic study of the New Testament, and fifteen or twenty
young men, after consultation with the school authorities, met with him twice a week for the ostensible purpose of acquiring that knowledge of Christianity which
should the better fit them to oppose its progress.   On
the 30th of January, 1876, about forty of these young

men went up on the Hanaoka mountain near the city and organized themselves into a Christian society under the most solemn mutual pledges to dedicate their lives to Christ. This stand was taken with a full knowledge of the consequences, for it involved not only the sacrifice of worldly considerations, and in many cases the abandonment of careers for which they had been preparing, but estrangement from friends and home, and bitter persecution. Early in January the Christian boys had begun to teach the lower classes, gathering in the school-room with their English Bibles. On complaint to the authorities Captain Janes advised the discontinuance of this practice, and an apology was offered to the school manager, but the meetings were still held at the house of Captain Janes, whose course was one of tact but firmness. He assured the manager that no Christian would disobey any rightful order, but that if such meetings were forbidden, then also the gathering of those who opposed Christianity and who indulged in threats of personal insult and violence should likewise be prohibited. The governor was one of seventeen who had attacked a party of Frenchmen, some of whom were killed, and had been saved from forced suicide only by the clemency of foreign officials after several of his companions had inflicted the necessary self-punishment of harakiri. The well-known liberal sentiments of the central government, and the alarm caused by the malignant form of private persecution adopted by the families of those who had embraced the Christian faith, probably account for the apparent indifference of the local authorities, who, for selfish reasons, were inclined to fear if not respect the policy of the Tōkyō statesmen. The rations of all who had openly professed Christianity were, however, promptly stopped by the school manager. This action threw many entirely upon Captain Janes for support. Sharing their slender means in common, they organized a mess under his direction, preparing and serving their own food in the school kitchen. Meanwhile the private persecution already referred to had been most bitter. When these young men arrived at Kyōto their English Bibles and the clothes they wore were their only possessions. They had been subjected to the most cruel treatment at the hands of their relations, and, outcasts from home, disowned by their friends, had literally abandoned everything for the sake of their faith. In proposing their admission to the Doshisha, Captain Janes wrote to Dr. Davis: —

"My boys and I have been passing through unusual events, and the mutterings of a sharp, vindictive, and exciting persecution are still in the air. They have four of my Christian boys still shut up in their homes. I think the little band is practically intact. No lives have been taken, although that was seriously enough threatened, and there are no cases of harakiri yet to report, although a mother in one family and a father in another took that method of driving their sons from the faith. The number of faithful to the end has been larger than I expected. I grieve over my imprisoned Christian boys. The physical strength of one is failing, and his unthinking persecutors may kill him. I understand there was an auto-da-fé of his Bibles a few days since."

Of Mr. Kanamori, subsequently pastor of the college church and succeeding Mr. Neesima as acting principal and president of the Board of Trustees, Captain Janes writes, June 25, 1876: —

"The bearer is one of the Christian company here, of whom I have written you. He must tell you his own story. I will only say that he is a graduate of this year, and had completed the regular course of study before he was taken from the school and subjected to persecution. He has received the most cruel and outrageous treatment at the hands of his brother, acting under the influence of the opposition party here, and has been practically a prisoner for one hundred and twenty days. He was made the slave of the servants of his family, who were instructed to treat him as one possessed of a devil, without human rights. He is now practically outcast. He severs his family connection finally and strikes for liberty. He is a shorn lamb, and leaving all."

Among other members of what came to be known as the Kumamoto band were Mr. Tokudomi, now a trustee, editor of "The People's Friend," a quarterly magazine published at Tōkyō, as also of a leading daily newspaper, an author also of national reputation and influence; Mr. Yokoi, also a trustee, pastor of a church in Tōkyō, and editor of "The Christian," the weekly organ of the Congregational churches in Japan, and of a literary journal, "The Rikugō Zasshi;" Mr. Kosaki, now at the head of the Doshisha as Mr. Neesima's successor; Mr. Ebina, afterwards pastor of a flourishing church in Annaka, and now principal of a large English school at Kumamoto; Mr. Morita, for eleven years a professor in the Doshisha, and Mr. Shimomura, at present professor of chemistry. Of the work done by Messrs. Kosaki at Tōkyō, Ebina in Kotsuke, Miyagama in Ōsaka, Kanamori in Okayama, and Yokoi in Shikoku, Dr. Davis says: —

"It has already changed the history of Japan. The

coming of these young men at that early day, with their earnest Christian purpose, gave a tone to the school; and their influence was felt in moulding the Doshisha morally and in shaping its course of study from that time. They have helped to make the school what it is, and they came to love Mr. Neesima and to be loved by him as brothers."

The record of the years intervening between 1876 and 1884, when Mr. Neesima revisited America, is one of failing health, constant trial and anxiety, but unfaltering faith in final success. The numbers in the school slowly increased, but for several years the local opposition was so strong that few of the students came from the immediate vicinity. The influence of the Kumamoto Band brought many from the island of Kyūshū; many anxious parents sent their boys to be taught in the "new way;" and the moral tone of the students, although they were generally despised as Christians, was very effective in spreading the reputation of the school.

In March, 1877, Mr. Neesima writes:—

"In the last communion season my dear father was added to our church. It was a most important event to us all when that aged man received baptism. He has been living in pagan darkness these sixty-nine years, and we had a constant fear that he might go beyond this world without the true light."

About this time a misunderstanding arose as to the amount of Mr. Neesima's salary, $500 of which it was arranged should be paid from the treasury of the Board, the remainder being supplied by Mr. Hardy. When the announcement to this effect was made to him he understood that his salary had been reduced to $500, and wrote Mr. Hardy:—

"I thought it rather strange that you should do so without giving me any notice or explanation. At any rate, I said, if the Prudential Committee think it best that I should live on a least salary and has reduced it down, and you think so, it must be obeyed. As I remain your ever obedient son I would not do anything contrary to my father's will. I told it to my wife, we put our heads together, and consulted how to reduce our expenses. We said, 'cut short this and that, give up our farmer who works for us in our garden when we need him.' After reducing many things we thought we could live on that salary. I felt it rather hard at first, for besides ourselves I have my parents and one invalid sister, but afterwards I felt very happy exercising self-denial for Christ's sake. I have not asked any missionary a reason why my salary was reduced, nor expressed my feeling to any one. But lately, I found it rather hard to live on that reduced amount and asked Dr. Davis whether he had heard anything about it. He explained to me that the Board authorized me to draw $500 annually from the mission treasury, and the balance will be sent to me from you. Then I found out what a mistake I had made. If, however, you say live on $500, I shall say yes, and shall be very thankful for it. And if you be pleased to give me balance, I shall receive it with a grateful heart. I have adopted Apostle Paul's doctrine: 'I shall be thankful for all things.'"

Exhausted by his duties, in the summer of 1877 he sought rest with his wife at Wakayama, from which place he writes July 12th: —

"We came to Ōsaka by rail, and hence to this quiet fishing village by jinrikisha. It is about sixty miles southwest of Kyōto and is somewhat warmer.

The famous orange growing country is only a few miles away. We came for the purpose of taking the sea-baths, and I find them beneficial. Here we have hired a small villa owned by a quite wealthy fisherman and are very comfortably situated. Fish and vegetables are plenty. Above all we are enjoying our quiet. I am hoping to go fishing as soon as the rough weather is over. I went up the surrounding mountains soon after I came and found the scenery wonderfully beautiful. As I was sitting down alone on a high mountain top, looking upon hills, rivers, plains, bays, promontories, islands, and open sea beyond, I could not help reflecting upon my past enjoyments which I had with you at Mt. Desert. Then I bursted out to tears and wept silently. Every enjoyment I had with you seems very dear and sacred. I suppose such enjoyment will never come to me again while I am in this world."

Early in 1877 Mr. Neesima had sent, through his brother-in-law, Mr. Yamamoto, some books to the inmates of the prison at Ōtsu. Among these books was a Chinese copy of Dr. Martin's "Evidences of Christianity," which fell into the hands of a prisoner who became so much interested in it that he undertook its translation into Japanese for the benefit of his illiterate associates. Mr. Neesima gives the following account of what transpired: —

"Most of the prisoners are uneducated, and petty thieves. A lamp was allowed for evening study. This was a great concession from the authorities, for the use of lamps had heretofore been forbidden. But one lamp proved insufficient for the large number of prison students. I believe they were eighty in number. Subsequently one more lamp was granted, then another, then another, till finally the room was fully lighted. He who taught his associates also began to preach to them every day. One day fire broke out in the prison, but there was no least confusion. He kept them in complete order. Under his direction each one worked nobly and soon the fire was extinguished. Afterwards the prisoners were inspected, and none of them had escaped. It was a wonderful thing. The authorities of the city were informed of the behavior of the prisoners and the reason for it, and their leader was released on account of his good conduct, although he had one year yet to serve. After his release he called on us and told us his story. He had killed a man ten years ago in a quarrel. He has since started a private school in Ōtsu, and Mr. Davis, myself, and some of our students have preached there ever since. This will soon result in the formation of a church there."

In March, 1878, while visiting Tōkyō on business connected with the school, he made a journey to Annaka, where he had first preached Christ on his return from America.

"Finding the Minister of the Interior so ill that there was no prospect of seeing him immediately, I made up my mind at once to go to Annaka in order to improve my time. After leaving that place some three years ago the people began to lose their interest in the truth, as there was no one to guide them. My letters written to them occasionally kept up the courage of a few. Last summer one of our brethren from Kyōto went up there and stirred up their almost fainting faith, and as they have more leisure in the winter than in the summer time, it was their especial request he should come again in the winter. When I arrived there I found them well prepared to be baptized. I held a meeting on the evening of my arrival, preached to a large audience the next day, and held an inquiry meeting in the evening. This was repeated the following day, and on the fourth day I baptized thirty persons and organized a church. It was the most solemn and yet most joyful event I ever witnessed. The people thus far have paid all expenses and have never received any aid from without. They take pride in doing so, and have already raised a fund for the support of their church. There is a rich merchant among them, the most influential man in the place, although quite young. He keeps the pastor in his home and does everything for his comfort. He also supports a free reading-room, where daily, weekly, and monthly papers, secular and religious, are kept. When I left the place, numbers came with me as far as the outskirts of the town and expressed to me their gratitude for my coming."

A school for girls had been opened two years before in Kyōto at the house of one of the missionaries, and had recently been removed to a building erected for this especial object. A similar school had already been established in Kōbe. The object of these schools was the fitting of young girls for the great work to be done among the women of the land. Nowhere outside of these "Homes" could the growing class of Christian workers find Christian helpmeets. Certain members of the Mission deemed this movement premature, but events proved that those who were sanguine were not sanguine enough. Mr. Neesima's visit to Tōkyō was for the purpose of securing permission for the residence of two American ladies as teachers in Kyōto. This permission had been refused by the governor of the city. "This," he writes, "is the gravest matter we have ever experienced. We will bear it with all the grace we have got, but if the despotic governor does not cease to ill-treat us we will burst out and appeal to the supreme power." On consultation with the American minister and the Japanese minister of foreign affairs he found the chief cause of complaint to be the fact that while the Doshisha was nominally a Japanese company, its funds were derived from foreign sources, and that in the name of education its real object was the extension of Christianity. The growth and prosperity of the school and the establishment of the Kyōto Home for girls had aroused the enmity of the local governor; the authorities at Tōkyō declined to interfere; Dr. Taylor had been forbidden to practice medicine even in his own house, and was finally ordered out of the city; the outlook was discouraging, and Mr. Neesima wrote a strong appeal to America for a permanent fund. "If we have such a fund," he said, "although coming from a foreign source and managed by foreigners, yet we can say that we support our teachers with our own money."

The refusal of the Kyōto governor to permit the entrance of the lady teachers was, after four months' delay, overruled by Count Inouye. "I conveyed to him," writes Mr. Neesima, "my idea, that it is impossible to check Christianity, because it is a *living principle*. If crushed in one city it will surely burst forth in another. The best way is to leave it alone, else Japan will lose her best patriots. The decision of the central government was in our favor and the plan of the local authorities was utterly defeated. Glory to our living God!"

Mr. Neesima was exceedingly tried at this time.

Mr. Yamamoto had lost his connection with the city government by reason of his active interest in the Doshisha. Every difficulty connected with the school, difficulties of internal management, as well as those arising from outside opposition, was brought to Mr. Neesima for settlement. He stood between the students and the foreign teachers, between his immediate associates and the general mission, between the school and the authorities. He was actively engaged in missionary work, and in addition to the cares inseparable from his connection with the Doshisha and Kyōto Home, were those growing out of the organization of native churches throughout the empire, and the formation of the Japanese Home Missionary Society, in the superintendence of whose work he took an active part for many years.

In the summer of 1878 he took a brief vacation in a suburb of Kyōto, from which he writes, August 16th: —

"My wife sent me off from home to this quiet village, which is only six miles away, and much cooler than Kyōto. Trees are plenty. It is shady everywhere. I came here three days ago and am now staying in a temple. I have hired two large, airy rooms, using one for reading and another for sleeping. The temple is surrounded by a very wide piazza, a part of which I use for my kitchen. You may ask whether I have brought a cook with me. I answer, no. I employ girls at home, but it would not do for me to bring a servant girl to such a place when I am alone. I am a person of wonderful adaptability, and can be both cook and boy. Dried meats, eggs, sweet potatoes, fruits, etc., are all provided. Now I have a chance to show forth my old skill which I practiced on the Wild River. Alas! none to see but myself. The old priest and his family are living in the back part of the temple. They are very quiet people and do not distrust me at all. I retire and rise early, finishing my breakfast before seven. I read till ten, and take an artificial salt bath for my health. Then I prepare dinner, take a little nap and a long walk along the shady valley.''

In the spring of this year he received a letter from Viscount Okabe, then studying in Springfield, Mass., where he had united with the Congregational church. Mr. Okabe, formerly Daimio of Kishinowada, province of Idzumi, and now vice-minister of foreign affairs, requested Mr. Neesima to send some one to preach to his former retainers living at Kishinowada, and in answer to this request Mr. Neesima at once visited that place in person. An account of this visit is given in the following letter to Viscount Okabe, dated August 16, 1878: —

TO VISCOUNT OKABE.

Allow me to write you a few lines to inform you of my experience in your old castle town. On receiving your letter I tried hard to send one of our best students to that place. Unfortunately they were all assigned to other places before the receipt of your letter, and I was obliged to leave the matter untouched for some time. Although much occupied with many things, I started from here on the 19th ult. and reached Kishinowada on the 20th. On arrival I sent for Mr. J., who promptly called upon me with Mr. M. I told him your special request and translated to them your letter. They were much pleased to see me, and through their prompt action I had the pleasure of delivering my first discourse to your people at Show-shia on the 21st. There were twenty hearers. I preached on seven consecutive days, the audience increasing to one hundred, all men and mostly of the samurai class. There were many schoolmasters and advanced pupils, most of whom were young and quite sharp. They raised up all sorts of questions, for the new doctrine I preached seemed to them very strange and doubtful. They had never heard of the doctrine of the immortality of the soul. They kept me pretty busy while I was there. They were ready to hear and ready to discuss; I was ready to tell. I forgot my strength as well as the time. Although I tried to get hold of these intelligent hearers, I did not neglect the uneducated. In my discourse I spent one hour for the former and another hour for the latter. Thus my discourse lasted two hours every day. To my great satisfaction the former began to read the gospel and "Evidences of Christianity," and found out their Creator and also immaterial soul existing in themselves, and the latter listened very attentively and some of them already began to reform. You may anxiously ask me whether one has begun to believe in the crucified Saviour. I cannot give you an affirmative reply yet, but I can simply tell you that through God's grace his humble servant has opened before them a new way to enter, and if I mistake not, some of them have already directed their faces towards it.

On the 25th I explained to them my desire to preach to women as well as to men. I told them men are not the only creatures to learn the way of salvation, but women also. While women are kept down like slaves, as in our country, the state of society will never be improved. On the contrary, if women are

Christianized, educated, and elevated, they will do more than men for the purification of society. Special meetings for women were therefore arranged for the evenings of the 26th and 27th. The audience was larger, over one hundred each time.

When I returned I found one of our students had just got back from Fukichigama, where he had gone to preach; having been obliged to leave on account of the strictness of the local authorities. So I sent him to Kishinowada to take up the work I left unfinished. Besides him, about twenty-six of our school have gone there to take sea-baths. They are mostly young fellows, and yet believers. I wish I could inform you more about our work, but I find my work almost beyond my strength, and am therefore obliged to write you hastily and briefly.

Mr. Neesima was often, and at this time especially, embarrassed by differences of opinion prevailing in the Mission. Obstacles of every kind were constantly arising, — obstacles which threatened the very existence of the school and all that had been previously accomplished. Every opportunity was taken by the anti-foreign and anti-Christian party to defeat his plans and arrest the growth of the Doshisha. The fact that, while nominally a Japanese company, the Doshisha was in reality supported by annual grants derived from foreign sources, was made the basis of an attack which very nearly resulted in closing its doors. The renewal of the passports of resident teachers was obtained only after long and persistent efforts, and the course of study was continually subject to the hostile interference of the local authorities. The condition of affairs was frequently so serious that the Mission lost heart entirely and was ready to abandon the contest as hopeless. Internal difficulties aggravated the situation. Some of Mr. Neesima's associates felt that too much prominence was given to the strictly educational work of the station. The entire separation of the native churches from the Board was openly advocated, a course which Mr. Neesima believed to be impracticable in the early stages of their existence. The settlement of all conflicts between the students and the faculty, between the native pastors and their foreign associates, between the Mission and the authorities, devolved upon Mr. Neesima, and he was often misunderstood and misrepresented by those whom he respected and loved. Many of his best Japanese friends criticised him severely for receiving money from Mr. Hardy for his support, — money which, in view of the slender salary paid by the Board, was indispensable, — and this criticism assumed at times the form of bitter personal attack. In addition to the cares inseparable from his position as head of the school, his activity in organizing the native missionary work involved so large a correspondence and such frequent journeys that for many years he was practically without rest or vacation. "O," he exclaimed at one time to Dr. Davis, "that I could be crucified once for Christ, and be done with it." And yet Mr. Neesima was exactly the man for the place. Anglo-Saxon straightforward methods of procedure, so foreign to the semi-indifferent, indirect Japanese mind, made a middle-man an absolute necessity, and both by nature and education Mr. Neesima was admirably fitted for this position. He knew enough of both parties to sympathize with each, and his great heart of love was ever between them to prevent violent conflict and unhappy misunderstanding. Many young Japanese educated abroad have returned so convinced of their superiority that all coöperation with them has been impossible. Mr. Neesima occupied a position of peculiar difficulty and temptation, and was subject to a cross-fire which tried his tact and patience to the utmost; yet he retained throughout the confidence of all in the singleness and sincerity of his purpose, and the simplicity of his Christian character.

In February, 1879, he was again in Tōkyō interceding with Mr. Mori, then vice-minister of foreign affairs, for the renewal of Dr. Learned's passport. His success in this instance is but an example of his general success in accomplishing what was regarded as hopeless by his associates. Although in this case the special object of his mission was secured, his interview with Mr. Mori convinced him that the safety of the school depended upon the creation of a permanent endowment, and he therefore wrote at once the following strong appeal to the Prudential Committee of the Board: —

"When I returned from my missionary tour to Kyūshū I was mostly used up by exposure to intense heat there. When I fairly commenced my labor there numbers of telegrams came informing me that I must return home as soon as possible to attend to grave matters. To my great regret I was obliged to give up my work and return homeward. Now I must inform you of the difficulty just hanging upon my shoulders, but I trust you will never be discouraged. I am fully convinced the Lord has designed me to bear all sorts of trials for extending his kingdom in my beloved country. No matter how heavy the cross may be, I am ready to bear, but what I fear is that I cannot picture out to you our present critical condition so that you could fully understand the impending difficulty and our pressing want.

"When I undertook to start our school in the city of Kyōto, I was rather compelled by law to ask permission from the central government both for establishing it and for employing foreign teachers. For foreigners are not allowed to remain in an interior city like Kyōto unless they are employed by natives. As my American friends gave me funds to start a school and the American Board agreed to furnish me teachers, I was naturally obliged to assume a position of proprietorship. My written application for a school was first presented to the educational department, with the approval of the Kyōto governor. But it was contrary to the regulation of said department to employ regular missionaries as teachers either in the public or private schools. It was my first obstacle. But through Mr. Tanaka's special favor I secured permission for Dr. Davis to enter the sacred and ancient capital of Japan. When it was done I rejoicingly said, 'Miraculous!' When we had fairly started our school we began to preach the gospel in a most quiet possible way. But the truth spoken in a private room became known throughout the city, and caused a great alarm among the priests in the region. They got up a great meeting and presented their united application to the governor to stop our preaching altogether. Then the governor summoned me to his office and requested me not to preach any more in my house. But I asked him, if a friend of mine comes to my house and inquires after a truth, would his Excellency intend to compel me not to give any reply? He answered in the negative. Then I asked him if two, three, or even one hundred friends come and ask me something of the Christian truth, has his Excellency any power to stop me telling them of it? He said no. Then, said I, if he has no such power I can keep on preaching in my house. Finding I was such a stiff-necked fellow he simply charged me not to teach the Bible in our school. It has been taught ever since without ceasing, even through many darkest periods. When one battle was over another battle followed. Then another, still another. It was rumored that our governor reported to the central government that I have started my school with the pretense of education, but my real design was to promote Christianity throughout the empire. Just about that time I presented applications for the entrance of Miss W. and Miss P. into Kyōto. It was refused without any reason being given. The next complaint of our governor was that although I am a nominal employer of foreign teachers, the school is really not a native institution but a foreign one, since it is sustained by the annual grant of the American Board. Our situation became much endangered. The minister at Tōkyō was ever trying to stop the entry of missionaries into Kyōto. When Mr. Learned's first passport was nearly out I applied for a second. Everything seemed dark and hopeless. I knew surely that a permission could not be had if I took an ordinary course. To make a bold strike was my inspiration. I called on our governor at his office and requested him to approve my application and to speak favorably of us to the Foreign Department. He promised to do what he could, but said everything depended on the Foreign Office. By this way I prevented his doing any mischief, and then started for Tōkyō to see Mr. Mori, and explained to him all about our school, — how it started and how it is sustained. His reply was, 'You have a right to exist and also to employ foreign teachers if you use your own fund instead of that of the Board. The Foreign Office objects to your depending upon the American Board altogether.' I told him this annual aid was a free gift, and that we made a good use of it. Is it forbidden us to receive any aid from a foreign nation? If so, the law ought also to prohibit us from aiding other nations. Did not our people send an immense quantity of rice last year to a famishing district in China, and can we not also receive some aid for our moral and intellectual famine? This argument was just enough to bring him around to our side, and through his kindness I obtained the extension of Mr. Learned's passport for five years.

"When I applied this summer for Dr. Gordon's passport there was a sharp discussion between Mr. Mori and the minister. I must inform you why the latter is so bitter against us. He is a hater of Christianity. He does not clearly discriminate between us and some native merchants who keep shops open for foreigners outside the concessions in Tōkyō, by using their own names although they are hired and paid by the foreigners. Such is strictly forbidden by the law of the empire, yet is done by shrewd natives. The minister ranks us with these merchants, and is ready at any time to drive us out from Kyōto. But Mr. Mori stood up for us nobly, and persuaded him to grant our application. At the same time he sent me word by a friend to be cautious, and advised me to raise a permanent fund at once. For if it be proved that our school is sustained by the Board, I shall be heavily punished, our work will be suspended, we shall be driven out of the city, yea, — all our effort thus far put forth will disappear like morning dew before the sun. Seeing such a dark prospect before me shall I lament like the old prophet Jeremiah? No, I am determined not to lament, but to fight through till we conquer. May God help us, untiring soldiers. Since I heard from Mr. Mori I have been seriously thinking how to escape the governor's iron hand. We are badly spoken of throughout the country and ridiculed as the cradle of Christian priests. If we lose our hold here how can we start in the interior again? Our missionaries do not fully apprehend our critical condition. Doubtless some of them have written to the Board about it. Will the gentlemen of the Board stand and see us perish without any fellow-sympathy? Is the policy of the Board so conservative that it cannot give us a permanent fund from the large legacy they have recently received? In time of need it is often desirable to create a new policy in order to boldly carry out God's work. It is time for them to consider whether they will attack or retreat. If they do not understand my aim, if they be still incredulous, I will come to Boston to explain. If they do not grant me the fund I will present my cause to wealthy individuals in the States. I will become a public beggar from city to city. In my situation I would not cease begging as long as I can use my tongue or my pen. For Christ's sake and my country's sake I will become a loudly crying beggar.

"In this connection I must mention the standard of our school. Our people are making a bold strike in educational affairs. The government institution of learning as well as some private schools are advancing above us. If we do not strive to improve we shall be left in lower strata of educational system, and fail to lay hold of the best class of students. Our good missionary friends have thus far tried to teach the Bible too much and neglected scientific teaching. Numbers of promising boys were much disappointed and have left us to go to the schools in Tōkyō, where they will have no Christian influence. We can't afford to lose these promising ones. We must tie them to our school by giving them a thorough, higher, and professional as well as Christian education. This, if I mistake not, is the keynote of success for Christian effort in Japan. Unless the missionaries find this keynote their work will be largely wasted and fruitless. To my great disappointment some missionaries do not take pains enough to adapt themselves to our way in this important respect. Hence they are getting quite unpopular and cannot get along with the natives quite smoothly. A chief reason is that they are still Americans. Their habits, ideas, and imagination are all American. What Americans regard as good the natives may despise. Something honorable in America is regarded dishonorable here. Petty troubles arise now and then between them and our Christians. They want to get too many foreign reinforcements instead of raising up native workers by their own hand. They cannot talk as the natives can. They cannot go about from home to home as well as the natives can. They cannot bear heat of the day as well as the natives can. They cannot live in a cheap rented house so patiently as the natives can. Their work should be a high spiritual brain-work. They should raise up the spokesmen instead of speaking themselves. If I were in the place of Dr. Clark I should put all my effort in founding a strong Christian university in Japan, in order to raise up Christian ministers, Christian physicians, Christian statesmen, and even Christian merchants. Christians must not be charged with being ignoramuses, or we shall not get the respect of the people. We shall be ridiculed for our ignorance as well as for our faith. It is well for us to remember and practice our Saviour's words, 'be wise as serpents.' Try to send out choice men, men of the New Testament spirit, of broad education and strong character, possessing the power of adaptability. And I earnestly beg of you to give us a fund to save the life of the Kyōto Mission and to raise our educational standard so as to make our school the centre of Christian power and influence. I have freely expressed my humble opinion. May God give you and the gentlemen of the Board help to see our present critical position, is the prayer of your unworthy child."

Throughout this whole period Mr. Neesima wrote fully and freely to Mr. Hardy of all his trials and perplexities, but his letters are absolutely free from personalities and contain explanations where one might look for reproaches. The spirit of hope and faith always dominated that of discouragement, and there is no trace of fault-finding. Stronger even than the testimony of his colleagues in the various missions as to his bearing under these trials is that of these letters written in confidence, wherein he poured out his whole heart as a son to his father. From these letters a few extracts are taken.

"I am staying in an old Buddhist temple in a suburb of the city. While I am at home I receive constantly visitors who take up my time. As a large portion of them come on business, I cannot avoid them conveniently. There is no vacation in this hottest part of the summer. My correspondence and these callers still keep me busy. I will try to get off from home as soon as possible, else it will kill me. With regard to my opinion on mission work, I think the plan of Mr. —— will cut it short. The native churches ought to be independent. Most of them are striving to be so quite hard. Here is no lack of independent spirit. But some churches are like babes. Mr. ——'s plan is to make men out of babes at once. He says the native churches ought not to receive any foreign money; that the native missionary society ought not to receive any aid from the Mission; that the Doshisha ought to be supported by the native churches; that the girls' school should be in their hands; that the theological school and newspapers ought to be sustained by them. It is hard work for most of these churches to support their pastors and defray all other necessary expenses, and too much for sixteen or seventeen poor churches to take so much into their hands independently of the Mission. None of us have any beggarly spirit, yet there are some things which we cannot efficiently do. If this plan be carried out our school will be weakened and the number of theological students diminished. I would call this a poor and short-sighted policy. To save money is to lose our best workers. We are hoping to start a vernacular theological course to educate some in Chinese and Japanese without English. Those who have a thorough English education ought to occupy central places, and those who are taught in Chinese and Japanese can be assistant workers. Since last May our Buddhist priests are wide awake. They have plenty of money to hire scholars to attack

Christianity. We must have men well furnished with scientific and Biblical knowledge for advancing Japan. We are now on a battlefield. Soldiers ought to be strong. Hereafter uneducated pastors will be thrown out of the market. Such will everywhere be disliked. The better preachers we send, the more money will the people raise.

"This is only leisure hour I have found since last April. I can only say to you that my life is like a race runner's. I find leisure hours only in summer. I devote these chiefly to my own study. I must keep pace with the advancing world. On the 17th and 18th I made a short visit to Kishinowada. My time was so fully occupied there that I could scarcely eat. While I was eating people were waiting in the room.

"I must be thankful for the wise management of the American Board in sustaining our Kyōto institutions. Let the present arrangement continue as long as it may be needful. According to your kind fatherly advice I will be careful and try to do all things in a perfect harmony with our missionaries. I shall be careful not to find fault in others. We were terribly attacked by some brethren in other stations. I attempted to defend our position. It is all over now. I shall say nothing about them, of them, or against them. There is now perfect harmony between the different stations of our Mission. The last two months were the hardest ones I have ever experienced since my return to Japan. I found myself in the lowest stratum, and received the whole pressure upon myself. A heavy trial with respect to the government, and grave troubles among our native brethren and also in our school. O, heavy burdens! I bore them chiefly on myself by His help, but I think I came pretty near to burst up my brains."

Mr. Neesima had been for some years looking forward with "a great delight" to a visit from Mr. Hardy. "It would seem to me a dream," he says, "to be permitted to shake your hand on this side of the water." He was also anxious that Mr. Hardy, then chairman of the Prudential Committee of the Board, should see for himself the exact need of the country. When he learned that his visit, so long anticipated, was deferred, he says: "I cannot speak to you of this disappointment; it is too great." He was then in the province of Hyūga, in Kyūshū, the most southerly of the four large islands of Japan, where he had gone at the request of a native physician to engage in missionary work. In the fall of this year his sister died of hemorrhage of the lungs, and on October 27th he writes: —

"Five weeks ago I went to Imabari, Shikoku, to organize a church and install a pastor. I was preaching to a large audience in the evening when I received a telegram from home. I hurried back to find my sister dying. We tried our best to save her. She gathered all her relatives about her and told them she might doubtless depart very soon from this world, and her best wish to them all was that they should walk with God and live on Christ daily as we live on food. When I was obliged to attend the annual meeting of our Home Mission Board at Ōsaka she knew I was hesitating to go there, and told me not to stay away from that important meeting on account of her illness, but to do the Lord's business first. By these brave words I felt much encouraged to go. During the past two weeks she talked and dreamed much of heaven. Her mind was full of it. One day she said to me: 'What free grace it is that I, a poor sinner, could find a hope in the eternal heaven. I am desirous to go there even now.' She dreamed much of persons in white singing beautifully, and since then has become very fond of singing, asking every Christian visitor to sing for her. Then she shook their hands and bade them farewell till they meet her in heaven. Two minutes before her death she asked my wife to sing one or two hymns, then passed away as if she were going to sleep. It happened I was away that morning. When I came home I found her countenance already changed, but she replied to me once when I called her name. I was unwilling to go to our school that morning, because there was such change in her face, but she said 'No, go, do your duty.' We miss her very much, but the very thought of her makes us feel that heaven is very near."

In November, on returning from Annaka, he received from Dr. Clark the glad tidings that the year's appropriation of $8,000 had been placed in the hands of the native society which he represented, to be used under his direction for the educational work in Kyōto. The relief from all embarrassments with the government afforded by this action was very great. To Mr. Hardy he writes December 27, 1879:—

"I found your last letter on my arrival home. When I read it I exclaimed, 'The good Lord has done it!' My rejoicing was mingled with running tears. I knelt down before the Lord with my wife and gave Him our heartfelt thanks. Next to the Lord, I must express my gratitude to you for your deep interest in us. I must also thank the gentlemen of the Board. Through this action I shall be relieved from grave difficulty. Step by step the plots of our enemies are defeated. 'Delight thyself in the Lord and He shall give thee the desire of thine heart.' 'Commit thy ways unto the Lord; trust also in Him and He shall bring it to pass.' O, what precious promises they are unto us. I am wondering why God has chosen a weak instrumentality such as I am, weak both in body and mind, for promoting his kingdom in this empire. I could simply say to Him: 'Here I am; employ me in thy vineyard if thou findest a pleasure in thy humble servant.' In my later experience I find more than ever nothingness in me."

It was very characteristic of Mr. Neesima, and thoroughly in line with his efforts to spread the gospel through an educated ministry, that in his missionary tours he always sought to interest the leading men of the town or district, as well as to reach the poor. In February, 1880, he writes, in this connection, from Okayama: —

"I find it very hard to reach prominent men in our society, because many of them are too proud to be taught. They are self-conceited and seek for no further improvement in their moral condition. They have also a strong anti-religious spirit. I find in them the strange notion that any religion, even Christianity, hinders the progress of nations and has nothing to do with modern civilization. On the other hand, I always find some brilliant man who comes forth boldly and manfully. There are doubtless some thoughtless boys with us, but none who speak against Christianity. I have to be pretty careful. They do not like oldest kind of theology. They cannot bear any stiffness. In the Government University of Tōkyō, where are about seven hundred students, is an infidel atmosphere. Some native and some foreign teachers exert bad influence. There are also anti-

Christian schools in Tōkyō. We shall get learned persons enough within a few years, but mere worldly wisdom will not help our perishing people. We need the broadest culture and strongest Christian faith to counteract the downward tendency of our educated youth. The works of Spencer, Mill, and Draper are their favorites. They look down upon us as bigots. We must raise our standard of education until they can no longer assail us. If we limit it simply to theology, the best self-sustaining students will not come to us. Only by making our school attractive by giving a good and broad education can we widen our Christian influence. Some of our dear brethren have got very strange notions, and think altogether too little of education."

The personal friendship between Mr. Neesima and his colleagues of the Kyōto station was very strong. For Dr. Davis especially, who had shared his burdens from the outset, he felt the warmest affection, and repeatedly ascribes success to his tact, courage, and counsel. He writes to Dr. Davis August 12, 1880:

"I must assure you we cannot get along without you. Doubtless the many troubles you have encountered these past years broke you down completely. I hope you will take the matter slightly easier and try to rest as much as you can. The mission work in Japan is not like child's play. You have many troublesome boys under your care. I fear I am one of them. What I feel keenly in myself is my imprudence in many things. Certainly it must have been a great trial to you. But I trust an imprudent child such as I am may grow wiser as he grows older. At any rate it is well for us to remember that the world cannot be converted in a day."

The year 1881 opened more brightly. The governor of Kyōto had resigned, and his successor proved to be a man of liberal ideas. "I am informed," writes Mr. Neesima, "that he intends to call upon me soon. He will then be quite different from the former one. When I see him I shall try to present to him a plan to revolutionize the system of education in this city. My aim is to start a Sunday-school for the teachers of the primary schools." One of the immediate results of this change in the local government was the permission granted to hold religious meetings in the large theatres of the city. The first of these was attended by four thousand persons, and was addressed by twenty different speakers. These meetings produced a profound impression. In an editorial, of which the following is a translation, the " Ōsaka Nippo," one of the most influential daily papers of Japan, asked: —

"Is it the hand of man or of Heaven, or is it the inevitable tendency of the age, or is it the freedom of the human mind that has advanced to such an extent, that, in the very heart of Kyōto, the original Head and Holy Seat of Shintoism and Buddhism, a great meeting for the preaching of the Jesus Way has been held without any opposition? We need not go back to the utter destruction of the Christians in the war of Shimabara, but confining ourselves to what we have observed, it seems like the things of yesterday, that law rigidly prohibiting Christianity, written in eleven characters, and posted high in air before all the people; and that other law of religious examination that required every one to be enrolled once a year as either a Buddhist or Shintoist. Now such laws have become the dreams of fourteen years ago, and have passed away forever from our loved Japan. . . .

"Six years after the Restoration (eight years ago) the government took the first step of silent toleration of Christianity by removing from the high places the laws against heresy. Since then this new religion, hand in hand with western learning and civilization, has been gradually spreading not only in the open ports, but even in the interior. Churches are being built with the cross of Christ erected over them, and our people are everywhere being publicly taught the Bible. Already among the believers there are countless numbers who, having learned the outlines of this religion, go everywhere preaching and admonishing, converting the people, and daily spreading wider and wider the truth.

"We remember that some six or seven years ago, when Mr. Nakamura of Tōkyō published a translation of Dr. Martin's "Evidences of Christianity," there was an anxious discussion in one department of our government as to whether such an act could be passed over in silence. But now everywhere there are stores where Christian books are on sale. We are apt merely to notice that Christianity spreads only an inch to-day, and an inch to-morrow; and so accommodating ourselves to its gradual advance, we do not wonder at its rapid march. But when we sketch on paper the steps of progress, we cannot shut our eyes to the marvelous manner in which it is taking root. And among all these progressive steps, that which seems to us the most astonishing is what is written in the opening sentence of this article: The preaching of the Jesus Way in every centre of Kyōto, the Holy seat of Buddhism and Shintoism, the place where the

people are the most given to superstitious ideas about
gods, where they hold in deepest reverence the departed spirits, and where but ten years ago the arrival
of a foreign ambassador gave rise to the thought that
the soil of the Capital of the gods was polluted, and
that the wrath of the gods and of Buddha would surely
fall upon the people!"

In his early school days at Andover, amid the influences of a Christian home and training, Mr. Neesima had first conceived the plan of a Christian university for Japan. When we remember the condition
of Japan at that period, before the restoration, and
his own position, an exile struggling with poverty
and ill-health, we are not surprised to find him referring to this project as a day-dream. Yet it was even
then more than a dream, it was an ambition and a
purpose. "I kept it," he says, "within myself, and
prayed over it." From time to time he confided his
thought to his friends, but met with no encouragement. On the eve of his return, in the presence of
an audience whose sympathy and interest were indispensable to success, the desire of his heart burst from
his lips, and in the appeal then made he laid the corner-stone of the Meiji University. Beginning, with
seven pupils, in two dingy rooms, a school which for
years was the object of contempt and ridicule, opposed at every step by the hatred of the authorities
and the prejudices of the people, his purpose never
faltered. The time had now come when he could appeal to a sentiment to whose development he himself
had largely contributed. Residents of Kyōto who
had formerly antagonized all his efforts, but who were
deeply interested as patriots in the general question
of education, had become convinced that the sound-

est learning rested upon the Christianity which they had despised. Dissatisfied with the results of the government university at Tōkyō, plans for an institution independent of the state began to be discussed, promises of money for departments of law and medicine were made, and Mr. Neesima was consulted with reference to the incorporation of these departments and the broadening of the curriculum of the Doshisha. With these brighter prospects opening before him he began the realization of his long-cherished plans and publicly announced his purpose. In the spring of 1884, the first of several meetings designed to call public attention to this movement was held in Kyōto. It was attended by the leading officials and business men of the city and was addressed by Dr. Davis, Mr. Neesima and others. In May the following appeal, prepared by Mr. Yamamoto and Mr. Neesima, was issued : —

"The recent political changes in Japan have swept away feudalism, for many hundred years the basis of society. Under the steadily increasing influence of these changes the transformation of society has been so great that we seem to live in a new Japan. On every side are those who insist upon the improvement of our political institutions, our educational methods, our commerce, and our industries. We heartily agree with them in the importance of these things, but when we examine the present condition of affairs we find one cause for sorrow. Do you ask what that cause is? It is that there does not exist in Japan a university which, teaching the new science, is also founded upon Christian morality. This is the foundation which our civilization needs. In natural advantages Japan is not inferior to Europe or America. Why

then is our civilization so different? It is certain
also that we have few men of earnest purpose. Hence
the necessity for universities. We can learn from
the example of Europe. In the sixteenth century,
Luther, the great reformer, said: 'Parents who refuse to send their children to school are enemies of the
state and should be punished.' Fichte, the German
philosopher, said: ' The reason why Germany stands
in the front of European civilization is found in the
power emanating from her universities.' The twelfth
century was the dawn of civilization in Europe.
Greek philosophy was then studied in the University
of Paris and Roman law in the University of Bologna.
Before the year 1600 the universities of Oxford and
Cambridge had been founded in England, those of
Edinburgh and Glasgow in Scotland, of Prague,
Heidelberg, Leipzie, Tübingen, and Jena, in Ger-
many. Universities have also been established in
Holland, Spain, Portugal, and Austria. Abelard,
Roger Bacon, Kepler, Galileo, Lord Bacon, Locke,
Newton, Milton, Leibnitz, Kant, Reid, and Hamil-
ton, were famous as great scholars in those countries.
Pym, Hampden, Pitt, Fox, Burke, Johnson, Wycliffe,
Luther, Calvin, and Knox, were reformers in politics
and religion. Through the influence of these univer-
sities philosophy and science advanced, despotism and
feudalism were checked and destroyed, the power of
priest and noble resisted, the desire for liberty and
self-government kindled. The Reformation and the
English Revolution changed the condition of Europe.
In 1800 there were over one hundred universities in
Europe, and that the march of civilization has been
hastened by their influence is an indisputable fact.
Look also at the colleges and universities of America,

numbering over three hundred, yet only eight of which have been founded by the government. Harvard, Yale, Princeton, Amherst, Williams, Dartmouth, and Oberlin, of which the first is the most famous, may be noted. Harvard has now 110 professors, a library of 134,000 volumes, and an endowment of $14,854,372. In 1872 there were in the United States 298 colleges and universities, and 66 were founded in the following seven years. This growth of the higher education in the United States is one of the wonders of the world. In the year 1620 the Pilgrim Fathers, seeking freedom to worship God, landed at Plymouth. They established a school founded upon Christian morality. For 260 years their descendants, inheriting the spirit of their fathers, have carried out their purpose. They have believed that such schools would diminish the number of evil-doers, and increase the number of those who do good; that they would foster the spirit of liberty and become the foundation of the state; that the Christian university was the safeguard of freedom; and we do not doubt that their free institutions are the outcome of this spirit.

"As soon as it saw the importance of the university our government established one at Tōkyō, and has also founded several academies. These will give us intellectual and material, but not moral growth. There are many who are seeking to improve the public morality on the basis of Chinese philosophy. But we cannot rejoice in their efforts, for the moral code of China has no profound hold upon the minds of men. All Oriental states are almost wholly destitute of liberty and Christian morality, and cannot therefore advance rapidly in civilization. It is the spirit of liberty, the development of science, the Christian morality, which has given birth to European civilizations. Trace the effect to the cause and you will find science resting upon the foundation of Christianity. We cannot therefore believe that Japan can secure this civilization until education rests upon the same basis. With this foundation the state is builded upon a rock. No sword can conquer it, no tempest destroy it, no sea overcome it. Resting on the old moral code of China, it stands upon the sea-sands, and, when the rough waves beat upon it, falls to ruin.

"We are, therefore, hoping for a university which teaches advanced modern science and which is founded upon a pure morality. We have been very earnest in this matter. In this spirit we established the Do-shisha school in Kyōto in the eighth year of Meiji. Its students have increased year by year and our aim has ever been the university. We made known our purpose publicly in April of the sixteenth year of Meiji, and received much encouragement. At this time we met our friends in Kyōto and named it the Meiji University. We have determined first to raise an endowment for the departments of History, Philosophy, and Political Economy, and subsequently also for those of Law and Medicine. This is not easy of accomplishment, for a large sum is needed for buildings and professorships. Being so few we cannot of ourselves furnish the needed money, but we will not abandon our purpose to found this university now. We must work for new Japan. All true patriots should do so. Help us, as far as you are able, to accomplish our purpose and do this great work. Without your help our purpose cannot be realized."

Mr. Neesima's personal activity in this matter was incessant, but the strain to which he had been subjected for nearly ten years had seriously impaired his health, which was now the cause of grave concern to his friends. Already in 1882 he had been urged to go to China for rest. This, however, he refused to do, writing to Mr. Hardy that "To go to China might possibly excite some jealous feeling among my home brethren, who have given up every earthly comfort for the Lord, and are suffering much pecuniarily. I must never be a stumbling-stone to my dear brethren in Christ. But I begin to feel that I cannot go on much longer, and must stop work. My head does not allow me to read or write, yet something is always at hand. So I have made up my mind to take a trip to the north where I can see no Christian friends."

This plan was carried out, and he spent part of the summer of 1882 in Wakamatsu, his wife's early home, following, mostly on foot, the great interior road known as the Nakasendo, and visiting Annaka and Nikkō. At Wakamatsu he wrote by request the account of his early life quoted in the beginning of this volume, and, in forwarding it to America, said: —

"I hope Mr. Hardy will pardon me for not doing it sooner. I am afraid he will call me a disobedient boy. Since I began my work here I found out more and more my unworthiness, and have trembled to write this sketch. I wish I could break down my too great sensitiveness on this point. Some time ago I thought I was something, but now I feel I am nothing."

CHAPTER VI.

SECOND VISIT TO EUROPE AND AMERICA.

ALTHOUGH relieved at this time from teaching and freed by his associates as far as practicable from routine duties, the general care of the school and his intimate connection with the work of the Mission rendered it impossible for him to secure the needed rest. To his own health, however, he referred but rarely. In a letter of January 14, 1884, Mr. Hardy proposed his return to America via Suez, saying: "You allude merely to your health, but the Mission writes seriously of it;" and in the spring he was formally requested by a vote of the Prudential Committee of the Board "to take a furlough for such period as may be needful." This proposition he finally accepted. "It has been very hard to get him started," writes Dr. Davis, "and we have been afraid that he would break down entirely before he got under way. The number of irons he has in the fire is amazing, and it has been almost impossible for him to find time to arrange for his leaving. As you value his life and work give him as long a rest as you can in Europe, before he crosses the Atlantic." In yielding to the solicitations of his friends Mr. Neesima wrote to Mr. Hardy from Kōbe March 9, 1884: —

Kōbe, *March* 9, 1884.

I am very much indebted to you for your kind invitation as to my return to my dearest America. It was a serious matter for me to decide. In the first place I feel it too great an offering. It has been my attempt thus far not to place myself on a footing with the missionaries lest I should prove a stumbling-block to my native brethren. In the second place the anti-foreign party might sharply criticise my going to America. But after serious consideration I have concluded to accept your great favor and visit you once more. I feel there will be no least objection on the part of my native brethren. Some eminent men in the empire outside the churches heartily sanction my going. My friends at Ōsaka urge me strongly to go. I came here yesterday and my friends are all glad of this great opportunity for my sake. It is not my usual custom to write on the Sabbath, but yesterday I found occasion to speak to two eminent men on religious matters, and I feel I ought to write you at least a line to thank you. Dr. Berry urges me strongly to start from here at once, but I have something on my hands to be attended to first.

FROM MRS. NEESIMA TO MR. AND MRS. HARDY.

To my two revered personages I desire to present this letter. While I was much perplexed on account of the serious brain trouble of my husband, you kindly invited him to come home to America. Though I think of the depth of your kindness like multitudes of mountains, I utterly fail to express it by my writing-brush. So I simply resort to God with my thanksgivings. I request you still farther to look after him. Please give him an opportunity to take a complete rest this summer, for he will be very busy when he comes home, and here is no possible chance for rest. As he is planning to enlarge the school, his care and labor will ever increase in the future. When I anticipate this matter I am greatly troubled thereby. Though I wished very much to accompany him and render him my service, I feared my going with him might possibly be more a burden than a help. Besides that, we have Joseph's aged parents still living with us and I must remain to serve and comfort them. Although it is very hard for me to be so long separated from him, yet I bear it rejoicingly.

O, what happy creatures we are! While God was utterly unknown to us, we are known to Him. He called Joseph out to your country and provided you to receive him, and through the help of many our Doshisha was founded. As for me I am born in Japan and am grown in ignorance. Hence it is. impossible for me to help my husband. However, I am endeavoring to be his helpmate in my service to God with a sincere heart. Lately I started a woman's meeting in a suburb of Kyōto. It has been attended by six, ten, and by thirteen. I feel I have no ability to lead these beloved sisters. I am but a child in faith. I wish to win one person to start with, and by and by another may be added unto. I wish I could meet your two personages at least once in this world to express my grateful feeling. And while I am unable to express it either by my tongue or my pen, I hope that I could have an abundant opportunity to meet with you and talk with you in the same language in heaven when we are called up there by His mercy. But on acount of the shortcoming of my faith I have some fear that I may not be permitted to appear there. I hope you will pray for me on this account. Hereby I send you these my requests with my query for your health.

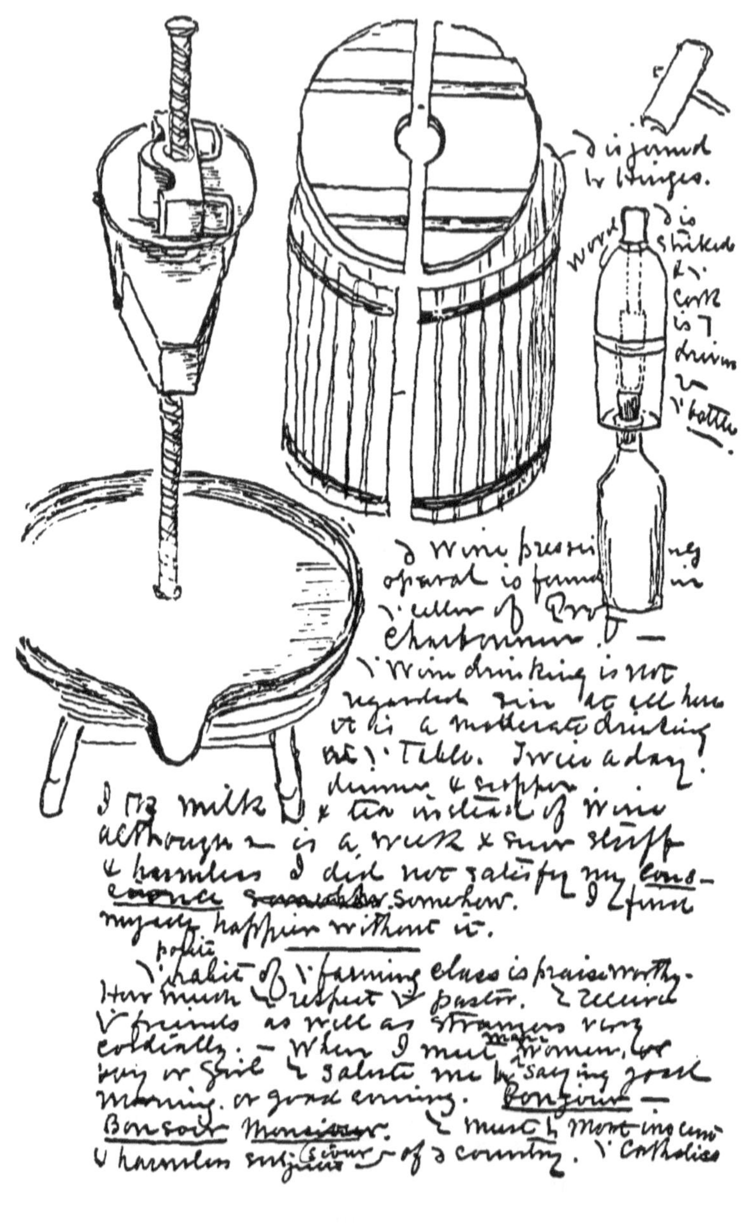

& Wine pressing apparatus is found in y cellar of Prof. Chautonin. —

y Wine drinking is not regarded sin at all here & it is a moderate drinking at y Table. Twice a day dinner & supper.

I try milk & tea instead of wine although it is a weak & sour stuff & harmless I did not satisfy my conscience somehow. I find myself happier without it.

y habit of y farming class is praiseworthy. How much I respect y pastor & record y friends as well as strangers very cordially. — When I meet women, boy or girl & salute me by saying good morning. or good evening. Bonjour — Bonsoir Monsieur. y must be morning custom & harmless religion of a country. y Catholics

The notebooks kept by Mr. Neesima during his journey reveal the variety of his interests. They are filled with historical notes, statistics, and memoranda of conversations with those to whom he had letters of introduction. He everywhere inspected the schools and colleges, recorded in detail their methods and results, and made plans of the buildings and apparatus. He describes minutely the architecture, agriculture, and manufactures of the localities he visited, and nearly every page contains drawings of the processes and implements described, or sketches from nature. It is the journal of a man of keen observation and wide sympathy, but of one more anxious to learn than to criticise. The following extracts are taken from its pages and from letters written by the way: —

April 6. Left Kyōto on the 5th inst. The whole school and other friends, including the members of three churches, came to the station to see me off. It was a great trial for me to leave home, and especially my aged parents (both of them now 78 years of age), my dear wife, and our school, to which I am so much attached. My wife accompanied me to the SS. Khiva in the harbor of Kōbe. I committed her to the care of Our Father, on whom she can rely far better than upon myself.

April 7. Prayer for theological students. We passed through the Straits of Shimonoseki at 5.30. The weather was fair and I was not sick at all.

April 8. Prayer for the fifth year class. We arrived at Nagasaki at 6.30 A. M. It is an excellent shelter for ships. The only defect of the harbor is its shallowness. The scenery from the steamer is fine. The harbor is surrounded by mountains, and the foreign residences are mostly on high ground. A boatman took me over all the important streets for 30 cents, and I saw some very fine tortoise-shell workmanship in the manufactory.

There are two Japanese youths on board going to Odessa with a Russian priest. The meals are excellent. The servants are Chinese and Hindoos.

April 12. We arrived at Hongkong at 10 A. M. I visited with Mr. H. the Anglican, Catholic, Chinese, and Mahometan cemeteries. The architecture of the latter is very peculiar. They are all handsomely and tastefully laid out. They seem a paradise in this world. Visited the Chinese quarters. At one place the wares were spread upon the ground. Public speakers, singers, and fortune-tellers were there. In one street many painted women invite passers-by into their houses. I visited a smoking gallery where were twenty Chinese in a small room smoking that cursed opium. I asked the editor of the 'China Mail' the proportion of opium smokers among the Chinese. He replied it was about the same as that of drinkers among Europeans. They smoke about 10 cents a day. To my surprise the Chinese are a great commercial people. They have splendid stores fully supplied with both Chinese and foreign articles. The stores on the Queen's Road are beautiful. Most of the houses are three stories high.

April 14th. I went to the union church yesterday. It was thinly attended. In the afternoon Dr. C. preached in Chinese. I also heard Bishop B. preach to the seamen. There are several mission societies working in Hongkong, — English, German, and one American. They have no regular Sabbath-schools established. Rev. Mr. Morrison commenced his missionary work in Canton in 1807. Bishop Burdon came to Hongkong in 1853. He has charge of St. Paul's College, about thirty pupils. His diocese extends from Foochoo to Hongkong. No self-supporting churches in China this side of Foochoo. The bishop has five pupils to teach one hour a day. A slow process! One hundred people belong to his church; one hundred people for thirty-one years' labor! He says the missionaries have not yet discovered a way to reach the higher Chinese classes. They are too proud of their own ways, and are not anxious to adopt western science or manners. In fact there is no movement among the higher classes towards European civilization either in social or political matters. Those who receive an education abroad have no voice. I see nothing in favor of the European way. It is discouraging to educate the Chinese, because they come to get English only and having got this, go away into business. China is honeycombed with secret societies. The people are tired of the government. If they found a capable leader they would rise. In one sense they are all united against foreigners, but it is almost safe to say that there is no public spirit among the Chinese. They are discontented with the government. They have an instinct for taking care of themselves. There are no public baths like ours. Being so filthy it is wonderful they are so thrifty. They are the Oriental Jews.

HONGKONG, *April 15.*

We left Nagasaki on the 8th inst. and had fine weather and calm seas nearly all the way to this place, which we reached on the 12th. I called on Rev. C. R. Hager, a missionary of your board, who secured a hotel for me and took me all over the city. So far as I can judge of the Chinese they seem to strive merely for money. For this they rise up early and sit up late; for this they would go without food and endure all manner of hardships. While here I think constantly of a nation for whose sake I am what I am. I called yesterday on the Bishop. He is somewhat discouraged and hopeless about the Chinese. But sooner or later China will move, though it may be slowly. I feel we ought to strike out from Christians' conversation and writing the terms "hopeless" and "discouraged." But hereby I do not intend to criticise the Bishop. I have full sympathy with him, and doubtless if I were in his place I might have become discouraged long ago. I find great comfort in that our God is not simply the only God, but our Father also. It is a great trial to me to leave Japan, but . . . I cannot write on this subject. I am glad to say that I can sleep much better and have experienced no sharp headaches; but I find it a hard thing to write much.

CEYLON, *April* 27, 1884.

We reached Singapore after a hot voyage of five days. I did not go ashore because it was the Lord's day, and passed a very uncomfortable night, as the steamer was taking on coal. Those who went ashore were equally miserable on account of the heat. Monday I visited the city, which is inhabited by mixed races, most of the shopkeepers being Chinese. About the wharf are small houses in which poor natives and Chinese live. They are one story high and supported on posts. The vegetation is splendid. We found a carriage and drove to the city. The driver was a great cheat. Groves of cocoanut-trees growing to enormous heights were delightful to us. I bought a weekly paper, resembling our "Japan Mail," which cost 40 cents; also a most delicious pineapple, of a naked boy. The road to the city was well laid out, and the botanical garden, planted with tropical trees, is well kept up. The Maharaja of Johore visited the steamer to bid farewell to some friends. He was dressed in the English style, and wore a colored band of silk about the waist. Singapore is an island of undulating ground. If the straits were fortified no man-of-war would be able to pass through. It is well situated for growth, and may in the future become of more importance than Hongkong.

April 23d. We arrived in the harbor of Penang this morning. The island is just west of the peninsula of Malacca; is about thirteen miles wide and nine long, and, except on the north, where the city is, hilly and mountainous. Owing to the intense heat of the tropical sun I did not accompany the few courageous ones who went ashore to visit the city.

Sunday, 27th. The English service conducted by the chief steward was thinly attended. The Catholics, Mahometans, and Parsees, were not, of course, present. The younger officers regard it as a stupid and tiresome thing. One of them said, we are soon to meet with storms because missionaries are aboard. On this account the sailors are much afraid of us. I dislike written forms of prayer, but I liked to be with Christians and enjoyed singing with them. We sighted the island of Sumatra on the afternoon of the 25th. To the northwest is the beautiful wooded Poolo Way. Splendid showers passed over its thick forests and a rare rainbow made me wish I was a painter. The heat is very oppressive. This morning we began to see the peaks of Ceylon in the distance, though I do not yet smell the odors of those famous spices! We shall change our steamer to-morrow at Colombo and may have a chance to see that famous prisoner Arabi Pasha, as also to visit the temples of Kandy. I feel more and more what a rare opportunity I am enjoying, and think of those Italian cities before me; but above all I am thankful that I am once more invited to my dear America to see you. My heart constantly goes back to my dearly beloved Japan. I can only say for her sake I am now here.

29th. We entered the harbor of Colombo early in the morning. The harbor is protected by a finely built breakwater on which is a railway and lighthouse. I drove with my Japanese friend to the house of Arabi Pasha. Leaving our carriage at the gate we entered the grounds. A young man came to ask us what we wanted. We presented our cards and told him we came to call upon Arabi Pasha. While we were talking we saw a tall man dressed in white walking to and fro under the palm-trees. The young man took us to that gentleman and presented him our cards. He was glad to see us and ordered chairs. We exchanged salutations in the Oriental fashion. He asked the object of our visit, and whether we were going to England. He asked, also, where we learned English. We informed him that English was extensively taught in Japan. He then inquired whether England had possessions in Japan. We replied, of course, in the negative. Our conversation was interrupted by a short visit from some English ladies. He seemed to take more of a fancy to us than to his English visitors, but when I came to draw out something about Egypt he showed dislike to any conversation on that subject, remarking: "We cannot tell what will become of Egypt. God only knows. He will take care of it." He asked how large a military force we had in Japan, also how many men-of-war. To our replies he said, "Very good." He advised us to maintain a good army and navy. He inquired about our educational system, and was much pleased to hear of our progress in that respect. Whenever our answers pleased him he said, "very good." I asked about the religion of the Arabs. He replied "Every Arab is a Mahometan." He was pleased when I informed him that I had a copy of the Koran. I have not read it yet, but will do so. He said the Mahometan religion was spreading quite fast in India, and also in China. He asked what religion I embraced, and my reply surprised him. He spoke through an interpreter, but occasionally he burst forth in broken English. His voice is tiger-like, but he has wonderfully pleasant features when he smiles. He is tall and rather fat; his face is full and his eyes comparatively small; his skin and hair are dark, and he wore a long white garment. He received profound obedience from his attendants, and seemed to be one loved and respected. When we bid him adieu he thanked us for calling upon him and gave us his autograph.

Then we drove through groves of palm trees, and the streets and market of the town. The native streets are dirty and dusty, and everywhere were bad odors; the shops are small, scantily supplied, and very inferior to those of Singapore and to the Chinese shops of Hongkong. Most of the houses are of mud, with but one story. The cottages without the city, surrounded by green yards and tall palm-trees, are very picturesque. We saw several nicely built churches of European style; these are Catholic. Numbers of natives crowded about us, showing us recommendations in English and Japanese, and saying, "Other people tell lies, but me tell no lies." They were like flies in midsummer, shameless and bold; they have no self-respect and are downright beggars. At the market were many fruits unknown to me; the oranges are not so good as ours. I wished to ask many questions, but we were surrounded by so many shameless beggars and found ourselves amid such bad smells that, after buying some fruit, we cleared out.

May 5th. We are opposite the island of Sokotra, which is seventy-one miles long. It is an English possession, inhabited by a few Arabian fishermen, and has a few valleys where vegetables can be grown.

May 7th. Quite early in the morning we reached Aden, but on account of the quarantine were obliged to remain on the steamer. The town is built on the barren hills; not a single tree in sight. In the afternoon we passed the Gate of Tears and saw the wrecks of six steamers lying not far apart.

May 13th. Suez is yet a miserable place. There are few respectable houses, the rest being low Arabian mud houses without windows or tiles. Some of them are not over seven feet high, the roofs flat or like beehives, covered with hay and rubbish to prevent leakage. The railway system is bad. There is no head manager. Near Alexandria our conductor and engineer had a terrible quarrel. Everything was in confusion. Time is nothing to these Egyptians.

May 17th. Arrived in Brindisi and took the train for Naples. The fields are in a high state of cultivation. Miles and miles of grape-vines and olive-trees. The farmhouses neat and picturesque. The stations

are substantial stone buildings and the second-class
carriages far better than those of Japan.

ROME, *May 20, 1884.*

I visited St. Peter's this morning, and was perfectly bewildered by its richness and vastness. It is
far beyond my description. I gave especial attention
to the few Raphaels there. But my desire for the
fine arts is too profound, and I must cut short my stay
in Rome, for I shall be tempted to overdo. I could
but pity those poor devotees who kissed the toe of that
bronze statue of St. Peter. While I was gazing this
afternoon at that beautiful interior of S. Paolo Fuori
le Mura I began to wonder and query what St. Paul
would say of the building, or rather of the builder, if
he should rise to-day. I should like to ask both
Peter and Paul their private opinions of these things
done in their honor. I am myself too radical and too
practical, and as I cannot get replies at once from
these departed apostles must be contented with my
own opinions and criticisms. I have called on our
minister and Rev. A. G. Gray; also upon the Minister of Public Instruction. The rector of the Collegio
Romano showed me over this Jesuit college, and I had
a long conversation with Dr. Ottavio Grampini, the
librarian. I have also visited several schools with the
director of primary instruction. So I do not devote
myself altogether to sight-seeing, but am trying to
solve problems about this nation, its future and draw-
backs. This is a great place to study humanity. I
find traveling and sight-seeing both expensive and fa-
tiguing, and shall try to find some good resting-place
in Switzerland or Scotland before coming to you. I

am now bound to get well. I am very careful about my expenses; a missionary ought not to travel like rich people. I must defer telling you my rich experiences in Naples and Rome. Some thoughts differ from the reality. I used to think of the clear and beautiful Tiber; but what a dirty stream it is!

TO MRS. HARDY.

TURIN, June 18, 1884.

I remained six days in Florence, and spent much time in those splendid Pitti and Uffizi galleries. But what interested me most were the relics of Savonarola, which are kept in an old cell where he used to stay. I had a most interesting interview with Dr. Villari, the author of Savonarola's life. I found him rather indifferent to religious matters. He adopts Cavour's principle: a free church in a free state. He hesitated to reply when I inquired his own religious views, but of Christianity he said, "It is an excellent thing for the country, and has a powerful civilizing effect." To my question whether the spirit of Savonarola still survived he replied in the negative, to my great disappointment. Savonarola is dead, indeed, and the square where he was burned is not ornamented in his honor, but with mythological emblems. Alas! the spirit of this monk may be dead in the hearts of Italians, but he still lives and preaches to those of the evangelical faith. I also called on Dr. Piccini, the Oriental scholar. He has many Chinese and Japanese manuscripts. I have visited many institutions of learning. I find the clergy of Italy less well educated than those of France and Germany. But I meet very many accomplished Oriental scholars, especially Dr. Teza of Pisa, who speaks German, Dutch, English,

French, etc., and reads Arabic, Japanese, Chinese, and many hieroglyphic languages. He is Professor of Sanscrit in the university. Social science and language is much studied at Pisa, philosophy in Naples.

I am quite free from the fever which I contracted in the Red Sea, and had courage enough to climb that famous tower. It was towards evening, — a calm and beautiful evening, too. In the west, over the Mediterranean Sea, there was a splendid sunset, and in the northwest the ragged peaks of the Apennines, while around me lay the city and the highly cultivated fields. I shall never forget that view in my life.

I visited Genoa hastily, and passing under the lofty mountains came through the beautiful valley of the Po.

I attended a Protestant service in Turin. About twenty poorly dressed, ignorant-looking people, mostly women, — a discouraging sight! The work in Roman Catholic Italy seems disheartening. Their faith is not in God, but in religious forms. In company with Dr. Torre I visited the university and St. John's Hospital.

People here have a most wonderful skill in taking money out from a traveler's pocket. I have decided to go to Torre Pellico in the Waldensian valley to rest three or four weeks. I have several letters of introduction to eminent English people, members of Parliament, the Archbishop of Canterbury, and others, and am perplexed whether I shall try to rest here or not. It may be best for me to do so, but the temptation to give this time to England is very strong. Although sight-seeing diverts my thought from Christian work, it is hard for me not to think of Japan. I hope I shall gain strength enough to labor for Japan many coming years.

TO MR. HARDY.

TORRE PELLICO, *July* 1, 1884.

This valley is directly west from Turin, and Torre Pellico is the largest community. Here is a college for young men and a school for girls. The population is of the Protestant faith. The American consul in Turin advised me to come here, because of the beautiful scenery and fine air. He said nothing of the community in this valley, but I knew something of it before and am much interested to know more about it and to study its history. You know what severe religious persecutions they have suffered. They are just well enough off to support themselves, but can do nothing else. But for their poverty they might be a leaven to Italy. I have already taken some excursions to neighboring high hills, and have made many acquaintances whose society I enjoy. I cannot read or study much yet. As my health has been going down some years it may take some time to build it up. In your kind letter you urge me not to think about money for our school in Kyōto. But, dear sir, I have no single day in which my thought could be free from Japan. My heart is in two places, — heaven and Japan, — yes, one more place, — America. I desire to raise some money in America to start a medical school, for which I have already written to you with Dr. Berry. In Japan I also began to receive some sympathy from friends in regard to founding some special chair in our school. The matter looks rather dubious yet, but I feel I must work for it. I must either sink or swim, succeed or die. But I must not write on this subject any more lest you send me a regular scolding. Allow me to send you my special request to pray for Japan intensely, fervently. My heart burns for her and I cannot check it.

Mr. Neesima became deeply interested in the Waldensians at Florence, where he visited their theological school, and remained over a month at Torre Pellico, studying their history, institutions, and manner of life. The following thoughts are from his journal of this period. Most of them were written from his bed, to which he was confined by a fever contracted on an excursion when, overtaken by a storm, he was compelled to pass the night in a shed on the mountains.

" *Silence.* Silence is one of the virtues. There is much safety in silence. Wise men never talk much. As the tongue was given us to use for good purposes, use it for such. Vain and senseless talking often injures our reputation and causes us to lose our manhood. I often noticed uneasiness and a chaff-like element in vain and talkative men. There is something noble and serene in silence. It does not imply concealment, for the wicked often conceal their deeds with words. Silence is a manly forbearance. A man of silence is a blessing to a family and to society. It ought by no means to be accompanied by a bitter countenance, but rather with a cheerful one. Vain talking disturbs, but silence soothes and heals. We can easily weigh a man of vain talk, but cannot easily measure the depths of mind of a wisely silent man. But do not keep silence if by speaking we can do good or bear witness for the truth. O, how large a portion of our talk we spend upon the vain things of the world, and how little for the truth! When a word goes out from our mouth it is like water spilled on a parched soil; there is no possibility of taking it back again. What is said, is said. It becomes a fact of our lives for which we must in the future give an account. But above all let us not harbor evil thoughts, for evil thoughts are the mainspring of evil and vain talking.

"Poor creatures! we plan much and can do very little. Our plans are often defeated by something.

"*Receive others patiently.* If one would be a hero, let him be patient. If any brother do not behave as he ought, wait for some occasion to drop a kind word, so as not to offend him. Never send away a brother in Christ when he comes. 'The sacred beast does not trample upon even a blade of grass,' — which means that no man, however stupid, no enemy, however bitter, is despised by the divine mind. Cause no man to fail. Bear the evils of others for God's sake, for He bears ours patiently. He does not correct us furiously, at once, but takes many occasions to heal us and many years to sanctify us. Let us by no means neglect our duty to others. Look at the ocean, — how beautiful it is! Yet it must receive many filthy things from the shores. It receives and purifies. We shall be happy men if we can be like it. Be minute for ourselves in everything, but when we come to deal with others, let us be careful not to offend them by a close calculation.

"*Roughness and Politeness.* A rough manner with a kind heart is far better than a petty artificial politeness with no least meaning. Japan is one of the politest nations in the world, but, alas! the heart is not in it. Artificial politeness is a national habit. This is not the result of a true sincerity. Politeness ought to be the necessary exponent of real love and kindness; but without sincerity it is a kind of deception.

"*Business Character*. The Italians appear to be polite, but they lack business character. They are by nature easy-going, and would rather postpone business if possible. They will not move unless they are pushed by some one. They do not know how to be prompt. They talk much and are easily excited. Time is not money for them. Do what is to be done promptly. Waste no time in talking. Do it, and it is done.

"*Man's Greatness*. Man's greatness does not depend upon his learning, but upon his disinterestedness in self. Those with much learning are apt to be more selfish than the unlearned. Let us look at Christ on the cross. He is our example. O how noble, how grand, how gracious, He seems to us! Let us forget self, and offer ourselves freely for the cause of truth. Let us also be truly penitent and humble. I call this man's greatness.

"*The True Hero-worshiper*. Most Japanese are hero-worshipers. They are a difficult people to manage except by a hero to whom they can look up. Yet they are very easily led away by a hero. They move on the sensational currents of the hero's opinions, and lack individuality. Most hero-worshipers are tinged with the same color as that of their hero. Their weak point is that they cannot rise above their hero. If he makes a mistake, or fails, they also do the same. If he falls, they fall likewise. This has been true of us, as close examination of our history will show. You will also find that there has been no hero in Japan who has done all for unselfish ends. He is apt to be more selfish than the common mass of the people.

If the mind of our people be directed to the Hero of heroes, the greatest the world has ever produced, I am sure it would revolutionize the future of Japan. He is far above Socrates and Confucius, yet He is the friend of the poor. He is far above Alexander or Napoleon, yet He shed his own blood for humanity, instead of shedding that of hundreds of thousands of the innocent for his own gratification. He had no selfish aim in his life; He was perfectly holy, yet perfectly simple; He had no place to rest his head, yet He sits for eternity on the throne of the universe. If the Japanese must have a hero, let them worship this one, the Hero of heroes. His worshipers will be tinted with the one best color, — the color of godliness. Within this bound there is ample scope for freedom: man can choose any profession except bad and harmful ones. In following Him we shall obtain true human liberty and certainly preserve our individuality. O how I long for our people to turn towards this Hero, so far above weak humanity.

"If I teach again I will pay special attention to the poorest scholar in the class. If I can do that I believe I can be a successful teacher.

"*A Policy for our Training School.* Let us be like an unpolished diamond. Never mind the outward rough appearance, if we can have the shining part within. Let these three factors be our perpetual mottoes: 1. Christ as our foundation stone. 2. Well qualified instructors. 3. Well selected library and thorough equipment of apparatus. These three factors will be the true shining part of our school. Too much of brick and mortar does not suit my humble taste. I am terribly craving for the inner polish. That will certainly command the respect of thoughtful Japanese far more than brick, stone, and mortar.

"Ordinary observers may take no notice of the unpolished diamond. A skilled jeweler sees at a glance what it is. Wonderful beauty within! Never mind if the world takes no notice of us because we do not shine in society. If we could only have that wonderful beauty within, that were enough for us. If we have the life and light of Christ within us, then we are most precious diamonds, though we may seem rather dull and unpolished outwardly.

"Always remember the disappointed.

"*Promises.* Fulfill your promises promptly. Never postpone till to-morrow, for we may not see to-morrow or may be fully occupied with something else. It is a sort of weakness and shame for a man to make all sorts of apologies to another. Let yea be yea, and nay be nay. Do, or not do. But never be sluggish or leave business half done. Earnestness is like a transparent crystal; but love is like honey, always sweet and without any bitterness.

"Try to say what we mean, and never anything which we do not really mean in our heart. It is a moral weakness to utter what we do not really mean. Straightforwardness is found mostly among the Anglo-Saxon races.

"I find some Christians narrow and stupid. Yet Christianity ought to produce great-heartedness, activity, and progress. Narrowness and stupidity are the results of a dead faith. Salt which has lost its savor is good for nothing.

"There is great danger of our forming an opinion of others by looking at them in one case. We should be careful, because some who are quite deficient in one respect may be very efficient in another. There must be some defect even in a so-called perfect man.

Discover his temper, his education, his surroundings, his circumstances in life. See how he behaves in some unusual case. Never criticise too soon, else we shall surely misjudge him. Judge with a Christian grace. Never be too harsh or too minute. Love others as our Heavenly Father loves us. If we have love on our side we shall lose all our petty criticising spirit. O, it is a most unhappy and unhealthy thing to have too critical eyes for others. When we discover some defect in others, take it as it were upon ourselves and try not to repeat it. When we see great success among our brethren, wish more success for them. Never look upon our dear brother with an envious eye. If he is good, praise him, pray for him, and follow his example. I observed often that when some one hears good news of his friend he would say, 'But he is so and so,' instead of rejoicing over his success. Weak human nature is prevailing everywhere. There is a great deal of competition among educated people. Note: Be especially patient when we are sick or feeling unhappy.

"Don't be a Jack-at-all-trades. In passing through some country towns I notice there are ever so many things shown in the shops, but when I closely examine each article I find the stock of each kind is rather scanty. It is well for us to be widely informed on many subjects, but do not imitate those country shops, — many articles, but a scanty supply of each. We ought to be well posted in at least one subject or professional study. It will be a rich treat to us. Success in our life will chiefly hang upon it. Let this be our defensive and offensive weapon on the battle-field of truth. Though our talent be small, let it be solid and weighty. Be single-minded for a single purpose. We shall sooner or later reach our mark. Never shoot one arrow into the air; aim at an object surely, and then let it go. If we miss, then repeat the process again and again until we can satisfy ourselves. I never knew of a single case of a talented, puffed up, yet unsettled man accomplishing anything noteworthy.

"Never miss a rare opportunity to do good. Let our guns be always loaded. When we meet our game, aim at it and shoot it instantly; for our game will never wait for us. When we meet with any occasion to do good to another, don't let it go; don't wait for to-morrow; do it at once, for we may never have the occasion again. To shoot wild game is a mere pleasure, but to shoot men for our Master is a grave business. Let our guns be first loaded with living powder and bullets from on high, and be always ready. Many hunters of men carry their guns unloaded. This explains why Christ's kingdom does not spread faster among men.

" *The Divine Fire.* Many Christian ministers may have highest culture, and may write their sermons with much skill and thought, — beautifully executed work, like a Grecian marble statue. Alas! there is no heat in it. Heat must be caused by fire; if there is no fire in the sermon to heat the hearer's heart, it is a serious affair. Divine fire is needed to heat men's hearts. This fire can only be got by daily seeking. Those who depend very much upon their talent and knowledge are very apt to forget to seek this much needed divine fire for themselves as well as for their hearers. How cold such a heart must be to a congregation! It is fireless and lifeless. If each professing Christian had this divine fire what would be the aspect of the Christian world! O Heavenly Father, give us this fire! However small we may be, if we have genuine fire we shall consume even the whole world. How small a spark burned up a vast forest in Canada! How small a lamp consumed two thirds of the great city of Chicago! Sometimes one may make an artificial fire in imitation of the divine, but his hearers will sooner or later detect it; it is a mock fire. God will not bless such. O let the divine fire be burning within us always.

"When we are successful in life let us remember Christ's words: 'It is I.' He is the cause of all true success. When we are frightened, or disappointed, or alone, let us remember how he said, 'It is I.' O the consolation of Christ's presence!

"When I awoke this morning I thought of some prayer for some important event in the world. A single prayer, a single word or deed, may exert some vast influence. O what responsible creatures we are! I wish I realized it more.

"'It is finished.' Was ever dying speech so bold!

"Is there any one in the world perfectly free from selfish ambition? How can one know that he is free from such? Or is there any one perfectly free from the slightest deception? Can deception ever be eradicated from civilized society? How many of us can say to God, 'I have lived my life without the slightest ambition or deception'? Has any one ever seen, or could we expect to see, such a perfect type of humanity among the race of Adam, except the Son of God? It is too foolish to entertain such a question, but I would like to meet such a person.

"To be aimless is to be lifeless. A doubting mind never accomplished anything. If we have a doubt then, first clear up the doubt. A half-way scientist, or scholar, or Christian, or statesman, or benefactor, is of no account in the world."

On the 5th of August, Mr. Neesima started from Turin for Switzerland by the way of Lake Como and the St. Gothard pass with Dr. Alex. Thompson, who had been laboring among the Jews and Turks for thirty-one years. At Göschenen he left his companion and proceeded on foot with a German gentleman whom he met at the latter place. What followed is best described in his own words.

LUCERNE, *August* 9, 1884.

I wrote these inclosed papers at the Hotel du Mont Prosa on the St. Gothard pass on the 6th inst., when I was greatly troubled by my heart there. I felt something quite wrong in my breathing just a mile before I reached the pass. I requested a German gentleman who accompanied me to leave me behind, because I could not keep up with him. Accordingly he went on. I stopped to take breath every ten yards, but after a great struggle I reached the hotel in the pass. After resting a while I took my dinner, but had no appetite, and also began to cough. After resting further on a sofa I felt myself growing worse and worse and asked for a doctor, but there was none. I took a tablespoonful of brandy, to arrest my chill, and also applied mustard. About this time I began to think that it might possibly be the Lord's will to take me away from this changeable world to that unchangeable and glorious one. At this moment my thought for Japan, my plan for mission work, my constant daydream to found a Christian university, my tender feeling for my wife and parents, my gratitude to Mr. and Mrs. Hardy, came up at once like a volcanic fire. Still above all these feelings I believe I perfectly resigned myself to the hand of my Heavenly Father, and asked him repeatedly to receive my soul to his bosom if it be his will. While I was suffering from a most distressed feeling in my chest, how happy and how thankful I was for the Father's kind care over me, and especially for his forgiving grace manifested through his son Jesus Christ.

Then I sat up in bed and wrote the inclosed will on two sheets of drawing paper which I then had with me for sketching. While writing that I almost fainted away. Towards evening I began to feel a little better, and took a cup of tea. I slept quite well. On the following morning I was still better, but had not strength to start for Andermatt, so I took a carriage from Airolo and reached Andermatt about dinner time, resting quietly there that afternoon. Desiring to see a doctor I started for Lucerne on the 8th. My chest was examined by Dr. Stocker. He warned me to keep myself quiet for a few days, as he found my heart out of sound state.

I desire to keep these papers, because I had then a most unparalleled feeling I ever felt in my past life. Since then I feel more and more my life is not for me. Whether I live or die I must live or die for Christ. May the Lord ever keep this sin-wounded soul under his protecting hand, and count me as a least one in his kingdom through the righteousness of Jesus Christ.

His most unworthy servant,

JOSEPH H. NEESIMA.

I am a native of Japan and a Christian missionary to my native land. On account of my ill-health I was obliged to leave my native land. I came from Milan to Andermatt yesterday and took a room at the Hotel Oberalp. I started on a trip to the St. Gothard pass with a German gentleman this morning. As I found myself unwell he left me here and went on to Airolo. I found myself hard of breathing. It must be some trouble in my heart. My goods are in the Hotel Oberalp with some money. If I die please send a telegram to Pastor Jurino, 51 Via Torino, Milan, and ask him to take charge of my body. May the kind Heavenly Father receive my soul to his bosom. August 6, 1884. J. H. Neesima. Whoever reads this writing, pray for Japan, my dear native land. I would ask the Pastor Jurino to bury me in Milan and send this writing to Hon. Alpheus Hardy, 4 Joy Street, Boston, Mass., U. S. A., as he and his wife have been my benefactors these twenty years. May the Lord give them ample rewards both now and hereafter. Send a telegram to Mr. Hardy at once. Please cut and send a little portion of my hair to my dear wife and aged parents in Kyōto, Japan. as a token of the inseparable bond of union in Christ. My plan for Japan will be defeated. But thanks be to the Lord that He has done so much for Japan. I trust He will yet do the wonderful work there. May the Lord raise up many true Christians and noble patriots for my dear fatherland! Amen and amen.

LUCERNE, *August* 17.

I bought an Alpinestock at Milan, intending to do much walking. But my plan is defeated. Still I take what comes to me. I have learned in my experience to make a resolution never to be sorry or discouraged. O hard resolution! I am now gathering materials on the Swiss higher education. Then I shall visit Prof. Christlieb at Bonn. While I meet these trials on account of my health, yet I find sunshine always before me. I have received a cordial invitation from the Mission House at Basle, and expect to go there next week.

On the advice of the physician consulted at Lucerne Mr. Neesima abandoned the walking tour he had contemplated in Switzerland and started for England via Basle, Wiesbaden, Bonn, Brussels, and Rotterdam. He remained some time with his old friends at Wiesbaden, and after a fortnight in London and a visit to the Universities of Cambridge and Oxford, sailed from Liverpool for New York, where he arrived September 27, 1884. On the way to Boston he passed a few days at New Haven with President Porter. His journal of October 1st contains the brief entry: "How happy I was when Boston came in sight, and I saw the gilded dome of its State House and the spires of its churches. How kindly I was welcomed there."

On October 7th he left Boston for Columbus, Ohio, to be present at the seventy-fifth annual meeting of the American Board of Commissioners for Foreign Missions, and made a short address at the evening meeting of the 10th. On his return to Boston he wrote an appeal in behalf of a higher Christian education for Japan. This appeal, indorsed by the secretaries of the Board, by Presidents Seelye and Hopkins, was printed for private circulation among the friends of education, and is given below, together with the letter addressed at the same time to the Prudential Committee.

To the Prudential Committee of the American Board of Commissioners for Foreign Missions.

Dear Sirs, — Allow me to submit to you the following statements to invite your attention to my humble scheme for the speedy evangelization of Japan. Before I dwell upon the subject just mentioned, I first beg your attention to the past and present condition of the country.

Japan, as you well know, was once opened to foreign intercourse, and also to Jesuit enterprise, in the sixteenth century. But for certain reasons the ports were closed to all western nations except the Dutch, and Roman Catholicism was checked by inhumanly persecuting and exterminating the devotees of the Cross, numbering probably more than 600,000. Japan thus became a hermit nation, so isolated and so exclusive. She would have nothing to do with the outside world. From that time it remained a rigid law of the country to fire upon every black vessel (as foreign vessels were then called by us) seen approaching our coasts, until we were compelled by your diplomatists to make a treaty with the United States. This was the day dawn of our history. The people were suddenly awakened from their profound morning dreams. Party spirit at once displayed itself. The commotion of the country was fearful. Bloodshed and assassination occurred here and there. Soon the late Revolution burst forth, the result of which was most marvellous even to our eyes. The despotic government of the Shogun was crushed, and the reigning power of the Mikado was restored in the sacred person of the present emperor. Those proud minds which had fought for the cause of the Mikado and had also determined to shut out foreigners from the coast, suddenly changed their views and turned out to be the most zealous advocates of western civilization. The anti-foreign spirit, which might have been a great barrier to progress, was crushed out by those strong hands. The affairs of the country began to be conducted on quite a different basis. Zealous, talented, and far-sighted patriots were appointed by the emperor to administer the nation's affairs. A cabinet was formed, and eight ministers appointed. All the feudal daimio gave up their possessions to the government for the common good of the nation. Their retainers, the proud samurai, were ordered to lay aside their swords. The etta, the outcast of society, were permitted to be numbered among the people. The military system of European nations was at once introduced. War vessels were built and purchased, dockyards were constructed. An active competition arose between native and foreign steamship companies. Post-offices were everywhere established, and telegraph wires were stretched throughout the country. The public schools were constantly improved. Tunnels were cut and railways were built to connect important commercial centres. The streets of Tōkyō began to be lighted by gas lamps, and foreign carriages ran in its thoroughfares. An American tramway was laid out in the capital. Many banks were organized on the European model. Chambers of commerce and houses of exchange were also started in several important cities. A police system was carefully wrought out and is well managed. Courts of justice were erected in the large towns, and the

rights of person and property became far better protected. The common and high school systems were
first started in the year 1872, and so far as outward
form is concerned, are now very successful. About
the same time the Tōkyō University was founded by
the emperor. There are now more than 2,000 students in its care. The printing press began active
operations, and newspapers and magazines were issued
with triple speed. Common intelligence is spreading
quite fast. Materialistic science is getting to have a
mighty sway to crush out the old superstitions. The
pagan religions are losing the support both of the government and the people. Public lecturers are diligent
in advancing their own political and scientific opinions
or theories. Self-government is becoming the topic
of discussion among inquiring minds.

All these material and social changes have sprung
up like magic within less than twenty years, and this
very fact has induced us to believe that the evangelistic work in Japan might as well be done in the same
way. Yea, the present changing condition of the
country has prompted us to desire that the gospel be
now introduced there with zeal and energy, else the
anti-Christian elements of materialism and socialism
will soon become the greatest barrier to its healthy
progress. Buddhism and Confucianism will not be
much in our way. But these modern unbelieving elements from abroad will certainly be our future foes.
The government has lately recognized the tendency to
lawlessness, discontent, and disorder. Some cry out
for liberty without morality, and eagerly run after civilization without religion. Crimes of all descriptions
are more frequent than ever before. The increase of
the police force is accompanied by an increase in the

number of criminals. The introduction of moral instruction in the schools is unavailing if the teachers themselves are without morality. Failing thus in every attempt to improve her subjects, the government has begun unconsciously to seek for something better than the mere product of human minds.

On the other hand, the Christian education carried out by your Mission in Kyōto has lately begun to show forth its great importance and its bright prospects. Though the institution is yet young it has already sent out forty-six graduates from the English, and twenty-eight from the theological course. These graduates, though they may be inferior to those who have studied at the government university of Tōkyō, yet in their high moral tone and zealous Christian character command the great respect of the people. The governor of a province remarked, after an interview with one of our graduates: "There is no young man like him within our province. What a pure aim and high moral tone that young fellow has!" The editor-in-chief of the Tōkyō "Weekly" is also one of our graduates. A few years ago he started that Christian paper in our capital with the feeble support of our young churches, and he was obliged to put in all his own private means. But he works on bravely for the sake of its utmost necessity, and not for gain; ready to confront any opponents who assail the Christian religion.

The moral victory manifested among the young students in our training-school is a great marvel in the eyes of our Kyōto citizens. It is truly an unprecedented fact in our national life. This Christian institution, so recently started there, has already shown forth its healthy fruit. We have never tried to make ourselves known much. But somehow we are known among the leading men of Japan. They begin to speak well of our school. Some of them have already sent their sons and friends to be educated under Christian influences, and they would the more gladly do so if we could raise higher the standard of our school. They urge us very strongly to found chairs for different professional studies on their account. They further tell us that if we will do so, we can save many, many youth from falling into bad company, youthful vices, and, finally, utmost ruin. It is a great disappointment to them to have to send their sons away to other schools to be further educated after finishing the five years' course with us. In Japan schools are generally most dangerous places for young men if there be no teaching of Christianity. Materialistic influence is inseparably combined with licentious practice. A rich merchant, who lives some way from us and who is quite unknown to us, visited Kyōto some years ago, and at the very first interview with a trustee of our school promised to furnish us at least 5,000 yen, if we would found a law school in connection with the Doshisha. He has been friendly to us ever since, and his two daughters are now being educated at the Kyōto Home sustained by your Mission. The cry for professional studies comes to us not only from outsiders, but also from our churches. They wish us to start a medical school in Kyōto. It was about three years ago, when Christian workers sent three delegates to Dr. J. C. Berry at Arima, his summer retreat, to request him to ask the American Board to found a medical school in connection with the training-school in Kyōto. They had found out that Christian physicians would be a great help to the cause. When we held the meeting of our Home Missionary Society at Kyōto last year, all the delegates of the churches connected with your Mission talked upon the subject again, and sent another united appeal to the doctor for the medical school. They all agreed that if he could obtain an appropriation from the American Board to start it in Kyōto, they would do something towards buying grounds and building edifices. Each expressed the necessity for such a school in the present stage of our Christian work. I am sure that if such an institution be founded on a Christian basis, as is the case with our school, it will greatly promote not only the work of evangelization but the general welfare of poor humanity. As Dr. Berry has already appealed to your public for this cause, I hope and pray he will be successful in raising a fund sufficient to carry out his noble purpose.

Just a few days before I left Japan for this country, about seventy eminent citizens of Kyōto held two meetings for the purpose of hearing us on the subject of Christian education. Dr. J. D. Davis and others were invited to address them on that subject. Accordingly we did so and won their hearty approval. They agreed to raise funds sufficient for the endowment of several professional chairs in our school in the year 1890, when our emperor will carry out his pledges relative to the formation of our Constitution. Their idea is to commemorate that important event in our political history. We expressed our gratitude for this noble gift, but refused to accept it unless we were given full liberty to dispose of it on a Christian basis. To this bold statement they made no objection. They requested us to take the matter into our own hands and to carry it out for them. We never dreamed of such a thing, even two years ago. It is a great wonder to us that the world begins to run after us with such confidence. However, we are not too sanguine. We will calmly wait and see what they will do for us.

A recent interview between some of our leading statesmen and missionaries indicates clearly that the former are anxious to know something of Christianity. I believe some of them feel keenly their treatment by foreign powers as a heathen nation. Recent news from home informs me that some political leaders and editors are beginning to cry out for religious liberty and have published very bold articles in favor of Christianity. The bold action recently taken by the government in severing its connecction with existing pagan religions has induced me to say with a profound awe that God is fighting for us.

With regard to our young churches, I think they are worthy of your notice. As everywhere else, they have been thus far despised and rejected. But within a year or two they have stepped forward to a front rank in society. The last report informs me that besides helping themselves they have raised nearly one thousand dollars for purely mission work, and some of them devoted more than a quarter of their income to this purpose. When we, the delegates from all the churches of the empire, met last year in Tōkyō at the third national conference, we participated in a most blessed revival then taking place in the bosom of those churches which welcomed us there. The spirit of the conference, kindled by this revival, toned us up and prompted us to hope that the 36,000,000 of our fellow-creatures might largely be reached within this century. Other revivals followed here and there:

especially one which burst forth like fire within the walls of our training-school and gave us fresh courage and conviction that the whole kingdom of the Rising Sun would become the kingdom of the Son of Righteousness and Peace. Ten years ago we prayed that doors might be opened, but now we pray that efficient laborers may enter doors so widely open. It is most painful to deny the Macedonian cry coming from all quarters. When we Christian laborers come together either accidentally or designedly we have no topic of discussion but the direct Christian work at hand. "What shall we do?" is the common phrase among us; and after long observation and careful consideration, we have come to the conclusion: *Educate and raise up efficient native preachers.*

I beg your pardon for dwelling so long upon the historical facts before presenting a plan for your consideration, but I felt it necessary to do so in order that you should see our present imperative need. I now beg your attention to the following scheme: —

First, the highest possible education should be given to the Christian ministry.

Second, the thorough education of Christian physicians would be of great auxiliary assistance.

Third, the foundation of chairs in Jurisprudence, Political Science, Political Economy, Philosophy, History, Literature, etc., would be a strong attraction to bring the choicest students under Christian influence.

I regard the first as a direct Christian work and expect to dwell upon it hereafter, and would also call the second of scarcely less importance; and the third I might call an indirect work, but it is a process silently leavening, influential and powerful. To direct preaching we may meet much opposition, but to this indirect effort none will object. It will be like a mother's gentle influence over her children, too dear to be refused and too impressive to be forgotten. However, it is not our aim simply to make them friends of Christianity, but also to win them to Christ so that they may have life. Why can we not endeavor to reach our future leaders? Why can we not be fishers for men of all grades? As the guns of our enemy are of modern improvement, we ought also to have the best possible guns to discharge the power given from on high. Who can subdue God's elect? We must fight under his banner; we must win the whole Japanese empire for Christ. At present the matter seems to us but a vague dream, but we look to God to help us to realize this dream. I know too well that you cannot undertake the second and third schemes without some special donation for those purposes, because your chief aim is the spread of the gospel. So, laying those aside for the moment, I beg permission to dwell upon the first scheme. This is the dearest to us and is not new to you. You have already carried out the plan at Kyōto and have successfully sent out a number of efficient native workers; and we gratefully acknowledge the boldness of the step you have taken. The establishment of theological schools by our Presbyterian, Methodist, and English brethren makes the education of the native ministry a prevalent topic among missionaries in Japan. The success your missionaries have had is largely due to their readiness to accept our participation in the work. Though they are Americans in citizenship, they are Japanese in heart. They stand affectionately by us and with us, and most of us appreciate this more and more. [Mr.

Neesima then proceeds to enumerate the special needs of the school and to detail his plans for its future.] Some of you may feel that we incline too far towards the intellectual side. But how, without Christian education, can a handful of missionaries reach so many swarming millions? You will surely find it a slow and discouraging process. They are not even allowed to live in the interior of the country. Let them cast their net where they can catch the best fish, — I mean the class of students belonging to the so-called samurai, the privileged bearers of two swords. [Here follows the description of this class, already quoted on page 170.] The success your Mission has thus far had in Japan is chiefly owing to the training-school which your missionaries so early established in the very heart of the empire, the ancient capital of the sacred Mikado. Without a single exception, the Christian laborers educated there and now so nobly engaged in the work belong to the samurai class. Surely you do not regret that bold enterprise. We do not ask you to sustain our primary schools, as is the case in Turkey and China, for our people take care of the primary education of their children. Neither do we ask you to help our churches, because most of them support themselves. It is also a shame to the red-blood Japanese to beg for money. But I willingly offer myself to bear it for the sake of giving the blessings of the gospel to my fellow-countrymen. But we are constrained to ask you for this special provision both on account of the mighty pressure upon us and the brighter prospect near at hand. We are now in a revolutionary and transition period. Never was there such an occasion in our past history, and doubtless never will there be such in the future. This may be the very appointed time of God to save our nation. If we lose this fairest opportunity we fear it will never come back to us again. If we do not discharge our duty now, what will they say to us in that awful day before the throne of judgment? When I think of it my blood boils within my veins and my heart aches. I admire your motto: "Strike while the iron is hot." Do intensify your force; do try to finish your chief work with a quarter of a century. Then you can apply the same force elsewhere. In the long run it will be more economical.

Dear Sirs: I fear I have detained you too long. If any of my remarks offend you, I earnestly beg your pardon. But as a humble missionary of the cross and a sincere lover of my native land I cannot keep silence within me; and if I do, I fear I will cry out even in my midnight dreams. Allow me to add further that I have poured out my heart and my prayers, as well as my tears upon these pages. I found it a risk to my impaired health. But it was my fixed determination to win your favor at whatever cost. So I sincerely and prayerfully request your attention upon these plans. May God show you his own way.

Your unworthy friend and fellow-laborer,

JOSEPH H. NEESIMA.

AN APPEAL FOR ADVANCED CHRISTIAN EDUCATION IN JAPAN.

Old Japan is defeated. New Japan has won its victory. The old Asiatic system is silently passing away, and the new European ideas so recently transplanted there are growing vigorously and luxuriantly. Within the past twenty years Japan has undergone a vast change, and is now so advanced that it will be impossible for her to fall back to her former position. She has shaken off her old robe. She is ready to adopt something better. The daily press so copiously scattered throughout the empire is constantly creating among readers some fresh desire and appetite for the new change. Her leading minds will no longer bear with the old form of despotic feudalism, neither be contented with the worn-out doctrines of Asiatic morals and religions. They cried out for a constitution a few years ago, and have already obtained a promise from the emperor to have it given them in the year 1890. The pagan religions seem to their inquiring minds mere relics of the old superstition.

The compulsory education lately carried out in the common schools, amounting in number to almost thirty thousand, is proved to be a mighty factor to quicken and elevate the intelligence of the masses. The Imperial University at Tōkyō is sending out men of high culture by the hundred every year to take some responsible positions either in the governmental service or private capacities. Another university will soon be founded by the government at Ōsaka, the second important commercial city of the empire, to accommodate the youths so anxiously craving the higher education. It will be out of the way for me to dwell here upon the material progress Japan has so recently made. But let it suffice to state that the waters of her coasts are busily plowed by her own steamers. Public roads are constantly improved. Tunnels are being cut here and there, and railways are being laid to connect important commercial points. Telegraph wires are stretched throughout the whole length and breadth of the empire. Surveying what she has accomplished within so short a period, we cannot help thinking that

she is bound to adopt the form of European civilization, and will never cease until she be crowned with
success in accomplishing her national aim.

In order to bring about the recent change and progress she has painfully sacrificed her precious blood
as well as her vast treasure. Indeed, her victory has
been dearly purchased. It was a quick work, and
was well done. It was a sudden movement, but to
our great wonder, very few mistakes have been made
in her past course. She has tried her best as far as
her capacity would allow. The most serious period
of our political revolution is nearly passed, and society as well as the government will soon precipitate
into some new shape. But what shape? To the
writer of this article our immediate future seems a
more serious problem than the past. The question is
necessarily rising among us, what will be our future?
True, she is destined to have a free constitutional
government; she is bound to have her people thoroughly educated. It will be a grand achievement if
a free constitution and higher education be secured to
her people. But these two factors may be proved to
be the very elements apt to bring out freedom of opinions, and hence the terrible battles of free opinions.
A fearful national chaos might be her fate if nothing
intervene to prevent it. If the nation be allowed to
take her own course as she does now, hope for her regeneration might forever be gone. But in the time of
need, Providence, which rules the nations with infinite
wisdom, has stepped in to save us from this national
calamity and despair. It was neither too soon nor
too late when the missionaries of the cross from America landed on our shore to proclaim the soul-saving
gospel to the people. Through their earnest labor and

constant prayers the foundation of the Christian church was soon laid.

After some years' experience all the missions engaging in the field unanimously adopted one general policy as the best possible method for prosecuting the evangelical work there; that is, to train the native Christians for the Christian ministry. There now are more than half a dozen schools of that nature in the country. Men thus raised on our own soil have gone out here and there to found new churches, and what they have already achieved in converting many souls to the new faith within a short period seems to us a fact greater than mere human agency could have accounted for. "God is fighting for us," might be our cry. The mission, started in the central part of Japan under the auspices of the American Board only sixteen years ago, has been much blessed and has lately reached the joy of a great harvest. The last report informs us that there were 33 churches with 3,000 communicants, 14 ordained pastors, and 9 acting pastors. A missionary in the field wrote to the Board last July, stating thus: "Six churches have been organized in connection with our mission since January, an average of one a month." Through the wise guidance of the brethren, the missionary spirit has been much fostered among these churches. They have already organized a Home Mission Society, and also an Educational Society, to coöperate with the mission of the said Board for carrying out the gospel work. It is a small start. But a desire for self-support is already manifested in their attempt. I am glad to mention here that most of our churches are self-supporting, and some of them have never received any pecuniary aid from the Mission from their very beginning. This is a brief summary of what the mission of the Board has accomplished since it gained its foot-hold in the country. But causes of its very success must not be neglected to be mentioned here.

Of course the fact cannot be denied that the field has been much traversed by the feet of those brethren who bore the glad tidings of peace to those anxious souls. But a good share might be attributed to the educational institution of the Board, established at Kyōto some years ago, for furnishing to the churches the most ardent and self-denying native brethren. This institution gives instruction five years in English and three years more in theology. It is quite young, and is not yet fully equipped, yet it seems destined to be the salt of the nation. It was founded thoroughly on the Christian basis, and is now publicly recognized by the people as a school of Jesus. It became a centre to attract many youths from all quarters of the country. Most of them come to the school unbelieving. Before they leave it, all, with few exceptions, become Christians.

As there is a constant demand for enlarging and improving the school, the Mission Board has recently taken an extraordinary measure to reinforce it with more men and more means. More edifices have been built. More apparatus has been purchased. More volumes have been added to the library. The preparatory course in English has lately been much improved. The theological course has also taken a bold step to enlarge its curriculum. Still there is much to be done. The present provision might do very well, if there were not any institutions of learning in the country much higher than our mission school. But the government's university has made a great advance in the latter years in sending out a large number of its graduates. The time will soon come with us when the poorly educated will be obliged to retire from the public service as leaders of society. In order to occupy a very front rank as Christian preachers in such a society, our young men must receive the first-class education. The ten years' experience in Japan has given us a strong conviction that the best possible method to evangelize her people is to raise up the native agency, and such an agency can be only secured by imparting the highest Christian culture to the best youths to be found there. It may be a costly work. But it will surely pay well at the end. Of course the mission work ought to be a faith work. But with us the intellectual culture cannot possibly be ignored. The better educated can do a larger work. Better qualified preachers can organize self-sustaining and self-propagating churches much faster than the ill-qualified. So imparting a broad culture to our best youths will be a most indispensable means to win and prepare them for the Master's work. Besides this great demand to carry out the evangelical work, there is another thing to be considered for higher education.

We have some youths with us whose circumstances do not allow them to become preachers, or who are not fit to be preachers. They come to us and take five years' academical course with us. But finding no provision in our school for higher courses other than theology, they are obliged to go somewhere else to pursue further studies. They are led to Christ while in the mission school, but there is danger of their forsaking Him as they go elsewhere. They are yet young in years. Their faith is not strongly confirmed. They still require further care. They are like treasures — too precious to be lost in the depths of unbelief. The institution to which they would be likely to go would be the Imperial University at Tō-kyō, where Christianity is entirely excluded, on account of its connection with the state. There their faith might be chilled. They might wander away from the path they once found. What shall we do with such? It is a serious problem to be solved. The only way we have found is to provide chairs for a few studies, by which they would be likely to be benefited for future usefulness. It would help and push our evangelical work if a medical school could be established, and Christian medical men raised in it to be sent out with Christian preachers, hand in hand, to carry out the Master's mission. For this cause a lately returned missionary, who spent in Japan more than twelve years, has made an urgent appeal to the American public. But as it required a large sum of money to start it, there has been no adequate response to his request.

There is another movement, started at Kyōto last year, to found chairs of Political Science, History, Literature, and Philosophy in connection with this school. Those who are connected with it were compelled to take this decisive step, because in the first place they felt they could keep those youths within the sacred walls of a Christian school for completing their special studies, and in the second place they thought they could attract those who would gladly come to the school if such instruction be given besides theology. It may seem to some friends here that we are getting out of the track, and starting something alien to the original plan of the school. We did not intend it at first, ourselves. But present circumstances have necessarily led us to take this step. It might also be charged by some that we are too ambitious to push the work. To such we would reply that we fear we are left behind the times. If we are destined to be the salt of the earth, we should not allow ourselves to be left behind. Why should not we attempt to win and foster the rising youths who may lead the nation in the future? What the people in the North have done for elevating the blacks in the South, and what the people in the East have done in rearing up the new people in the West, by planting strong colleges and seminaries, besides sending them missionaries, may point out the true way for lifting up the coming race in Japan. If we confine ourselves simply to theological instruction, the sphere of our influence in society may be limited only to Christian churches. But if we give them some studies other than theology, under thorough Christian instructors, there will be a grand chance for us to grasp a certain class of the youths, and evangelize them within the school walls, whilst there might be no other ways to reach them.

We believe Christianity is intended to benefit mankind at large. Why should we not undertake to extend our influence toward the higher sphere as well as toward the lower, that we might win all men to Christ? Why should we seriously object to raise up Christian statesmen, Christian lawyers, Christian editors, and Christian merchants, as well as Christian preachers and teachers, within the walls of our Christian institutions? It is our humble purpose to save Japan through Christianity. The souls and bodies of our Orientals ought to be thoroughly purged, and consecrated to Christ for establishing his glorious kingdom in the earth as in heaven. If we do not raise up men after God's own heart in the different spheres of our society to leaven the whole lump, we fear the seed of destruction will be soon sown by other agents while we make this delay. Remember what our Saviour said in Luke xvi. 8: "For the children of this world are in their generation wiser than the children of light."

There might be some undue fear that such a provision of those higher studies would naturally draw away ambitious students from the theological course. It may be, but we trust we shall receive a larger supply of students in the academical course, so that some could be spared for other studies without much loss to the theological department. On the contrary we may possibly attract some students to it from the other courses. Some evil may arise in such an undertaking, but it may be overbalanced by the good accomplished by it. Now allow us to state a few reasons for this undertaking: —

1. Such a provision will detain the youths for further studies in the school after finishing the academical course. It will help them to develop and strengthen their Christian character.

2. Such a provision will accommodate some thoughtful parents, who may naturally desire to send their boys to a school where their moral character is carefully fostered and will be likely to be developed so strong as to be a safeguard against youthful vices and corruption.

3. The youths who have thus received a broad culture will certainly have a grand opportunity to influence society for good. Words and deeds of well-educated, earnest Christians in different spheres of society will help the cause very much either directly

or indirectly.   Sometimes indirect efforts produce more speedy results than direct.

4. This provision will surely benefit and tone up the theological course, instead of causing any serious harm to it.

5. We desire to lay down a broad basis for Christian education by encouraging post-graduate studies.

The time is just ripening for us to take this step, so as to attract thereto the best and most talented youths in the country and foster and fit them for the highest good and noblest purpose.   We are thus compelled to attempt this broad sweep to reach and win thirty-seven million precious souls to Christ.   Seeds of truth must be sown now.   Undue delay will give a grand chance to unbelieving hands to make thorough mischief and render that beautiful island empire hopelessly barren and fruitless.   O Japan, thou the fairest of Asia!   "If I forget thee, let my right hand forget her cunning and let my tongue cleave to the roof of my mouth."

As I mentioned above, a movement was started at Kyōto last year to raise some money to found chairs for those special studies.   But our friends are very few yet.   The people are now pressed hard on account of the business stagnation, and a most destructive flood lately visited the country.   So we cannot expect to receive from them any large donation. When we met a number of the eminent citizens of Kyōto last year for this specific purpose, we urged them to give us a fund before the year 1890, so that when the emperor gives us a constitution in the same year, we might found a university to commemorate the most extraordinary period of our political history. This appeal created among them a great enthusiasm.

Some of them gave us their hearty pledge to do their share. So we may possibly realize some gift just sufficient to support a few native professors. But it is beyond our expectation to receive a fund large enough to sustain even a few American professors. So if a few professorships should be given by some American friends to found chairs of Political Science, History, Literature, Philosophy, etc., it will help the cause grandly. Some people in this country may hardly realize how dangerously our shores are visited and washed by the strong tide of modern European unbelief. But to a native of the country, who has been seriously watching and observing the course recently taken by the people, the present time seems grave. The future battle in Japan may not be with any foreign invaders. But it will certainly be between Christianity and unbelief.

Shall we remain at peace and unequipped because God would fight for us for his kingdom's sake? We fear He will not help us unless we do our part. It is the time for us to make an extraordinary effort to push evangelical work as well as Christian education in Japan in order to save her from corruption and unbelief. The American Board has done for us in the educational line as much as it can wisely do. Yet there remains much to be done in order to carry out our work more efficiently. The Lord's army must not be hampered there while the battle is fairly commencing. Strong means must be provided there in order to furnish to the field strong men from time to time.

Now who will step forth in this grand republic of America to render us timely help to save us from this impending national calamity? Here may be some

friends seriously considering how their property might
be best disposed of for benefiting poor humanity.
With such we would earnestly plead and loudly cry,
"Remember us." Would that God might touch the
hearts of some individuals to give us a portion of their
blessings, and establish chairs for advanced Christian
education there as a perpetual monument of peace
between the United States of America and Japan,
through which the millions of our people and their
posterity might be blessed.

Mr. Neesima's visit to America did not relieve him
from the cares and anxieties inseparable from his position. The outlook in Japan was broadening beyond
expectation, and with greater opportunities came the
ambition to profit by them. The necessity for higher
standards of education in the Doshisha, for a native
Christian press, for all that machinery, in short, which,
if secondary to direct preaching, becomes more and
more indispensable as such preaching is successful,
was keenly felt by the young graduates of the Doshisha. With all these needs Mr. Neesima was in full
sympathy, but he was in a far better position than his
native associates to estimate the difficulty of obtaining
financial aid for enterprises which, however important
in themselves, were not the first care of the Board of
Missions. Its treasury was inadequate to meet the
wants of the world. Pressing demands upon that
treasury did not come from Japan alone, and the ap-
portionment of its resources necessarily involved disappointment to young and earnest workers in special
fields. A plan for the foundation of a medical school,
to which Mr. Neesima alludes in the foregoing papers,
was being vigorously pushed; urgent calls for aid

were received in behalf of a religious paper recently established in Tōkyō; efforts were made to secure funds which should enable certain of the native teachers in the Doshisha to fit themselves for the better discharge of their duties by courses of study in America; the occupation of Sendai and other centres was pressed upon the attention of the Board; and in all these plans, as in that of placing the Doshisha upon a university basis, Mr. Neesima was looked to as the main channel of communication between Japan and the sources of supply. He was constantly working for all these interests, by written appeals to the Board, and by conversations with its secretaries and members of the Prudential Committee, as also with others interested in philanthropic enterprises; but his efforts were not always appreciated by his zealous associates, and he received many letters whose criticism tried his patience. Of one of these, from a native pastor, he writes, December 15, 1884: —

"Our young men are too zealous for the cause, and are apt to be impetuous sometimes. They see the machinery absolutely necessary for the present stage of the work. If there be the slightest friction I know they will rise up instantly to lubricate, and move on again. If anything stands in the way they will attempt somehow to clear the obstacle. In this respect they possess a revolutionary character. For the common cause they are perfectly independent and frank to criticise. What I wish for them is more patience and grace. They are splendid fellows and will grow wiser by and by. I have been through such a hot fire these past two years that I am not afraid of them at all. I love them, can bear with them, and forgive them. But what I feel anxious about is that they may assume an unpleasant attitude towards your Board, not because they are ungrateful to you, but are so zealous for the grand cause of our common Master."

Of another letter from one of the Mission, relative to a serious misunderstanding of his position and action with respect to an important matter then before the Board, he wrote to Dr. Davis: —

"It is the most insulting letter I ever received in my life. I am sorry to say it is thrown into the waste basket. When I read it I said within myself, 'What! have I lost a sense of honor?' But I knelt right down for God's grace to preserve me in his hand. I am all right now. Please do not mention it to any one."

After explaining his action he continues: —

"My aim was to reconcile two parties. However, I believe my attempt was terribly misunderstood in Kyōto. Then I said calmly and sorrowfully, I supposed our good brethren had more confidence in me. Have I acted as their traitor? God forbid that I should ever betray our dear brethren. How sad and discouraged I was then I cannot describe. My only comfort was that the matter could be explained afterwards. I believe I am blamable for my writing too impetuous letters to you. I was too anxious to reconcile two parties too soon. It is a humiliation to me that I have made numerous mistakes. It is better for a sick man to hold his tongue. Allow me to assure you I shall ever abide *faithful* to your mission."

It soon became apparent that Mr. Neesima could not obtain the rest he came to seek unless he was completely withdrawn from all that tempted to activity. Accordingly in December, 1884, he started with Dr. Clark for Clifton Springs, New York, where he remained three months at the Sanitarium. He attempted at first to give up thinking of Japan; and devoted himself to study. Le Conte's "Geology" and Newcomb's "Astronomy" were among the books read during this winter. But in his journal he frequently exclaims, "Of what use is it to try not to think of my dear Japan!"

Difficulties of every kind were referred to him for solution, and he seems to have come to the conclusion that he could not escape the responsibilities of his position even on the plea of ill-health. His journal of March 10 contains the entry: —

"A broken cup! Though thou regainest thy shape by being put together, thou art no more fit for thy Master's use. Thou art now merely a vessel existing in thy Master's house. However, thou mayest be a warning example to others, that they may never follow thy footsteps. So being, thou canst still do thy duty. Be thou dutiful still."

Somewhat better in health, and greatly cheered by the news of the appropriation of $50,000 to meet special requests received from the Japan mission, he left Clifton Springs in March, 1885, and passed the following three months in visiting his friends in Boston, Amherst, New Haven, Andover, New York, Brooklyn, Philadelphia, and Washington. At Andover he excited a very deep interest in Japan, an interest which resulted in the formation of a Missionary Circle, and twelve members of the seminary pledged themselves to that field of labor if the way was opened to their entrance. At New Haven he arranged for the reception of one of his associates on the faculty of the Doshisha who was anxious to complete his scientific studies in America and to fit himself more thoroughly for his position as a teacher in the new scientific department. In his journal, dated New Haven, he writes: —

"Will they be tired of this poor begging Japanese? I may die as an unceasing beggar for Japan. It is the whole burden of my soul."

In Brooklyn and New York he had long conversations with Drs. Storrs, Taylor, Behrends, and others, and raised considerable sums for the library and the purchase of scientific apparatus. At Washington he devotes twenty pages of his journal to conversations with Professor Baird and other officers of the Smithsonian Institution relative to physical training in the Doshisha, the fisheries of Japan, and other scientific matters. At Baltimore he was the guest of President Gilman of the Johns Hopkins University.

While at the home of Mrs. Walter Baker of Dorchester, where he enjoyed a month of rest and quiet, he received the news of the baptism of Mr. Yamamoto, his wife's brother. "This," he says, "is startling news. How thankful I am I can hardly express. It will have a great effect among the influential citizens of Kyōto."

The summer months of 1885, Mr. Neesima spent at West Gouldsborough, Maine, on the north shore of Frenchman's Bay. Mrs. Hardy had placed at his disposal a large and pleasant farmhouse which she had purchased as a retreat from the busier life of Mt. Desert, and here Mr. Neesima found the rest and peace he so much needed. The house stood alone in a field sloping to the inlet. From its door one looked out over the islands of the harbor upon the shining waters of the bay and the distant summits of the mountains. These were days of restfulness, broken only by the arrival of the yacht from the opposite shore bringing provisions, letters, or, best of all, the friends he loved. Yet even here was opportunity, however humble. July 28th he writes to those across the bay: —

"The air is sweet and refreshing, particularly in the morning. The calm water of the bay, the sweet and melodious songs of some wild birds, seem to me most wonderfully soothing and fascinating. Everything tells me here, as Mr. Hardy says, ' peace! peace! ' I watch the white sails of the Ianthe as she moves slowly out from the harbor. She lingers within my sight as if Gouldsborough could not spare her, and when she returns, first a speck in the distance, she does not fly fast enough to receive my welcome.

"I went to church here last Sunday. After the service I asked for the Sunday-school. To my surprise the reply was negative. I thought it too strange and too bad that these young folks should grow up here without it. A thought came to me at once, why cannot we start a Sunday-school here? I proposed to a lady here that we should offer ourselves as teachers. I thought I would not show forth myself as the originator of the idea, and tried to put the preacher forward to execute it. He was most too glad to do so. I took the responsibility of getting the Sabbath-school papers for them, because I have no least doubt you will take a share in the work and get others interested in it."

In his subsequent letters from Japan, when burdened with many cares, and feeling the hand of death not far from him, Mr. Neesima asks again and again, "How is my Sunday-school getting along?"

CHAPTER VII.

During the last ten months of his stay in America Mr. Neesima was busy in presenting his plans for the Doshisha to the churches. He sailed from San Francisco in November, arriving at Yokohama December 12, 1885. On reaching the railway station at Kyōto he found over five hundred friends, — students, teachers, relatives, and prominent citizens of the city, — assembled there to greet him. On the following day the tenth anniversary of the foundation of the Doshisha was celebrated, and Mr. Neesima laid the corner-stones of two new buildings. As one reads his account of this joyful home-coming, and sees him alighting from the train in this once secluded and holy city of the empire to receive the welcome of so many friends, one remembers the poor boy who, twenty years before, in opposition to those claims of filial duty so strong to Japanese hearts, stole away by night from a remote seaport in the north, a lonely exile under penalty of death. December 23d he wrote to Mrs. Hardy: —

" How happy I was then to be received by so many greetings I cannot express. At home I found my aged parents impatiently waiting for me. My wife had prepared a regular Japanese supper, and we sat on our heels in the Japanese fashion. It was a happy day with us indeed. When I attempted to translate your kind letters to my wife and parents I was obliged to pause many times before I could read your most tender and motherly words. My profound affection for you is not to be diminished by these thousands of miles which I have traversed. All my past with you is a real and substantial present, so sweet to look back and reflect upon. I believe I am not dreaming, but thinking upon a reality — love begotten by love. My heart does not permit me to write upon this sub ject. It begins to throb and beat fast as soon as I attempt to do so. Many, many thanks for all you have done for me."

The anniversary exercises above referred to had been postponed a few days, and were held immediately after Mr. Neesima's arrival. The corner-stones of the new buildings — one a large chapel, the other a library, museum, and laboratory — were laid in the morning. In the afternoon the anniversary exercises took place in the gymnasium, the largest room at that time in any of the school buildings. It was beautifully decorated with evergreens and chrysanthemums. His Excellency the Governor of the Kyōto Fu was present, and the large room was crowded with students, graduates, and friends of the school. The historical address was made by Dr. Davis. In the evening the grounds were brilliantly illuminated by colored lanterns, and a meeting of welcome to Mr. Neesima was held, when addresses were delivered by representatives of the students, the faculty, and the Kyōto churches. An alumni association was organized the next day. The school was then in a flourishing condition, one hundred and twenty applicants for admission having presented themselves at the opening of the year, of whom eighty passed the examinations. The local interest in the establishment of additional departments, in the raising of the standards of instruction and the increase of material outfit was thoroughly aroused, and Mr. Neesima began at once to prosecute his plans with vigor.

He had been the recognized head of the school from its foundation; but, while accepting the responsibilities of his office as president, had always been reluctant to assume its rights and privileges, and could hardly be prevailed upon to occupy the president's chair on the chapel platform. In one of his letters he says: "Since I returned here I have found something hard to bear. The faculty call me president of the institution. I wish I could get rid of this name. It may be an honorable title to somebody, but I feel I am utterly unworthy to be called so."

Two years later, on learning that the honorary degree of doctor of laws had been conferred on him by Amherst College, he writes:—

"Some one told me of this while I was at Ōsaka. I said it must be a mistake. I could not believe in such a report. When I came to the seashore, where my wife was staying, I found there an official letter from the college. Then I began to understand it was a true fact. I was quite hesitating whether I could accept it or not. What shall I do with it? I felt I was utterly unworthy of it, and wrote to several friends asking their opinion. I was then thinking to decline it, but they advised me to accept it by all means. So I have decided to do so with a most grateful heart. I cannot discover any tact, power, or ability in me to come through the path of these last twenty years. When I think of it I am utterly overwhelmed, and at the same time I am encouraged to stand and face the world."

In the spring of 1887 Mr. Neesima went to Tōkyō to secure the exemption of the Doshisha from the conscription law. Under the provisions of this law all students except those connected with the government schools were liable to military service, and many had left the Doshisha in order to escape the draft. The law was subsequently modified so as to include among the exempted schools such as should fulfill certain prescribed conditions. To meet these conditions an additional endowment fund of $50,000 was necessary. By a vote of the Prudential Committee, May 17, 1887, an income of not less than $2,500 per annum, the interest on the above sum, was assured to the Doshisha. Mr. Neesima received the news of the vote, together with that of Mr. Hardy's last illness, at Sapporo, the new capital of Yezo, whither he had gone in accordance with a resolution of the Kyōto mission relieving him from his duties and advising rest. From Sapporo he writes to Mrs. Hardy : —

" July 30, 1887. Mr. Hardy's letter informing me of the action of the Prudential Committee was received here with a grateful heart. Alas ! the intoxication of this joy was soon dampened by the telegram telling me of his serious illness. I had some fear of it since receiving your last favor. How greatly I am troubled I can scarcely state here. I wish we could have some sort of medium to convey our messages every hour. Oh, how anxiously I feel about him. He has sown with us, and I earnestly wish he could reap much more fruit here in Japan with us before he departs in peace. Besides, I do own a real affection for him, and think I love both of you more than my own parents. I am begotten of you by your love. Pure love kindles love of the same kind. Noble affection binds us much firmer than some natural ties. Here I am, far away from you. I wish I could appear before him even in his dream."

" August 24th. I am all confused when I attempt to write to you. I have many things to say to you concerning Mr. Hardy's departure for another world. But when I attempt to write, alas! I find everything chaotic. I sit by my table, I hold my pen, — but I can do nothing further. Of course I know that our Heavenly Father wished him to come to the blissful heaven. I know most too well we must submit all our affairs to his hand. I know also Mr. Hardy may be far better off than in this troublesome world. But I miss him very much. I feel quite lonely. I feel my real father is gone ; yea, he has been to me more than my father. I believe that he knew me more than all my Japanese friends here. I have lost the friend of Japan. My heart is darkened like the total eclipse so recently happened here. Cheerfulness and brightness are suddenly disappeared. Alas! the total darkness. The air is chilled, the temperature is fallen. This solar eclipse lasted only for a while, but my heart's eclipse may continue so long as I live. I cannot finish even these few lines. I am too sensitive just yet. Besides this sensitive feeling I have another, my sympathy with you. You must miss him beyond a measure. His cheerful voice cannot be heard any more. My heart aches in your behalf. However, I rejoice with you that when he departed from you he must have commanded you to trust, and rely upon another arm, ever strong and everlasting. I will try and write you much oftener than before, but at present I find it a hard work to write to you."

" September 4th. It is quite rainy this afternoon.

I am undisturbed by any visitor; my thought turns to Boston. My reflection about you and Mr. Hardy is taking hold of my heart very strongly. This is the fifth Sabbath since he left us, but with him it must be the continual Sabbath. We who are left behind weep and mourn, but he rejoices. All the mysteries here may be no longer any mysteries to him. How grand that must be! While I am sadly missing him, and at the same time cheered up by the idea of his most holy, happy, and blessed state, I have a mixture of contrary feelings. We all feel we have lost the father of the Japan mission. Some sent me telegrams to console my sorrow, others wrote me letters to express their own. Now we have got to go on without his advice and support. At this critical hour I simply cry out, 'God help us.' I would like to write you some things I have observed in this island. At present I have no courage to do so. I have received your letter telling me of his most loving memorial to me. Now I must say what a touching thing it is that he should remember me so far away as he did. I shall never, never forget it. Through God's help I will try to follow his example, and to hand over to my fellow-creatures as he has handed over to me. Doubtless your letter was written with many tears. So it is with mine. My heart is still burning like a volcano with all sorts of plans for our work. But my wife is my constant guard to check me and take away my control. She works like a policeman to remove my pens and papers, and requests visitors to cease their conversation. I told her that I cannot hide myself anywhere in Japan now, and I am thankful for it."

"March 5, 1888. Our Christian work is gaining

much ground here. At the last communion we received over forty new members into our chapel church, and we may receive about thirty more at the next communion. There is no least sign of excitement. It may be called a steady spiritual growth. Our weekly prayer-meetings fill the chapel. It is a grand sight to see five hundred young people gathered there. A week ago I married a warm friend of ours, the head of the Yokohama bank. He gave us, last summer, one thousand yen for our preparatory school, and last week four hundred yen for the completion of a dormitory which is to bear his name. His young wife was formerly a pupil in our Kyōto Home, and is the eldest daughter of a wealthy merchant. The wedding took place in the largest hotel in the city, and was a grand ceremony. The wedding procession was very gay. The bride was accompanied by our governor's wife and six maidens, and the bridegroom by the ex-lieutenant-governor of Shiga, an adjoining province. Many people of rank were present, and the solemn ceremony of a Christian marriage made a deep impression."

In April, 1888, a meeting was held in the great Buddhist temple of Chionin in Kyōto to consider the question of a university endowment. It was attended by the officials of the province and city, the leading bankers and merchants of Kyōto, and after addresses by the governor, mayor, Mr. Neesima, and others, a committee was appointed to take the matter actively in hand. Mr. Neesima's views as a Christian were, of course, well understood, and the whole aim and spirit of the Doshisha were known to all. Its marked success had stimulated the friends of education in other centres, and the training-school at Sendai, organized under Mr. Neesima's supervision, grew out of the desire of its founder to create a second Doshisha. The presence of such an audience for such a purpose in the hall of one of the most magnificent shrines of Buddhism shows the change which had been wrought in public sentiment. The son of the governor was at that time a student in the Doshisha, and his two daughters were being educated in the Kyōto Home. Mr. Neesima's connection with the Iwakura Embassy in 1872, his efforts for the school during the early period of opposition, the prominent positions taken by its graduates in public life, had called attention to the work in which he was engaged. He himself had repeatedly declined all offers to enter the service of the government, but he had always cultivated his acquaintance with the influential men of his time, and his earnest, self-sacrificing devotion commanded their respect and sympathy. In July a dinner was given him by Count Inouye, late Minister of Foreign Affairs, in order that he might present his cause to a number of distinguished guests. He was then nearly worn out by his efforts, and fainted away while speaking. The result of this meeting was the pledge of about $30,000, as stated in the following plea for the university, prepared by Mr. Neesima and published in November in twenty of the leading newspapers of the empire : —

"It was long ago that I formed the intention of establishing a University in Japan, and for many years I have been earnestly laboring to accomplish this purpose. Now the current of public opinion has become so favorable to my plan that the present time seems to be favorable for making my purposes known to the public and soliciting their help in accomplishing this great enterprise. I wish therefore to explain what led me to undertake so great a work and what is the design of the proposed institution.

" About twenty years ago, at a time when our country was greatly excited over the question of intercourse with foreign nations, having the desire of studying in western countries, I went to Hakodate; and from thence, in violation of the law which forbade Japanese to leave their country, I succeeded in getting passage on a merchant ship, and arrived in Boston after a year of hard life as a sailor. In Boston, happily for my purposes, I was welcomed and aided by a well known American gentleman, by whose kindness I was enabled to study in Amherst College and Andover Seminary. During the more than ten years of my student life in America, observing the conditions of western civilization and having opportunity to meet and converse with many leading men, I became gradually convinced that the civilization of the United States has sprung by gradual and constant development from one great source, namely, education; and also I was led to reflect upon the intimate relation between education and national development. Hence it came to pass that I resolved to take education for my life-work and to devote myself to this undertaking.

" In the 4th year of Meiji (1871), while I was studying at Andover, Mr. Tanaka, Minister of Education, came with the late Mr. Iwakura, Ambassador, to observe the condition of education in western countries, and I received an official invitation to accompany them for this purpose. After visiting the famous academies and universities of the United States and Canada, we traveled in Germany, France, England, Scotland,

Switzerland, Holland, Denmark, and Russia, and I had opportunity to carefully examine the state of education and the condition of the schools in these countries. The result was that I became more and more convinced that education is the foundation of western civilization, and that, in order to make our Japan a nation worthy to be counted among the enlightened countries of the world, we must introduce not only the externals of modern civilization, but its essential spirit. Accordingly I was the more strengthened in my resolution to establish a university after my return to my home, and thus to discharge my duty to my native land.

" In the 7th of Meiji (1874), as I was about to return to Japan, and was present at the annual meeting of the American Board and made a short address at the request of many friends, I said that my country was in a disorganized condition, that the people were wandering in search of a light which might guide them into the right way, and that true education was the only means by which the people could make progress both in knowledge and morality. In speaking of this I was so much moved that I could not refrain from shedding tears. Taking one step more in my speech, I said that on returning to my native land I should surely devote my life to educational work, and begged my hearers to help me if they approved my purpose. No sooner had I thus spoken than a number of ladies and gentlemen in the audience signified their approval of my request by contributing several thousand dollars on the spot.

" In the last part of the 7th year of Meiji (1874), after an absence of ten years, I returned to my home, cherishing in my bosom this one great purpose. In the following January I met Mr. Kido, counselor to the Cabinet, and told him of my purpose, who approved of it and gave me much aid in accomplishing it. I also received much aid from Mr. Tanaka, the Minister of Education, and from Mr. Makimura, then governor of the Kyōto Fu. The result was that, in company with Mr. Yamamoto, I opened a school in Kyōto on the 8th of November, 1875, which was the beginning of the present Doshisha College.

"Thus the Doshisha was established; and its purpose was, not merely to give instruction in English and other branches of learning, but to impart higher moral and spiritual principles, and to train up, not only men of science and learning, but men of conscientiousness and sincerity. This we believe can never be attained by one-sided intellectual education, nor by Confucianism, which has lost its power to control and regulate the mind, but only by a thorough education founded on the Christian principles of faith in God, love of truth, and benevolence to one's fellow-men. That our work is founded upon these principles is the point in which we have differed from the prevailing views on education, and owing to this we failed to gain the sympathy of the public for a number of years. At that time our condition was very weak, with almost no friends in the whole country, with our principles of education not only despised by the ignorant, but treated with contempt even by men of enlightenment. Nevertheless, being convinced of the ultimate victory of truth, helping and strengthening each other, we proceeded on our way with a single eye to the end and with strong determination amid the greatest difficulties.

"Fortunately general opinion has now changed respecting religion, so that even those who do not themselves believe in Christianity are ready to acknowledge that it contains a living power for the regeneration of men. Thus society has been prepared to welcome us. At the same time our Doshisha has come to be appreciated and respected, and people have begun to recognize that we are giving our students a sound and well balanced education both intellectually and morally, so that our school is one to which parents may send their children without hesitation. Meeting with such favorable reception, our school has steadily advanced both in number of students and in grade of its curriculum, and ever our friends have urged us to furnish higher and higher courses of study.

"Especially in the 14th and 15th years of Meiji (1881 and 1882) such requests began to come in upon us, and we felt that we must proceed to lay the foundations of the future university. Yet the establishment of a university is one of the greatest works that can be undertaken in this country, one in which we need many helpers and much money; and what was our condition at that time? Having a few friends and helpers, we were not so entirely neglected as at first, but still we were in an isolated condition. What then could we do? Yet never for a moment did we falter in working for our purpose. We sought those who might favor our plans and help us, and, finding several who gave us assurances of aid, we held several meetings, to which we invited the members of the Kyōto Fu Assembly and asked their coöperation. Receiving the approval of the leading members of the Assembly, we published a tract 'On the Establishment of a Private University,' and set forth in it the purposes of the proposed institution. This may be called the first step in the undertaking of the work. Nevertheless, although many gentlemen gave assurances of help, as it was a time of business depression nothing was accomplished towards raising money, and our plans seemed to come to a stop for a while. Also I was obliged to go to America for a time and to leave the work in the hands of friends during my absence, so that the whole amount raised until April of the present year was only about 10,000 yen.

" During the present year we have especially devoted ourselves to this work, and good results have been accomplished. In April we called together over six hundred of the prominent people of Kyōto and explained our plans to them, at which time Mr. Kitagaki, the governor of the Kyōto prefecture, not only approved our purpose but himself made an address urging the people to help in the work. Since then several meetings have been held, and a committee is collecting money, and we have reason to hope that our confidence in the generosity and public spirit of the people of Kyōto will not be disappointed.

" And I have worked in Tōkyō as well as in Kyōto. Counts Okuma and Inouye and Viscount Aoki and others, to whom I have explained my plans, have expressed their approval of them, and especially Counts Okuma and Inouye, after visiting the school and personally inspecting its working, have given it their warm recommendation and encouraged us in our purpose of establishing higher courses of study. Besides these, other gentlemen and business men of Tōkyō and Yokohama, after hearing my plans, have given the following sums since April of the present year : —

	Yen.
Count Okuma	1,000
Count Inouye	1,000
Viscount Aoki	500
Mr. R. Hara	6,000
Mr. K. Iwasaki	3,000
Mr. K. Okura	2,000
Mr. H. Tanaka	2,000
Mr. Y. Shibusawa	6,000
Mr. Y. Iwasaki	5,000
Mr. H. Hiranuma	2,500
Mr. K. Masuda	2,000

Counts Ito and Katsu and Viscount Enomoto have also signified their approval of our work and have promised to aid us. In addition, some friends of mine in America have promised $50,000 towards the endowment of the present school, and another friend has recently promised $15,000 for a Science Hall.

" In view of this, since our work has now progressed for twenty years or more, and has gained so much approval in many quarters, and since we are now beginning to meet with so much success, I think we must now be diligent to seek out many helpers, for the institution of a university is a great undertaking and needs much money and help of all kinds. Such an opportunity as we now have, if once lost, may never be found again, and therefore we must not waste a moment. Also when we consider the present state of the Doshisha, we feel sure that our purpose is not in vain. We have increased the number of trustees of the Doshisha Company, perfected its constitution, and thus established the government of this educational work upon a firm basis. At present we have a preparatory course, an English collegiate course, a theological course, a girls' school, and a hospital and nurses' school. The following table gives a few statistics in regard to each : —

	Regular teachers.	Assistant teachers.	Pupils at present.	Graduates.
Preparatory department	1	13	203	108
Collegiate department }	17	6	{ 426	80
Theological department }			{ 81	57
Girls' school	13	2	176	21
Nurses' school	3	2	13	43
	34	23	899	309

" The school has thus attained so advanced a position that we expect to make the course of study in the collegiate department equal to that of the government's Koto Chu Gakko (colleges) within the present year. We feel, therefore, that it is necessary to add the university course to the present school; that the time has come for the establishment of the university. Since the university is the place for thorough training in special studies, those who graduate from our collegiate department should have university courses open to them to carry on their studies in such special departments as they wish. To leave the collegiate department without the higher courses of the university is like building an arch and leaving out the keystone. Thus we are such that the establishment of the university cannot be postponed.

" We have hitherto spoken of the motives which have led us to undertake this great work ; now we wish to mention the ends which we have in view. We do not believe that it is fitting to commit education entirely to the hands of government, because the education of our young people is our own duty, and we not only are able to discharge this duty ourselves, but can do it with more activity, thoroughness, and economy. In this way our Doshisha has attained its present prosperity, and in this way — with the help of others — we hope to enlarge it into a university. We think it not well to rely on a single university under government control, however high be its grade of culture; and we conceive that the reason which led the government to establish the university was not that they wished to take higher education entirely into their own hands, but that they wished to give us a model to follow. How long, then, shall we be content with merely looking at and admiring the model without making any effort to imitate it? We, of course, see the advantages of the Imperial University, and recognize its superiority in endowment and equipment, but we also believe that it is our special work to nourish the spirit of self-reliance in our students' bosoms and to train up self-governing people.

" Education is one of the most important works of a country, and it gives us great sorrow to see the people commit it entirely to the hands of government in timid indolence, for such conduct clearly betrays a shameful spirit of dependence on the government.

" The enlightenment of a nation is not a work which can be accomplished in a day. In New England Harvard University was founded within fifteen years after the Pilgrims landed on the stormy and desolate shore of the Atlantic ocean. Now it has 110 professors, over 200,000 books, and nearly fifteen million dollars of endowment. We have no doubt that the living power of such institutions is one great cause of the spirit of self-government which prevails so generally among Americans. In Germany, since the times of Ashikaga (three hundred and fifty years ago), one university has been established after another

until now there are thirty or more that are flourishing. In Italy there are seventeen. Now if we look
at our own country and find only one university, and
that under the control of the government, can we
say that this is sufficient for the enlightenment of
the people? Must it not be said that we are greatly
lacking in provision for the education of the people
and in preparation for the future welfare of the country? Such considerations as these have forced, and
are forcing, us to attempt so great an enterprise.

"What is the true end of education? We understand it to be the full and symmetrical development
of all our faculties, not a one-sided culture. However much students may advance in the arts and
sciences, if they are not stable and persevering in
character, can we trust them with the future of our
country? If, in consequence of principles of education which shoot wide of the mark, our young men
are moulded and trained in a one-sided and distorted
manner, no one can deny that such principles are extremely injurious to the country. Such students, in
their search for western civilization, choose only the
external and material elements of civilization — literature, law, political institutions, food and clothing,
etc., and seem not to comprehend the source of civilization. Consequently, blindly groping for light and
wandering in darkness, they are misled by selfish and
erroneous principles in the use of their acquired
knowledge. And though there come some who wish
to reform these evil tendencies in education, they
only make the evil worse by resorting to measures
of oppression and restriction instead of training up
noble and high-principled students whose minds are
free and broad as well as disciplined, and who govern

themselves and follow the right way with self-determining conviction. We would hold our peace were it not that these thoughts make us anxious for our country and people.

" We think that western civilization, though many and various in its phenomena, is in general Christian civilization. The spirit of Christianity penetrates all things even to the bottom, so that, if we adopt only the material elements of civilization and leave out religion, it is like building up a human body of flesh only without blood.

"Our young men who are studying the literature and science of the west are not becoming fitted to be the men of New Japan, but are, we regret to say, wandering out of the true way in consequence of their mistaken principles of education. Alas! what a sad prospect this offers for the future of our country.

" We sincerely confess that we are of ourselves unworthy to undertake so great a work, but, with God's blessing and the help of our patriotic fellow-citizens, we will forget our own weakness and even venture upon this great task.

" To express our hopes in brief, we seek to send out into the world not only men versed in literature and science, but young men of strong and noble character, by which they can use their learning for the good of their fellow-men. This, we are convinced, can never be accomplished by abstract, speculative teaching, nor by strict and complicated rules, but only by Christian principles — the living and powerful principles of Christianity — and therefore we adopt these principles as the unchangeable foundation of our educational work, and devote our energies to their realization.

" Notwithstanding that our work is based on these principles, if any one says that our purpose is the propagation of religion and the culture of Christian ministers, we must tell him that he knows us not at all, for we went to work with a broader purpose than what you ascribe to us. Our work is not for the propagation of a religion, but for the imparting of a living power ; not simply for giving culture to young men, but for fitting them to lead and influence others by their work and conduct. Therefore, by the side of the theological course already established, we wish to establish courses in politics, economics, philosophy, literature, law, etc., thus making a true university. If we are not able to establish all these courses at once, we will organize them one by one according to our ability and their relative importance. Thus it is plain that our university is not intended as a means of propagation of any sect or party, either religious or political.

" By making known our purpose to the public, and by gaining popular sympathy and aid, we hope earnestly to accomplish this work. Some of our graduates will enter the political field, some may be farmers or merchants, and some may devote themselves to science. Though their occupations are different, it is our hope that they will all be true patriots, each doing his part towards the welfare of the country. Since the security of a country depends not so much on its possessing a few great men as upon its government being in the hands of intelligent and public-spirited people whom we may call the conscience of the country, the education of such people is the great and pressing need of Japan. Looking forward to the coming epoch, Meiji 23d [1890 — the year fixed for the opening of the National Assembly], we feel

more and more the need of such an institution as we
are planning ; for, as constitutional government takes
the place of the present system, and as the people
come to share largely in_political rights, the most important need will not be perfect laws or institutions,
but self-governing and intelligent people.

" This being my purpose, when I consider my own
strength I find it far short of accomplishing so great
a work ; but I cannot be silent, — the needs of our
country and the urgency of my friends forbid me to
decline this task. Thus being stimulated and urged
on by the condition of the times, forgetting myself,
I devote myself to this work, and I pray that with
God's grace and the help of my fellow-citizens this
university may be successfully established. — *Kyōto,
November*, 1888."

Mr. Neesima's health during the summer of 1888
was very precarious. He was warned by physicians
in Tōkyō that he had not long to live, and by their
advice was taken to Ikao, a mountain resort, in a
kago, being too weak to travel even by jinrikisha.
Many causes had operated to discourage him. While
at Andover in 1885 he had kindled a strong interest
among the seminary students, and he had long been
looking for the advent of several who had pledged
their lives to the work in Japan. This movement
had been checked by the action of the Prudential
Committee in its refusal to appoint candidates for the
foreign field who failed to conform to its views upon
certain theological speculations then under discussion.
The resignation of Mr. Hardy, chairman of the Prudential Committee, still further depressed him, and
his death a year later was a blow from which he
never recovered. His own father also died the same

year. The plan proposed in 1887 for a union of the
Congregational and Presbyterian churches of Japan
had also greatly troubled him.   He was not opposed to
the general principle of alliance and coöperation, but
he did not favor an organic union, and thus found
himself at variance with many long cherished friends
and co-workers.   Under the shock of his physician's
warning he writes Mrs. Hardy, from Tōkyō, July 4,
1888 : —

"Allow me to send you my compliments for this
glorious day of your nation. I came here on the 11th.
My wife is with me.   She is a sort of policeman over
me, watching me lest I overdo. Though I am slightly
gaining, I believe I shall never get well again. My
doctor says my heart is enlarged and will never resume its original size, and that at any time my bodily life may soon cease. Of course I bore it rather
bravely, but to my wife it seemed almost unbearable.
She was warned to keep it a secret from me. But, a
poor creature! she could not keep her secret. I tried
to comfort her and told her all my future expectation.
However, I found it a hard work to quiet down my
own sensitive feelings. Since then she stays with me
and does not give me a chance to write much. Just
now I sent her off for a few minutes in order to write
this letter. Though I am absolutely prepared to resign my future into the tender hand of the Heavenly
Father, yet when I think of you, all my past affairs,
your motherly and unceasing love, comes at once to
my precious memory, and I weep like a babe. I dislike to pass off suddenly without a good-by to my
dear friends. Therefore, though it may be useless to
inform you of such a matter beforehand, I should be
sorry to leave this world without sending you my last

farewell, with my unspeakable thanks for all you have done for me. I owe you all, and have nothing to pay back but my thanks and daily prayers for you. If I fail to send you my last farewell by reason of passing off suddenly, as my doctor described to me, please regard this as my last word to you. I wish I could write as I feel, but I cannot express myself at all. I trust you can guess at it. What I cannot say I hope I shall say in another world. With regard to my tender feeling to my dear wife and aged mother you may sympathize with me. You know also how much I am interested in our Kyōto schools and the gospel work throughout this island empire. I am willing to leave all these interests behind. I am thankful for what has been done for my beloved country. What now shall I hope or expect to receive? As you know, I have a desperate will and plan to make our Kyōto school a Christian university. For this cause I came to Tō-kyō. For this cause I became ill and fainted away. For this cause I am still staying here. However, I am very careful. I fear I cannot write you much here-after. If I pass off I hope you will not feel too sorry. I fear this may not be a very complimentary letter to receive on your fourth of July. But so long as I am prepared to resign myself to His hand I like to tell my sympathizing mother and ask for her prayers for my soul. My wife has returned and warns me to stop. What I write here is not revealed to her. Please keep this secret from other people. I am still hopeful to live, but am prepared to go also."

TO MRS. HARDY.

IKAO, JOSHU, *August* 13, 1888.

My friends have held a special council to see what
they can do for my poor health. They consulted with
Dr. Baelz of the Tōkyō University, who urged me to
come to this bathing place. Their plan is to keep me
away from Kyōto lest I should be worried about our
school. I am enjoying the quietness of this place. It is
cool and pleasant, and nearly 3,000 feet above the sea,
the road ascending gradually from Mayebashi, a railway terminus, where we have a church of two hundred
members. I am surprised to find how fast a mountain town like this is Americanized. We can get
good milk, meat, and tolerably good bread. I have
hired a small cottage, although there many hotels well
filled in the bathing season. This little district is
honeycombed by the gospel, and is one of the
strong proofs of my humble theory, — *educate the
natives*, and they will take care of themselves and
start self-sustaining churches. I wish I could visit
these churches. Alas! it may be His will to keep me
ill and teach me His way. I am trying to rest; I
walk little, eat slowly, talk little, read and write spar-
ingly. I have read Victor Hugo's " Les Miserables "
and "Ninety-three," and the Life of Dr. Franklin. His
precepts are good, but his example might mislead
many. I suppose you are now at Mt. Desert. If I
might sit down on your piazza I would talk with
you and listen to you, hear gentle sounds of the surf
and see the Ianthe in the bay. Alas! with this pleasure, something would be missing. A year ago I received Mr. Sears' telegram about Mr. Hardy's death.

What I felt then I feel now keenly and will feel it forever. I have pressed for you a petal of a sweet-smelling wild lily, a token of my profound respect.

During the year 1889 Mr. J. N. Harris of New London, Conn., who had previously given $15,000 for the erection of a building for the scientific department of the Doshisha, increased his gift to $100,000. In acknowledging this gift in behalf of the trustees of the university Mr. Neesima wrote to Mr. Harris: "A donation like this is unknown and unprecedented in our country." Referring to this donation he says in a letter to Mrs. Hardy: —

"Our trustees recently held a meeting in Kyōto to talk over financial matters. The Buddhist priests are making an utmost effort to check our growth, and are bringing all sorts of bad names against me. They think I am the leader of the Christian movement. Through God's hand I am still protected; my life is in his hand and I am not nervous at all. This sum came in just a right time to relieve me from an intense anxiety. When I left Boston in 1874 I bought a single mattress, supposing that I might be obliged to live a single life and even be killed for His name's sake. You may laugh at me for my thought when I bought that mattress with such a martyr-like spirit. During this pioneer period the Lord has blessed this poor fellow beyond my comprehension. You know how ill and weak I am, unable to engage in any vigorous work. Even in this weakness He still uses me. This is a perfect wonder to me. I write this private matter to you and request you to rejoice with me."

Mr. Neesima seemed much better during the summer of 1889, and after having seen the foundation of the new science building laid, went to Tōkyō in October to work for the university endowment fund. Count Matsugata, Minister of Finance, became much interested in his projects, but owing to the attempt on the life of Count Okuma, Minister for Foreign Affairs, and the unsettled condition of politics, not much was accomplished. Mr. Neesima therefore went to Mayebashi for a brief rest. Here he contracted a severe cold, but returned to Tōkyō and resumed his work. A relapse followed, and in a weak condition he went with his clerk to Oiso, a health resort on the seashore, about forty miles southwest of Yokohama, where he died. The last letter he wrote to Mrs. Hardy was from Kyōto, October 5th, just before leaving for Tōkyō.

"Your favor written at West Gouldsborough was at hand yesterday. A precious memory is connected with the house where you wrote it, and whence you doubtless looked down from time to time on the calm expanse of that picturesque bay, spotted here and there by white sails. The memory of it is as fresh to me as if I saw it yesterday. It is so sad, and yet so sacred.

"It is quite warm to-day and the doors of my study are wide open. As the weather is calm I could not help being calm also. Here I am reflecting upon the past, the past connected with you. My thought is flying far off to a distant land, a celestial spot on earth. It is almost immaterial to me whether it be on the earth or in heaven. Where my thought goes there is something sweet and sacred.

"Since I had my serious heart attack I cannot engage in any vigorous work. But my thought is busily engaged with the idea of our future university and of building up Japan. The Christian work is somewhat neutralized now on account of the union question.

There is also great political excitement. The people are earnestly discussing the revision of the treaties, and political parties are using this question to gain ascendancy. The excitement will be greater next year when we come to elect representatives to the National Assembly. It will be a great epoch in our political history. The world is moving in Japan, so we are bound to push forward our educational work, and to get hold of the conscience of the people. Alas! why can we not make an utmost effort to take up Japan and humbly offer it to Christ?

"Some scholars in Tōkyō are endeavoring to check the progressive party and the Christian work. I suppose they will be a power for a while. They are positive, but narrow and exclusive. The movement is a semi-political one. The petty politicians wish the support of the Buddhist priests. The latter hope to maintain their position through the help of these narrow-minded and short-sighted politicians. Let us wait and see how long they will survive against the light of the world. At such a time we ought to make a union effort to keep our *front* strong. But the union attempted is the centralization of the power of our local churches. Our simple-minded people rather favor this union because it looks broad and is presented in a tangible form. The union I would favor is rather spiritual. I am a lover of democracy. It is not an easy task to occupy the position where I am. When anything happens I am apt to receive the hardest blow. But I don't mind it at all. I have chosen a policy in which church autonomy is recognized and every member can have his voice in the management and government. If the terms of the union are based on this condition I have no least objection to it; but I confess I am careful not to rush forward without any conditions. I beg your pardon for speaking of such unpleasant affairs. But have no least fear. We must go through some fire in this world, but time will heal all petty feelings and misunderstandings. Alas! I must go back to West Gouldsborough to calm down my feelings. Laying aside such thoughts for awhile to engage in meditation on the past seems to me a very part of heaven. What will be my thought when I step forward to the future immaterial heaven! Though I am often disgusted with this world's affairs, I am bound to live through and push through all I can for Christ."

On learning of his retirement to Oiso, Mrs. Neesima became anxious and desired to join him. He, however, urged her to remain with his mother, then eighty-four years of age, reminding her that "in olden times the samurai did not take his wife with him into battle." No serious apprehensions of a fatal result were at first entertained, and during the first week of January there were signs of improvement. On New Year's day he wrote a short poem of which the following is a literal rendering: —

> Seeing the old year go,
> Do not lament over the sick body;
> For the cock's crow is the harbinger
> Of happy times at hand.
>
> Although inferior in ability,
> Poor in plans for the good of my generation,
> Yet still cherishing the greatest hope
> I welcome the spring.

The first days of the new year he passed in studying the missionary problem in Japan, writing long letters to several of the leading native pastors and workers, in which he urged the occupation of certain new centres. He was never a random sower of seed. Thoroughly conversant with the characteristics of the people of the various provinces, and watching carefully the opening of the interior to foreign influences, he planned his campaign like a general, marking on a map of the five provinces the strategic lines of advance, and indicating by different colored inks the relative importance of the places he wished to have occupied. On January 10th he seemed as well as usual, and passed the evening with two of his associates on the Faculty in the discussion of plans for the new school of science. Professor Shimomura, seeing the discomfort of his life in a Japanese inn, urged his return home, but he characteristically replied: "I have here a debt of $20,000, and cannot leave until it is paid." On the following day he had an attack of intestinal catarrh, which rapidly developed into peritonitis, and on the 17th physicians were summoned from Tōkyō and Kyōto. To the suggestion that Mrs. Neesima should be sent for he replied: "No, wait a little." His disease, however, made rapid progress, and on the 19th a telegram was sent to his wife, who, with other friends from Kyōto and Tōkyō, hurried to his bedside. On the 21st, referring to friends expected from Kyōto, he said to Mrs. Neesima: "If they come, please encourage them and tell them not to weep for me, for I also am a man of feeling. I might be moved by their sorrow, and increase it by my own."

The Japanese inn where he was lodging being without modern conveniences, a mattress and bedclothes were procured; but to these slight provisions for his ease he objected, saying he was not worthy to die so comfortably. His pain was at times severe, but his mind remained clear to the end. On January 22d, he was told that he could not live, and was asked if he had any directions to give. He replied: "Not to-day; let me rest." The next morning he sent for the maps which he had been studying, and with these spread before him he explained his plans for the extension of the mission work, and dictated the following messages: —

"The object of the Doshisha is the advancement of Christianity, Literature, and Science, and the furtherance of all education. These are to be pursued together as mutually helpful. The object of the education given by the Doshisha is not Theology, Literature, or Science, in themselves; but that through these, men of great and living power may be trained up for the service of true freedom and their country.

"The trustees should deal wisely and kindly with the students. The strong and impetuous should not be harshly dealt with, but according to their nature, so as to develop them into strong and useful men.

"As the school grows larger there is danger that it will become more and more mechanical. Let this be carefully guarded against.

"Every care must be taken to unite the foreign and Japanese teachers together in love, that they may work without friction. I have many times stood between the two and have had much trouble. In the future I ask the trustees to do as I have done.

"In my whole life I have not desired to make an enemy, and I look upon no one with hatred. If, however, you find any one who feels unfriendly towards me, please ask his forgiveness. I find no fault with heaven, and bear no malice towards my fellow-men.

"The results which have been accomplished are not

due to my labors, but to yours; for all I have been able to do has been done only through your earnest coöperation. I do not regard it as my work at all, and I can only thank those who have so zealously labored with me.

"My feeling for the Doshisha is expressed in this poem: —

" When the cherry blossoms open on Mt. Yoshino,
Morning and evening I am anxious about the fleecy clouds on its
summit."

To Mrs. Hardy: "I am going away. A thousand thanks for your love and kindness to me during the many years of the past. I cannot write myself. I leave this world with a heart full of gratitude for all you have done for my happiness."

To Dr. Clark: "I want to thank you most sincerely for your confidence in me and in all I have undertaken. I have been able to do so little, owing to my feeble health."

Among his last words to Mrs. Neesima were these: "Do not erect a monument after my death. It is sufficient to have a wooden post stating on it, 'The grave of Joseph Neesima.'"

At two P. M. on January 23d seeing the end near, Mr. Kanamori, subsequently acting president and pastor of the College Church, said to him: "Teacher, please go in peace. We will do our best to carry on your work." In great pain, Mr. Neesima raised his left hand with a smile, saying: "Sufficient, sufficient," and at twenty minutes past four, with the words, "Peace, Joy, Heaven," on his lips, entered into rest.

Less than a month before, in a mountain village of the provinces, a band of children were going about the streets, their cheeks rosy with the cold.   To a traveler who asked what they were doing they answered with sweet smiles, "We are paying Christmas visits to our friends and relatives, gathering presents; and when Mr. Neesima comes we shall give them to him for the university."   Dearly beloved children!   He for whom you so eagerly waited will come no more.

On January 24th the body was taken to Kyōto for burial.   The train did not arrive until nearly midnight, but a thousand persons, including over six hundred students, were waiting at the station.   On receipt of the news that Mr. Neesima was dangerously ill, the students had been with difficulty restrained from proceeding to his bedside in a body, and the earnest appeals made in the prayer-meetings held for several days before his death testified to the strong affection between the teacher and his pupils.   The night was stormy and the streets were deep in mud and half-melted snow, but they allowed no one else to touch the bier, carrying it themselves by relays, changed at every block, the three miles which separated the house from the station, so eager were all to share in this sacred service.   On Sunday, the 26th, memorial services were held in the chapel, that of the morning being conducted in Japanese, and that of the afternoon in English.   All day long hundreds filed by the casket to look for the last time upon the face of him they loved.   "It touched my heart," a young Japanese said to me, "to see among many who came to take their farewell look at his face, the chief judge of the Kyōto court, a pleasant gentleman, always ready to say something amusing.   He entered the house very softly, and before passing into the room where the casket was, took off his outer garment, so that I saw he wore his ceremonial dress. He came in very gently and made a most profound bow; then, as if speaking to a live person, he said: 'Mr. Neesima, while you were living I was much indebted to you. I am sorry I have not accomplished more. In the future I will try to do better;' and, shedding tears like a child, he left the room. The next day, as the coffin was being borne away, I heard him say, 'The Marquis —— and Mr. —— were carried to their graves by the public undertaker; but Mr. Neesima is taken thither on the shoulders of those who will do great honor to their country.'" The two persons referred to were the late prime minister and the wealthiest merchant of Tōkyō.

The funeral services took place on Monday, January 27th, in the presence of the school, graduates from all parts of the empire, the provincial and city authorities, and representatives of the foreign missions. A large tent had been erected in the college grounds, as the chapel could not accommodate the assembled crowd, which numbered over four thousand. The walk leading from the gate to the chapel was lined by fifty of those immense bouquets of flowers and evergreen of which the Japanese are so lavish on ceremonial occasions. The bier was hidden in flowers. A brief sermon was preached by Mr. Kosaki, Mr. Neesima's successor, from the text: "Except a corn of wheat fall into the ground and die, it abideth alone; but if it die, it bringeth forth much fruit." The procession, a mile and a half in length, was formed in a heavy rain, the students again acting as bearers. They had from the first insisted upon doing everything possible with their own hands, and had themselves prepared the grave. Japan is essentially a land of contrasts, and as the procession, with its flowers and banners, files through the beautiful grove of the Buddhist temple on the slopes of San Jo, where lies the body of Mr. Neesima's father, but where burial was refused the son because he was "the very head of Christianity in Japan," one is astonished to see in its ranks a delegation of priests, bearing a banner with the inscription, "From the Buddhists of Ōsaka."   Among other banners was one from Tōkyō, with the device, "Free education, self-governing churches; these, keeping equal step, will bring this nation to honor," — one of Mr. Neesima's last utterances.

No private citizen has ever died in Japan whose loss was so widely and so deeply felt as that of Mr. Neesima.   "Who is this man," exclaimed a native of Oiso, "whose name I have never heard, with whom the rich and the great not only hold communication, but for whom, in his extremity, they also sorrow?" His death was deplored by the press throughout the country as a national loss.   Hundreds of letters and telegrams were received from men of all ranks and classes, and no just estimate of the esteem and love in which he was held by his countrymen can be formed without some knowledge of the many touching tributes elicited by his death.   For, under circumstances in which one of his persistent purpose and firm conviction might well have created enemies as well as opponents, he retained the respect and even won the affection of all.

Count Inouye had telegraphed to Oiso, "You must keep him alive." Viscount Aoki wrote, "I have lost a great and good friend."   A letter from the governor of Shiga contained, with its message of sympathy, the sum which had been promised for the university fund.

In a letter addressed to his followers and family, a Buddhist priest wrote: —

"Having learned from the papers of the death of your honored President, Mr. J. Neesima, I lament exceedingly. Being in my religious belief a Buddhist, I always opposed him and often attacked his cause. Meek, noble, patient, and earnest as he was, I doubt not he proclaimed what he believed, and this greatly helped to awaken the religious thought of our people. When I first met him I was moved by his kindness and love, and in two hours felt as if we had long been friends. Oh! had I not believed in Buddhism, I would have followed him and believed in Christianity. And I distinctly remember saying to myself, he that works for religion should be like this man. I had afterwards several interviews with him, and each time I saw him my respect for him increased. On hearing this sad news his gentle face rose before my eyes, his words of love sounded again in my ears, deepening the feeling of loss. From the paper I learn he was of the same age as myself. This and many other thoughts come crowding upon me unbidden. I sent you a message of consolation by telegraph, but wishing to express my feelings more fully, I send you these humble words."

In the "Woman's Magazine" (Tōkyō) Mrs. Toyoju Sasaki gives the following account of an interview with Mr. Neesima a month before his death: —

"Mr. Joseph Neesima, the pole star of our religion, the founder of the university in Kyōto, died January 23d, in the 23d year of Meiji, at the age of 47. We-sorrow over his death, not only on our own account but for the education of Young Japan. He was overflowing with love, full of virtue and of the spirit of consecration. His departure on the eve of the completion of his great work is especially lamentable. His life is well known to the world, and any attempt to narrate it on the part of my unworthy pen would but mar the perfect gem. So I let that pass, wishing only to place before you some words of his which I wish thus to preserve as an incentive to my own spirit.

"About fifteen years ago, on his return from America, he preached frequently in Tōkyō and Yokohama, and also delivered several lectures. He deeply impressed all who heard him, causing them to look upon him as the father of our people. I was one of his listeners, and from that time tried to see him as often as I could. Gradually his name became known, and he recently set about his plan to establish a university. I rejoiced in this undertaking, and to show my interest in it, with other sisters gave a musical concert, the proceeds of which, a widow's mite, we forwarded to him. He sent us a letter of thanks, but we felt unworthy to receive even this from him.

"Last winter he came to Tōkyō. It was on the 23d of December. I had the pleasure of having a long talk with him. His face was gentle, but indicative of will. Though a man of few words, yet every one he uttered carried incalculable weight. He received me as a father receives his child, with overflowing love, yet with a delicate reserve. 'Believing this is the best opportunity,' he said, 'I wish to ask a favor of you. There is a work to which I desire you to give yourself, an important one at this juncture. Among the reasons why there are so few great men among us, why national morality is so low, I believe the greatest to be the existing inequality in the rights of man and woman. Therefore the first thing to im-

press upon the minds of the young girls in our classes
is the fact that they have individual rights and duties,
that we may thus enlist their interest in the cause of
religion. I have seen many girls who, after four or
five years of study at the expense of much money and
sacrifice on the part of their parents, enter married
life to conduct themselves as if they had had no education. They do nothing for society. They are under the rule of their husbands.—They have no opportunity to show their ability, but are condemned to
things in which they have had no schooling, — the
kitchen and the care of children. This is deplorable.
It is sad that their husbands, in the treadmill of petty
conveniencies, do not realize it. It may be the result
of custom, but it is a hindrance to the progress of civilization. In matters of social reform woman's influence is greater than man's. Her power is indeed
great. But in our country we still find conservative
and obstinate-minded men who cling to the old order of
things. Looking back over my own life I find great
troubles. A man whom I thought my sincere friend
and to whom I yielded my secret, turned out to be my
enemy. For what I undertook, believing it to be for
the best, I received sneers and hatred. There are
unspeakable troubles in our path. Equally great are
the trials which the women of to-day must meet. To
ask you the favor of doing for this cause may be asking you to shorten your life. But we do not live for
selfish ends, and you and I, being the servants of
God, do the duties appointed for us. Therefore we
must not be surprised at the sneers and evil tongues
of the world, for we must not forget that the greater
the trials we endure the greater shall be our reward.
This that I now say is foolishness in the judgment of

the majority; for looking at the great men of the past I find that all had to endure the sneers and attacks of their contemporaries, and even to sacrifice life. No wonder that Christ had to suffer the Cross. He, therefore, who wishes to be a leader must be ready to sacrifice his life.

"'I add one thing more, and that is of the Christians of to-day. Being fed and clothed by God they are just like dead matter. This is because they do not understand the words of God. Among many sad things this is the most deplorable. Even if 39,000,000 of people become nominally Christian, this will not suffice to purify society. This should not be lightly thought of.'

"His words pierced me through. Some time had passed, so I rose to leave, promising to see him again with Miss Ushiwoda. On my going he presented me with his photograph, saying, 'I give you this that you may not forget what I have asked you to do.' Two days later I visited him with Miss Ushiwoda. Though very busy, he received us, saying many things to us which I cannot speak of here, feeling my inability to express his thought rightly. But one sentence I shall not forget so long as I live. 'Let neither of you ever despair. Persevere. Dare to become reformers, yea, the renewers of this generation, and work on.' He seemed to be greatly moved as he uttered these words, and we left him in tears. His last words to us were: 'This may be the last time I shall see you, so please pray for me and for the Doshisha.' We went out of the door looking into his face, and sorrowfully gained our homes.

"From that time we prayed daily for his recovery and for the university, when unexpectedly we heard the sad news of the 23d. We did not know even how to lament, it was so unexpected. It was the 23d of December when he talked with us, — but thirty days between these two 23ds. Who could dream that those words were the last that he should speak to us? When I look back upon that day I recollect that his face showed traces of suffering, but he spoke to us as if he were unconscious of pain. Oh, his words! Even now though I shut my eyes I see his face clearly, and I can relate but little of what he said, for my feelings overwhelm me."

To those familiar with the national movement of the last thirty years in Japan Mr. Fukuzawa's name is well known. Like Mr. Neesima he was of the samurai class, and by his pursuit of western knowledge estranged his family and subjected himself to persecution and obloquy. On his return from America, which he visited with the first Japanese ambassador, he published a work entitled "The Condition of the Western Nations." This book was a revelation to Japan, and in those days of bitter feeling Mr. Fukuzawa was intensely hated by the anti-foreign party. In 1866, he visited Europe, and on his return issued "The Promotion of Knowledge," whose first edition exceeded half a million copies. In all questions of religious, political, and social reform, Mr. Fukuzawa has been the recognized independent leader of Young Japan. Like Mr. Neesima, also, he has steadily refused all political preferment. As journalist, lecturer, author, and especially as teacher, he has, in the words of a Japanese writer, "done more toward the growth of western civilization in Japan than any other man." The extract given below is from an article in the "Contemporary Review," of which Mr. Fukuzawa is editor.

"It is reported that Mr. J. H. Neesima died of heart disease on the 23d inst. in a hotel at Oiso.

"There is nothing more lamentable in human experience than death. But the death of Mr. Neesima is especially to be lamented as a loss to society. If we examine the state of society we see men attaching toc much weight to everything official, as if there were no position of fame or honor outside of the government. This is the natural outcome of the feudal system. To be a government official is to be on the road to sure success. And because of this belief the avenues of official patronage are crowded. In education and religion, as well as in politics and commerce, every eye is turned towards the government as the central source of prosperity. The existence of this tendency is disgraceful. Many things go to make up society, and of these government is one, but not the only one. In the lower stages of civilization extraordinary powers are vested in those who govern. Such a state of things would, however, be a blot upon this enlightened century, and those interested in educational and religious movements should aim at independence both for themselves and these enterprises. But is this the fact with us to-day? How many men are there among us who, free from selfish interests, seek the true independence of society? Now and then we hear a remark on this subject; but of what avail is it unless accompanied by individual illustration and example? It is as if a man who himself drinks to excess should preach temperance to others. Independent men make an independent society. Mr. Neesima, living in a corrupt age, was not corrupted by it. Working earnestly in the cause of education and religion, his purpose was ever single. He was indeed an example of independence. His body perished, but his name is beyond the reach of oblivion. Many of the coming generations will hear of him, to take heart and follow him. This may perchance be a comfort to his spirit. Learning the sad news of his death we lament the loss to society of a true freeman, and present herewith our humble condolences."

Mr. Jichiro Tokutomi, who is preparing a life of Mr. Neesima, to be published in Japanese, wrote in the "Nation's Friend," of which he is the editor: —

"Lamartine tells us that, next to his blood, his tears are the most precious things a man can give. Individually we have lost him to whom we looked as to a father and teacher, for strength and light and love, — Mr. Joseph Neesima. As a society we have lost the leader of the cause of moral reformation in Japan. We have done our best to keep back our tears, but in vain. It is now no time to express our sorrow, for it cannot to-day be contained in letters and words. Nor is this the time to eulogize him, to analyze his character. . . . Not only brave men, but those soulless waves which wash the shores of Oiso seem to mourn for him. But his spirit of consecration still lives, and shall not we who enjoyed his personal teaching take courage and work on after him in this spirit? An elaborate eulogy, a magnificent funeral, a splendid monument, these would not please him. Far better is it for us to do our daily duty, to help forward little by little with our whole heart and life the moral regeneration of society, that our land may be the home of men and women loving liberty, truth, charity, and God. This, indeed, would be pleasing to him, and let him who admires his character and deplores his death think of these things. You, preachers, make your church a self-supporting one. You, teachers, make your schools training places of character. You, students, seek for the spirit and energy of those who, loving liberty, can contribute to their country's welfare. You, editors, proclaim the truth fearlessly, to your enemies as to your friends. And you, all men, with all your soul and strength love God, truth, each other."

On February 21, 1890, a large audience gathered at Kōseikan, where the great public meetings of Tō-kyō are held, in commemoration of Mr. Neesima. The following is an extract from the address delivered by Mr. Hiroyuki Kato, President of the Tōkyō University: —

"You have assembled to-day to pay a tribute to the memory of Mr. Neesima. I have been requested to be present and to say something. I declined at first, for I never even met Mr. Neesima and have had no relations whatever with him. I am not a believer in Jesus. Those who have already addressed you are all, I believe, his followers. I alone am not a Christian. Neither am I a Buddhist. I am a man of no religion. . . . Yet, being urged to speak, I would like to make a simple statement. From what I have heard of Mr. Neesima I know very well what kind of a man he was, — one greatly to be honored and respected. All who have spoken unite in ascribing to him an invincible purpose. It is this unconquerable spirit of his which I honor. I do not praise him because he was a Christian. I care not whether he believed in Jesus or not. I praise him for that steadfast spirit, so essential in every sphere, of religion, learning, politics, or trade. I believe this spirit a great necessity in this country, although it is of course everywhere important. We are a clever people. Western nations commend us in this respect, and they are doubtless right. Within twenty or thirty years we have, in virtue of this quality of smartness, appropriated much from the west. It is a good thing to be clever, but to be clever only is to lack strength. Cleverness and steadfastness of purpose rarely go hand in hand. The former is apt to taper away into shallowness and fickleness, and the fickle, shallow mind can rarely carry through to its end any great undertaking. While there are undoubted exceptions, yet I think this is our weakness, that we have not the endurance, the indefatigable spirit, of the men of the west. In the case of Mr. Neesima, however, from the very first, when he decided to go to America, to the close of his life, this invincible spirit was conspicuous. Such success as he attained cannot be brought about by mere cleverness.

"We are praised for the enormous progress we have made during the last thirty years. Many who, not long since, despised foreigners as barbarians, now almost worship them. From regarding them as beasts of the field they have come to consider them divine. This transformation has been wrought by the genius of cleverness, and it is well that it is so; but a more steadfast spirit would have brought about the change more gradually. . . . Foreigners criticise us for our mobility, and in itself mobility leads to no good results. . . . Without other qualities we cannot compete successfully with the west. Even if in actual hand to hand conflict we should conquer, in the competitions of peace we would be worsted. For the west is not only clever, it is strong. . . . I do not say that we are altogether destitute of this element of strength, for if this were so the future would be hopeless. But I do say that for the young, Mr. Neesima is in this respect a great example. Not only those who follow him in his religious faith, but all, — merchants, statesmen, scholars, — should strive to acquire his spirit. It is well to understand in this age of the survival of the fittest the necessity for this capacity to endure, and I earnestly desire that more men of his temper may be raised up among us.

"In this audience there are Confucianists and Buddhists as well as Christians; but I think the latter are in the majority, and I would therefore take this opportunity to make another suggestion in respect to which also Mr. Neesima is an example. . . . A belief in Christianity seems to weaken patriotism and loyalty to the emperor (some applause, with cries of 'No, no,' from the audience). This is the opinion of some, and I think it is confirmed by the conduct of some Christians. I hear a great many 'Noes,' and I am glad if this charge is not true. There is no reason why belief in Christianity should decrease loyalty to country, but as Christianity is of foreign origin men of other faiths naturally bring this charge even if it be only in defense of their own creeds. During the Tokugawa dynasty, when Confucianism was in its prime, a great scholar asked his disciples what they would do if Confucius and Mencius should lead a hostile army into Japan, and they made no answer; failing to perceive the simple truth that whether it be Confucius or Jesus who comes to invade the empire, it is our duty to defend it. . . . Whether there be any such feeling to-day or not, Christians will be open to this accusation and should be careful to give their opponents no ground for attack at this point. Nothing of this sort can be charged to Mr. Neesima, and therefore I have not hesitated to speak of it and to commend him in this respect also as one to be honored and imitated."

At the same meeting, Mr. Takegoshi, editor of "The Christian," said: —

"In this large audience of the aged as well as the young, of men and women, sitting shoulder to shoulder, there are doubtless atheists as well as Christians, theists, Buddhists, and materialists, and certainly many who never knew Mr. Neesima. Why have so many unacquainted with him assembled here with those who knew him well? To honor his memory. And how shall we do this? Shall we honor him as president of the Doshisha? The Doshisha University is so firmly established that we need not grieve on its account. Shall we honor him then as a Christian? But this atheist, this materialist, and yonder Buddhist, how can they honor him for this reason? Why, then, are they here? This great assembly has gathered, I think, to commemorate Mr. Neesima as one of the great men of this century whose extraordinary character is the common possession of the people. It is, therefore, more fitting to speak of him on this occasion as a hero than to relate the history of his work or to tell the story of his faith. And there arises in our mind first the question, What is a hero? Man is a being who worships heroes. The universe is the temple of hero-worship. The history of the thousands of years since man first inhabited the world is the history of this worship.

"Carlyle asserts that the worship of a false hero is the evidence of weakness, and that the homage paid the true hero indicates a great people. Yet even great nations often bow down to the false and fail to notice the real hero who lives and dies in their midst. It is a great and glorious thing for a nation to recognize and appreciate its true heroes, and if the character of Mr. Neesima satisfies our ideal of greatness, his fame is the common glory of the nation. If a hero is one who can command an army, who rides among flying bullets and glittering swords, then Mr. Neesima was not one. If a hero is one whose eloquence like a mighty wind sweeps away all opposition, or whose fluent speech and practical tact insure success in every undertaking, he was not one. But if he is the hero whose life is a poem, a lesson which can be sung, and which is capable of stirring the enthusiasm of future generations, then Mr. Neesima may well be given that title. Does any one charge me with extravagant praise? I can say only what I believe. Often the fame of great men is larger than the reality. The shadow is greater than the body itself. So that on drawing near the reality disappoints us. For this reason great men are often compared to a picture which must be observed from a certain distance. But this was not the case with Mr. Neesima. Great as was his fame, when we approach nearer, to see and speak with him, he wins a larger respect. Those who knew him personally testify to his gentleness and meekness. But there burned within him a fire of mighty power. It is a very rare thing to see these two traits in a single individual. A merely good man is often weak-minded, while ability frequently leads to rashness and imprudence. Gentleness and force coexisted in Mr. Neesima to a rare degree.

"In one of his letters to me he wrote: 'Young man, fighting once, do not stop there. Fighting the

second time, do not stop there. Do not stop even
after fighting the third time. Your sword shattered,
your arrows all spent, yet do not stop fighting till
every bone is broken and every drop of blood is shed
for the truth. Yes, if we do not fight for the truth
is not our life a useless one?' These words rouse
me to action. When I read them I sit upright.
Within, his spirit raged like the billowy sea, but it
flowed out calm and peaceful in a meek and gentle
conduct. So a mighty river foaming with a power to
move mountains while in its bed, when it reaches the
sea spreads tranquilly over the vast surface without
a ripple. The secret of this combination of gentleness and strength was his confidence in heaven. He
intrusted all to God. He used. to say, 'The grasses
do not thank the spring breeze, nor the falling leaves
complain of the autumn wind.' Autumn wind and
spring zephyr were alike to him. He neither strove
to win fame nor to avoid misfortune. If joy and
pleasure came, he did not refuse them; if they passed
by, he let them go and did not run after them. He
left everything to its natural course. And thus on his
death-bed he said: 'I do not complain to heaven, nor
find fault with any man.' He began by trusting in
heaven, he ended by enjoying it. What a sublime
life. Nor did he, like an idle preacher, think lightly
of his high calling. When he was in Kōbe for his
health, being in Ōsaka I went down to see him. Forgetful of his own illness he conversed with me a long
time, asserting that the progress and prosperity of a
nation at any epoch was to be measured by the number of its great men, and went on to speak of the scar-
city of men devoted to the cause of humanity. After
an hour's talk he was tired out, and fearing that he

would injure himself by so long a conversation I entreated him to stop. But he would not consent, and went on speaking as if perfectly well. The transformation of this self-seeking world into a realm of freedom and righteousness, where the old should help the young and the young care for the aged, in which the rich and the poor should cease to antagonize each other, where labor should have its due reward, and peace and prosperity brood over the entire community, in a word the realization of the great possibilities of humanity, — this was his constant preoccupation and aim. Morning and evening, awake and dreaming, it never left his heart. To this end he strove to add morality to education. The great enterprise of his life had the same object in view. Riu Gen-Toku said ' Cho-un is all courage.' So it has been said of Mr. Neesima, ' he was all fire." And this fire burned to bring forth a peaceful, prosperous nation. His tears, his prayers, his philanthropy, yea, his sickness even, were all devoted to his country. His was a vocation ordained by Heaven, and to build up on earth the Kingdom of Heaven he conceived to be his highest duty. We can readily understand now why he believed in himself and assumed so great a responsibility.

"If it be possible to combine truth and humanity, a bold spirit and a meek character, to show practically by one's conduct what Christianity is, without help from the dignitaries of the state or the powerful of this world, Mr. Neesima has done so. He was the Puritan of the nineteenth century. His life is like a poem which has the power to thrill and awaken. It is a precept to be followed. Such a character as his is indeed to be respected, and it is an honor to the nation to possess it.

"Ladies and gentlemen, Mr. Neesima is no more. As a mortal man, as the Puritan of the Orient, the leader of humanity, the man of independence, the lover of children, the teacher of the young, the friend of woman, the comforter of the old, he is no more. His body is buried, as was the body of the thief. But he still lives.   He lives in the memory of his fellow-countrymen, in the cause of truth and humanity, in the grateful thought of the nation.   You who commemorate him, endeavor to follow in his footsteps, consecrate your energies to make this nation strong, upright, and noble.   This is the best way to honor his memory."

Few men give serious thought to the condition of the society of which they form a part, and of those who lament this condition fewer still are ready to consecrate themselves to the cause of social regeneration. Criticism and complaint are more common than self-sacrificing effort for reform.   But Mr. Neesima does not seem to have thought of self even in the early period of his discontent and restlessness, for the motives which led to his flight were distinctly patriotic.   Such they remained throughout his life; but, as his horizon widened, so also did his ambition.   Beginning with the desire to make his country strong, he ended by seeking to make it Christian.   When the embassy at Washington sought his services his allegiance had already passed from the empire of Japan to the kingdom of Christ.   In many of the elements which contribute to what we call success and constitute worldly greatness he was lacking.   He was not a learned man, nor a profound scholar.   He possessed neither great tact nor large executive ability.   He was too modest and retiring to attract general attention, and as a public speaker was deficient in those gifts which produce instant impressions. Nor did personal contact with him reveal those masterful qualities to which, as indicative of a profound confidence in self, success is often ascribed. But while he seemed to remember self only to become conscious of his own deficiencies, he had an immovable faith in a Divine Worker; and this faith carried him through discouragements and disappointments which faith in self only cannot survive. With the modest estimate of his own powers which gave his presence so rare a charm, was blended a trust in a higher Power working through him, and this trust was the source of his own courage and of the inspiration he imparted to others. He had a large heart, and in such an enterprise as that in which he was engaged, this quality of great-heartedness is more effective than those more negative ones of shrewdness and tact. Some of the attributes which go to make up the brilliancy of leadership, he did not possess, but those which make examples and inspire imitation, singleness of purpose, loyalty to duty, self-abnegation, gentle conduct, and overflowing love, were his to a marked degree. It is difficult to analyze that personality which lies behind a word or an act, insignificant in themselves, to lift them out of the commonplace. In his quiet personal intercourse with men, Mr. Neesima possessed this power of investing a common thing with an uncommon meaning, and by right of his absolute sincerity could do what a more prudent but less loving heart would shrink from.

On one occasion, when a rebellious spirit calling for severe discipline was manifested among the students, he acquiesced in the infliction of the penalties voted by the Faculty, but, in the presence of the

school assembled in the chapel, declared with deep
emotion that the existence of this spirit was proof of
a defective government, for which he was responsible,
and for which, therefore, he also deserved punishment; and taking a cane proceeded to strike his own
hand with a force that brought tears and indignant
protests from the entire school. This incident illus-
trates forcibly how intimate is the union of love and a
real justice. Mr. Neesima's love knew no limits. It
is easy to love our friends, it is possible to love our
enemies; but it is rare to find one who loves the great
multitude of the unknown. In a conversation with
one whom he was urging to take up work in the provinces, he quoted the poem written by the wife of one
of the earlier Shoguns:—

"However glad the city's spring may be,
  The thought of fading country flowers deep sadness brings to me."

Mr. Neesima's monument is not the simple stone
which marks the grave on the slope above Kyōto; it
is the university on the plain below. Every one who
visits Japan is impressed by the results it has already
wrought. A Russian nobleman, high in station in
his native land, after meeting Mr. Neesima and inspecting the Doshisha in 1887, said: "He is one of
the most wonderful men in some respects I have ever
known, and this institution would be a blessing to any
nation. There are no schools in Siberia to compare
with it, and I wish that some of the energy and force
and wisdom which have been displayed in its foundation might be devoted to the work of lifting up my
countrymen who are scattered through that broad
Asiatic empire which we possess." Yet even the university itself, the visible outcome of Mr. Neesima's

life, does not represent the sum of his activity. For beyond all the energy and self-sacrifice involved in its foundation are these personal and indirect influences upon men and society, which cannot be estimated, which cannot be adequately represented by a monument or an inscription, and which widen "with the process of the suns."

APPENDIX.

THE Doshisha School was established in 1875. The first class graduated from the Theological department in 1879, and from the Collegiate department in 1880. The Girls' School was opened in 1877; the Preparatory department and the Doshisha Hospital and Nurses' Training School were opened in 1887. The Harris Science School was opened in September, 1890, and the trustees have voted to open the department of Political Science in 1891. The name "Meiji" University, proposed in 1884, was changed in 1888 to Doshisha University. The Board of Trustees is composed of ten Japanese, residents of Kyōto, Tōkyō, and Ōsaka; there are also three foreign associates, and one honorary member. The catalogue for 1890–91 shows a Faculty of Instruction of thirty-four members, twenty-three of whom are Japanese, and the following courses of instruction : a Preparatory course of two years; an Academic course of four years; a Theological course of four years, candidates for which must have completed the Academic course or its equivalent; a Special Theological course of three years, established in 1882, with provision for one year's preparatory study ; and a short Vernacular course of two years, designed for such as cannot take the full course, but desire to engage in evangelistic work. The Harris School comprises two departments, one of pure science (university courses), and one of applied science (technical courses). The number of students entered in 1890 was : —

Preparatory	76
Collegiate	376
Scientific	33
Theological	85
Total	570

The Doshisha now comprises about twenty buildings, including thirteen dormitories accommodating seven hundred students, a gymnasium, a chapel for the Preparatory department, and four brick buildings, namely, a chapel with a seating capacity of seven hundred, a library which also contains six recitation rooms, a recitation hall with eight rooms, and the new Harris building with lecture-rooms and laboratories.

www.ingramcontent.com/pod-product-compliance
Lightning Source LLC
Chambersburg PA
CBHW051121120726
47905CB00005B/1366